RESTAURANT
NATHAN
OUTLAW

To my son Jacob, my daughter Jessica
and my wife Rachel. Without their
support Restaurant Nathan Outlaw
would not exist. I love you all xx

RESTAURANT NATHAN OUTLAW

Nathan Outlaw

photography by
David Loftus

BLOOMSBURY PUBLISHING
LONDON • OXFORD • NEW YORK • NEW DELHI • SYDNEY

Ma Cornwall. Gorgeous memories of Cornwall have always come easy to me. Clattering the cobbled lanes of Clovelly, attempting to board surf upon Bude's sunny beaches, being baked lobster-rouge after falling asleep down on the amphi-steps of the mystical Minack Theatre and even breaking my foot along the ancient and most slippery harbour of Mevagissy. Life in Cornwall was just one huge delicious pasty, with a few generous scoops of clotted cream ice cream to follow, bliss.

More recently my Cornish culinary adventures have taken a slightly more serious turn. I met The Outlaw a few years ago whilst he was treading the boards of his Rock hotel, and I fell in love with that giant of a Jedi over a wonderful plate of grilled buttered local lobster. Since then me and my dearest ones have tasted the delights of the teen-weeny Fish Kitchen poised snugly next door to Port Isaac's RNLI home, and the refined new dwelling of Restaurant Nathan Outlaw on top of the cliff, where the freshest of Poseidon's daily offerings are gently tweaked into works of art.

Nathan, my Cornish Jedi brother from another mother – I await your fish and chip shop.

Paul Cunningham
Chef, Henne Kirkeby Kro

My wife and I visited Cornwall and Restaurant Nathan Outlaw for the first time a few years ago and immediately got the feeling that Nathan had put a very special mark on his own precious corner of the world. The spectacular views in the nicest of settings obviously add to the experience, but the real star of the show was the incredible food we had. Every ingredient on the plate had a reason and a place to be there. It was a truly memorable meal. We left Cornwall in a bubble of fishy happiness.

Tom Kitchin
Chef, The Kitchin

Restaurant Nathan Outlaw is the one place where I confidently leave the choice of everything I eat and drink up to the restaurant. Damon's skills in selecting wines include the rare and little heard of that take you on a journey that perfectly matches the food. Nathan's menus are created with whatever seafood is at its absolute best that day.

I'm happy to enjoy the full tasting menu which is served with little fuss and at the right pace with no intrusion. I marvel at the precision of each plate, the simplicity of presentation, the cleanliness of flavours, the unique textures of cured fish and the mix of flavours from the subtle to the bold all in the right balance.

For me everything is perfect, it's food prepared by the hands of a chef with heart and a deep understanding and connection with each different fish, whose skills bring out the best of the differences between them all. I've not come across another restaurant where seafood is served with such skill and finesse. It is precise cooking that achieves the simple, uncomplicated and exhilarating joy of fresh seafood.

Mitch Tonks
Chef, The Seahorse

It's more than twenty years since I first tried Nathan Outlaw's cooking. Over the years and a number of restaurants, I've watched his passion for the breadth and quality of Cornish fish develop into a unique style that seems to get better and more original as time goes by. It's what makes Nathan such a renowned name among chefs. I've been racking my brain to no avail, trying to think of another restaurant that delivers such simply glorious seafood and well-honed hospitality. When it comes to a modern dedicated seafood restaurant, Nathan Outlaw does it best.

Elizabeth Carter
Editor, *The Good Food Guide*

We've been very fortunate to have eaten Nathan's food since he was at The Black Pig, but one of the most special and memorable meals was when he established himself at Restaurant Nathan Outlaw. As we didn't have much time for long holidays when we first opened The Hand & Flowers, we would take a couple of days to head down the M5 to Cornwall for a holiday. As you can imagine, everything was first class, stunning food with an elegance of simplicity. The crab risotto blew Beth's mind, it was so good that we had to go back the next day so that she could have it again!

Nathan is unquestionably one of the finest chefs this country has produced, and has a sublime and gentle touch on produce as delicate as fish. Which for those of you that know him, or have met him, may find quite surprising as he is just such a giant bear of a man!

Tom Kerridge
Chef, The Hand & Flowers

It was at The Black Pig, Rock that I first encountered the cooking of Nathan and although we didn't actually meet on that occasion and the cooking was extremely good – and won him his first Michelin star – it didn't fully reveal the exceptional talent that would later become evident when his love of seafood would emerge and define his destiny.

Our subsequent meetings at the Marina Villa, Fowey, St Ervan's Manor, Padstow and Restaurant Nathan Outlaw, Rock are where this prodigious talent blossomed. Nathan's ability with seafood is all too rare – especially as we are an island nation – and his fundamental understanding and mastery of flavours, textures and letting the main ingredient speak for itself is what sets him apart.

Since retiring from Michelin in 2010 I've had the pleasure of visiting Nathan in his latest – and hopefully final – eponymous restaurant in Port Isaac. His cooking now embodies everything I best like in food – quality and simplicity – and nobody is a better exponent of this than the gentle giant that is Nathan. This is simply the best seafood being served in the UK today.

Derek Bulmer
Former Editor of the *Michelin Guide – Great Britain & Ireland*

I've known Nathan for almost fifteen years, and I'm a big fan of his simple but beautiful cooked and presented food. His knowledge of fish has made him an authority on the subject and many of us admire his tenacity to produce a single-minded approach to fish cooking.

I remember going to Rock with Amanda and getting the small ferry from Padstow across the water. Still a wonderful memory of a warm spring and sea mist. (Amanda just said it was miserable and wet – it's funny how time can distort!)

What was incredible about Nathan's approach was that he was doing a tasting menu based only on what was surrounding him from the sea, which was very brave but so obvious at the same time.

I remember looking out his window and him pointing to a boat and saying that's where I get my mussels and I get my lobsters from over there and so forth; it's every chef's dream to have that kind of quality literally on your doorstep.

We had several brilliant meals there, in the small intimate dining room, and one thing always stood out: the quality of the produce. Nathan has an innate quality to allow the incredible produce to speak for itself, and that may seem easy or simple but in fact takes great skill, craft and expertise. I believe he is one of the UK's best cooks that just happens to cook fish and that makes us all very lucky indeed!

On another trip to Cornwall, we had arranged a little gastro tour and was told by Nathan to pop in and have tea and cake before he had to shoot off somewhere, so me and Amanda set off extra early from Nottingham, I think 4am to get there at a nice time to enjoy this incredible cake made by one of the best chefs in the world. So as we get past Bristol and heading into Cornwall, all giddy and excited I thought I'd ring him to say we were not far away. He replied, 'on your way to where!?????!' Yes, I'm afraid to say, he had completely forgotten about us! I was devastated as I'd made Amanda get up early and leave at silly o'clock to get this bloody non-existent cake, and he was at some country fayre signing books for excitable old ladies and got his dates mixed up!

So I hope you enjoy his book (and I hope you never have him suggest he make a cake for you!).

Sat Bains
Chef, Restaurant Sat Bains

It's always a pleasure to be boarding the train to head west for Cornwall and Port Isaac. The prospect of Nathan's cooking, the happy welcome of his restaurant folk and the fact that Nathan is a king of fish, happy in his habitat, is a joy.

The level that Nathan sets himself and the team come with a generosity and a smile is never too far away. A necessary attribute when Cornwall is wearing its winter coat, when in fact there's no better time to make that journey – it is a commitment rewarded!

In the land of lighthouses, Nathan's restaurant is a beacon, a singular place beyond Dartmoor where the Atlantic rolls in and the winter storms are as important as the summer beaches.

Nathan is a king of the fish and a magician in a far flung peninsular. His menus are a delight, they come from a profound local knowledge where taste and a customer's smile have not been forgotten. To be there is a joy almost elemental one might say, given that weather!

Trevor Gulliver
Restaurateur

Monkfish, mackerel, bass and turbot all startlingly fresh were on the menu in December last year. Cured, soused, grilled and roasted, every course seemed to bring out the very essence of the fish but the dish I remember best was scallops with red wine. Just a brilliant menu built round the best seafood that north Cornwall has to offer.

Rick Stein
Chef, The Seafood Restaurant

I have followed Nathan's career with great admiration and respect his dogged pursuit of a time and place for his cookery, and his celebration of all that is good about Cornish ingredients is incredible.

When I was lucky enough to eat at his place in Rock for the first time, I knew he was going to go on to greatness. He has an ability to take anything he touches to a new level. I remember eating an oyster as the first course and I said, 'my goodness Nathan, where are those oysters from?', and as he towered over me he just lifted his finger and pointed out of the window and said, 'right there'.

I am very lucky to call him a friend and share many food memories together, and in this book people at home will get the true Nathan Outlaw, someone who is a genius with fish but also humble, a true leader and simply a top guy.

Jason Atherton
Chef, Pollen Street Social

Eating at Restaurant Nathan Outlaw was such a joy; truly one of the best meals of my life! Plate after plate of the most wonderful culinary journey. Lip-smackingly amazing food, real simplicity and killer combinations. The seafood was so sublime and fresh, the wine and the service off the hook and the most important ingredient to me, confident restraint, letting simple ideas be big and bold.

Jamie Oliver
Chef and Restaurateur

RNO
Realising a dream

It didn't just happen overnight, Restaurant Nathan Outlaw has been the culmination of many years of work and development. During the early years of my career, I was privileged to work with some of the very best chefs, learning from them the skills needed to become a successful chef and restaurateur, and sometimes learning what not to do! Of course, back then, I dreamt of owning my own restaurant, that would enable me to develop my own ideas and aspirations.

My first restaurant, The Black Pig in Rock, was a joint venture with my brother and sister-in-law. Money was very tight, so we did all the initial decorating and preparations ourselves. We saved money wherever we could – I even remember cutting down plastic milk cartons to make food containers!

We couldn't afford to waste expensive foods if customers didn't order them on the day, so I had to use a little imagination and create dishes that would utilise luxury ingredients in a more affordable way. So, for example, instead of serving up a lobster whole, I used the succulent meat to make a flavourful risotto. The lobster risotto that features on our restaurant menus now, from time to time, harks back to this early dish and is always a favourite with customers.

The Black Pig proved to be popular, receiving excellent reviews and gaining a Michelin star after being open for just eight months. However, the seasonal nature of the restaurant business in Cornwall took its toll and the restaurant closed after two and a half years.

Restaurant Nathan Outlaw, as we know it today, came about in 2007 in Fowey, and moved to St Enodoc Hotel in Rock in 2010. At that time, I was running two separate restaurants within the hotel, Outlaw's Seafood & Grill, which catered for hotel guests and served breakfast as well as lunch and dinner; and Restaurant Nathan Outlaw, an intimate restaurant offering fine dining.

It was at St Enodoc that I took the risky decision to offer a seafood tasting menu only, in the fine dining restaurant, coupled with service that was relaxed and friendly, albeit of the highest standard. It was quite unlike most other restaurants of a similar calibre. The gamble paid off and soon after opening the restaurant was awarded two Michelin stars – the first exclusively seafood restaurant in the UK to achieve this accolade.

During our time at St Enodoc Hotel, I set about building a high-quality core team, many of whom are still with me today. I came to realise that to have the best staff, I needed to offer opportunities for training and education for young chefs and front-of-house staff.

In 2015, by coincidence, a restaurant building in the nearby fishing village of Port Isaac became available. We had opened a small restaurant, Outlaw's Fish Kitchen, in the picturesque spot a couple of years earlier.

The cliff-top location, overlooking the bay where local fishermen can be seen working, made it the ideal place for customers to be eating the very best, locally caught fish and seafood available. It was time for me and my wife, Rachel, to branch out on our own.

Since Restaurant Nathan Outlaw first opened its doors to customers I've kept to my vision of offering high-quality, relaxed hospitality and a menu which brings out the best of our seafood and other local ingredients. It is cooking that seems overtly simple, but it is actually pretty complex in its flavour combinations. Customers are treated as old friends, and seeing them enjoy not just the food but the whole experience is of paramount importance to me and my staff.

And the rest, as they say, is history!

Nathan Outlaw
Port Isaac, 2019

Early Spring

In the early part of spring, I like to make the most of herring before they disappear from our waters for a few months. The first outdoor rhubarb also appears at this time of the year. Its natural acidity and sweetness make it ideal to turn into a ketchup, and you can prepare this a few days ahead. A great canapé to kick off a meal.

PICKLED HERRING, RYE AND RHUBARB KETCHUP

To pickle the herring and rhubarb
Lay the herring side by side in a dish that is big enough to hold them snugly (covered with the pickling liquor). Sprinkle them all over with the coarse sea salt and leave to stand for 20 minutes. Wash off the salt and pat the herring dry. Lay them back in the same dish.

To make the pickling liquor, put the shallots, garlic, chilli flakes, juniper and bay leaves into a pan. Add the cider vinegar, sugar and orange zest. Heat gently to dissolve the sugar, then simmer for 2 minutes. Pour over the rhubarb slices and leave to cool.

Once cold, remove the rhubarb slices and set aside. Strain the pickling liquor over the herring and cover the surface closely with cling film, to keep the fish submerged. Place the herring in the fridge and leave to pickle for 24 hours.

To make the rhubarb ketchup
Place a large pan over a medium heat and add the olive oil. When hot, add the onion, pepper, garlic and chilli and cook for 4 minutes until the onion is translucent. Add the tomatoes, rhubarb, sugar and rosemary and cook gently for about 20 minutes until the fruit has broken down. Add the balsamic vinegar and anchovies and stir well. Simmer to reduce until the liquor is thick and syrupy.

Transfer the mixture to a blender and blitz until smooth, then pass through a sieve into a bowl. Season with salt to taste. Cover and leave to cool.

To make the rye bread
Using a stand mixer fitted with the dough hook, mix all the ingredients, except the salt, mixed seeds and rye flakes, together on a high speed for 6 minutes. Add the salt, seeds and rye flakes and mix for 2 minutes. Transfer the dough to a floured bowl, cover with a damp cloth and leave in a warm place to rise for 1 hour.

On a floured surface, knock back the dough then shape it into a loaf and place on a baking tray. Cover with a damp cloth and leave to prove in a warm place until doubled in size (this should take 45 minutes–1 hour).

Meanwhile, preheat your oven to 230°C/Fan 220°C/Gas Mark 8. Sprinkle the loaf with a mixture of equal quantities of rye and white flour. Bake for 25 minutes until the loaf sounds hollow when tapped on the base. Place on a wire rack and leave to cool.

To assemble and serve
About 30 minutes before serving, take the herring out of the fridge, lift them out of the pickling liquor and let them come to room temperature (to enjoy them at their tastiest).

Thinly slice the rye bread and cut into bite-sized pieces. Cut the pickled herring into similar-sized pieces. Place a few pickled rhubarb slices and ½ teaspoon of rhubarb ketchup on each piece of bread and top with a slice of herring. Finish with a garlic flower, a drizzle of extra virgin oil and a sprinkle of salt. Serve at once.

Makes 16 canapés

4 very fresh herring, scaled, gutted and filleted
4 tablespoons coarse sea salt
2 shallots, peeled and finely sliced
2 garlic cloves, peeled and crushed
1 teaspoon dried chilli flakes
2 teaspoons juniper berries, chopped
2 bay leaves
500ml cider vinegar
200g caster sugar
pared zest of 1 orange
1 rhubarb stalk, thinly sliced

For the rhubarb ketchup
50ml olive oil
1 red onion, peeled and chopped
1 red pepper, cored, deseeded and chopped
1 garlic clove, peeled and chopped
1 red chilli, deseeded and chopped
200g tin tomatoes
500g outdoor rhubarb, roughly chopped
100g caster sugar
a sprig of rosemary, leaves finely chopped
120ml balsamic vinegar
50g tin good-quality anchovy fillets in oil, drained

For the rye bread
200g rye flour, plus extra to sprinkle
50g white bread flour, plus extra to sprinkle
125ml water
7g fast-action dried or 20g fresh yeast
50g black treacle
7g fine sea salt
35g mixed seeds
35g rye flakes

To serve
wild garlic flowers
extra virgin rapeseed oil
Cornish sea salt

This fresh-tasting dish always goes down a storm with our customers. It's an unusual way to serve gurnard and so colourful it makes a huge impression when you first set eyes on it. Based on the excellent Peruvian ceviche technique, the fish is marinated for just 10 minutes before it is presented. If you can't get gurnard, then very fresh mackerel, bream and monkfish work well treated the same way.

MARINATED GURNARD, FENNEL, BLOOD ORANGE AND CHILLI

Serves 4 as a starter

4 very fresh gurnard
   fillets, about 150g
   each, skinned and
   pin-boned
Cornish sea salt

For the chilli paste
olive oil for cooking
2 shallots, peeled and
   finely chopped
2 garlic cloves, peeled
   and finely chopped
3 red chillies, chopped
   (with seeds)
2 tablespoons water

For the marinade
juice of 3 limes
30g freshly peeled root
   ginger, grated
1 garlic clove, peeled
   and crushed
1 lemongrass stem,
   chopped
1 tablespoon chopped
   coriander

For the orange oil
finely pared zest of
   4 oranges
400ml light olive oil

For the garnish
1 fennel bulb, outer
   layer and fronds
   removed, finely sliced
4 radishes, finely sliced
   (on a mandoline)
1 red onion, peeled and
   finely sliced
1 blood orange
coriander leaves
fennel herb leaves

First make the orange oil (a day ahead)
Put the orange zest and olive oil into a blender or food processor and blitz for 2 minutes. Pour into a bowl, cover and leave to infuse in the fridge overnight. The next day, pass the oil through a muslin-lined sieve into a clean container. It is now ready to use and will keep in a sealed container in the fridge for a couple of weeks.

To make the chilli paste
Heat a frying pan over a medium heat then add a drizzle of olive oil. When it's hot, add the shallots, garlic and chillies and sweat for 5 minutes, stirring often, until softened. Before the mixture starts to catch, stir in the water and 1 teaspoon salt. Scrape the mixture into a blender and blitz until smooth. Transfer the chilli paste to a container, leave to cool, then cover and refrigerate until needed.

For the marinade
Combine all the ingredients in a bowl and leave to stand for 30 minutes to allow the flavours to mingle. Strain the marinade through a sieve into a bowl and refrigerate until required. Discard the contents of the sieve.

To prepare the garnish
Immerse the fennel, radishes and red onion in separate bowls of ice-cold water for 15 minutes to firm up and lose the raw edge to their flavour.

To marinate the gurnard
While the garnish veg are soaking, slice your fish into thin, even slices, no more than 5mm thick. Place in a bowl, pour on the marinade and mix together well, adding a pinch of salt. Cover and place the fish in the fridge for 10 minutes.

To prepare the orange
Using a sharp knife, cut away the peel from the blood orange, removing all of the white pith, then cut out the orange segments from between the membranes.

To assemble and serve
Drain the garnish veg and season with salt and a drizzle of orange oil. Drain off the marinade from the fish. Add 1 tablespoon of the chilli paste to the fish and mix through carefully so as not to break up the pieces.

Arrange the gurnard on individual plates and drizzle 1 teaspoon of the orange oil onto each plate. Top with the fennel, radishes and red onion. Finish with the blood orange segments, coriander and fennel leaves. Serve immediately.

Every year when we come back from our winter break, I start looking forward to spring and the arrival of the first asparagus from St Enodoc, which is just up the road from the restaurant. It seems to take forever to appear and then it's only in season for about six weeks. At the same time, superb-quality crab starts to become available in Port Isaac. All I need to do is get them together on the plate in the best way possible.

CRAB AND ASPARAGUS

Serves 6 as a starter

1 large live brown
    crab, about 1kg,
    placed in the freezer
    for 30 minutes
    before cooking
salt

**For the asparagus
mousse**
3 sheets of bronze leaf
    gelatine, soaked in
    ice-cold water
25g unsalted butter
325g asparagus
    spears, trimmed of
    any woody parts
150ml double cream

For the mayonnaise
2 large egg yolks
1 tablespoon brown
    crab meat (from the
    crab above)
juice of 1 lemon
300ml light olive oil
Cornish sea salt and
    freshly ground pepper

For the asparagus salad
12 perfect asparagus
    spears, trimmed of
    any woody parts
1 tablespoon chopped
    chervil
40ml agrodolce vinegar
100ml good-quality
    olive oil

First make the asparagus mousse
Soak the gelatine in a shallow dish of ice-cold water to soften. Meanwhile, place a large pan over a medium heat and add the butter. When melted and starting to bubble, add the asparagus and cook for about 3 minutes until it softens and starts to collapse. Pour in the cream, bring to a simmer and cook for 3 minutes. Season with salt to taste. Squeeze out the excess water from the gelatine then add it to the asparagus mixture. Immediately tip the contents of the pan into a blender and blend for 2 minutes until smooth. Transfer to a jug. Carefully pour the mixture into 6 individual serving dishes and place in the fridge to set.

To cook and prepare the crab
Bring a large pan of water (big enough to hold the crab fully submerged) to the boil. Season the water generously with salt, to make it as salty as sea water. Once it comes to a rolling boil, lower the crab into the water and cook for 14 minutes.

Carefully lift the crab out of the pan, place on a tray and leave until cool enough to handle. Remove all the legs and claws from the cooked crab, by twisting them away from the body. Now, holding the crab in both hands, use your thumbs to push the body up and out of the hard, top shell or carapace. Remove and discard the dead man's fingers, stomach sac and hard membranes from the body shell.

Using a spoon, remove the brown crab from the carapace and place in a bowl (you won't need it all for this dish, so save to eat on toast or freeze it).

Cut the body in half, using a sharp knife, to reveal the little channels of white crab meat. Use a crab pick or the handle of a spoon to pick out all the crab meat from these crevices and put it into a separate bowl.

Using a heavy knife, break the claws with one hard tap if possible and pick out the white meat, prising out the cartilage from the middle of the claw. Do the same with the legs to extract the meat. Once you have extracted all the white meat, with clean hands, pick through it to search for any shell or cartilage. Refrigerate if preparing ahead or set aside while you make the mayonnaise.

To make the mayonnaise
Place the egg yolks, brown crab meat and lemon juice in a bowl and whisk to combine. Slowly add the olive oil in a thin, steady stream, whisking constantly until it is all incorporated. Season with salt and pepper to taste. Add enough of the mayonnaise to the white crab meat to combine.

For the asparagus salad
Carefully slice the asparagus spears lengthways on a mandoline. Add the chopped chervil and dress well with the agrodolce vinegar and olive oil, but don't overdo it (the dressing will soften the asparagus).

To assemble and serve
Take the asparagus mousses (and crab meat if chilled) out of the fridge 20 minutes before serving. Top each mousse with a pile of crab meat. Arrange the shaved asparagus salad on top and serve straight away.

Cuttlefish is very underrated but it doesn't deserve to be: it's versatile, tasty and sustainable. Ok, it's a bit messy to prepare, but that is part of the joy for me! A friendly fishmonger should be happy to help you out if needs be. In the spring, cuttlefish has a way of getting itself caught up in lobster pots in Cornwall, so at this time of year when our lobster fisherman bring in lobster and crab, they'll often have a few live cuttlefish too, and I'm always pleased to take them. At first sight, the black fritters can be something of a shock, but inside the crust is a flavour bomb that is guaranteed to satisfy.

CUTTLEFISH FRITTERS AND **WILD GARLIC SOUP**

Serves 6 as a hearty starter or light lunch

For the black bread
125g white bread flour
30g fermented starter dough (see page 290)
50ml water
7g fresh yeast
10g unsalted butter
5g sea salt
50ml squid ink

For the cuttlefish fritters
1kg cuttlefish, cleaned
light olive oil for cooking
2 white onions, peeled and chopped
4 garlic cloves, peeled and finely chopped
2 red peppers, cored, deseeded and finely diced
3 teaspoons smoked paprika
600ml dry cider
450ml fish stock (see page 288)
150g unsalted butter
120g plain flour, plus an extra 50g for coating
2 large eggs, beaten
sunflower oil for deep-frying
Cornish sea salt and freshly ground black pepper

For the wild garlic soup
light olive oil for cooking
1 small onion, peeled and finely chopped
1 medium potato, peeled and finely sliced
1 litre vegetable stock (see page 288)
250g wild garlic, plus a few flowers for the garnish (if available)

For the lemon and garlic oil
2 garlic cloves, peeled
2 lemons, finely zested
400ml light olive oil

First prepare the lemon and garlic oil
If possible, do this a day ahead. Put the garlic, lemon zest and olive oil into a blender and blitz thoroughly for 3 minutes. Pour into a container and leave to infuse in the fridge for at least 6 hours, ideally overnight.

To finish the oil, decant it into another container or bottle, leaving the sediment behind. Cover and refrigerate until needed.

To make the black bread
Put all the ingredients, except the salt and squid ink, into a stand mixer fitted with the dough hook and mix on a high speed for 6 minutes. Add the salt and squid ink and mix for another 2 minutes.

Transfer the dough to a floured bowl, cover with a damp cloth and leave to rise in a warm place for 30 minutes.

On a floured surface, knock back the dough and shape into a loaf. Place on a baking tray, cover with a damp cloth and leave to prove in a warm place until doubled in size (this should take about 40 minutes).

Meanwhile heat your oven to 230°C/ Fan 220°C/Gas Mark 8. Sprinkle the surface of the loaf with flour and bake for 25 minutes, or until it sounds hollow when tapped on the base. Transfer to a wire rack and leave to cool completely.

To make the breadcrumbs
Slice the bread and lay on a tray in a warm place to dry out. Once dry, blitz in a food processor to rough breadcrumbs. Set aside ready to use.

To cook the cuttlefish
Cut the cuttlefish into 2cm slices, pat dry and season with salt and pepper. Heat a large frying pan and add a drizzle of olive oil. When the oil is hot, fry the cuttlefish in 2 or 3 batches to avoid overcrowding the pan, for 1 minute, turning occasionally. Add the onions, garlic, peppers and paprika to the pan and cook, stirring often, for 2 minutes.

Return all the cuttlefish to the pan, pour in the cider and fish stock and bring to a simmer. Cook gently for 1 hour until the cuttlefish is tender. Remove the cuttlefish from the pan with a slotted spoon and set aside on a plate; strain and reserve the liquor.

To prepare the cuttlefish fritter mix
Melt the butter in a saucepan over a medium heat. Stir in the flour to make a roux and cook, stirring, for 5 minutes. Gradually whisk in the reserved liquor, keeping the mixture smooth. Continue to cook for a few minutes until you have a smooth, thick sauce. Remove from the heat.

...continued on page 24

Chop the cooked cuttlefish into smaller pieces and stir into the sauce. Taste for seasoning, adding salt and pepper if you think it needs it. Spread the cuttlefish mixture out on a tray and leave to cool, then cover with cling film and place in the fridge to chill thoroughly for at least 2 hours.

To shape and crumb the fritters
Spoon the cuttlefish mixture into 18 equal-sized mounds on a tray or plate and then, using wet hands, roll the mounds into balls. Place the balls back in the fridge to firm up.

Put the extra flour into one bowl, the beaten eggs into another and the breadcrumbs into a third bowl. Season the flour with salt and pepper. Take the cuttlefish balls from the fridge. Pass them, one at a time, first through the flour, then into the egg and finally into the breadcrumbs, turning to coat thoroughly all over, then place on a tray. Once all the cuttlefish balls are coated, place the tray in the fridge if preparing ahead, or leave to one side if you're cooking the dish straight away.

To make the wild garlic soup
Heat a medium saucepan and add a generous drizzle of olive oil. When it is hot, add the onion and cook for 1 minute, without colouring. Add the potato and then pour in the vegetable stock. Simmer for about 10 minutes

until the potato is cooked. Tip the contents of the pan into a blender.

Place a frying pan over a medium-high heat and add a little olive oil. When it is hot, fry the wild garlic in a few batches for about 1 minute until wilted and add to the blender.

Blitz everything together until smooth, then season with salt and pepper to taste. Unless serving straight away, chill the soup over ice to retain its vivid green colour.

To cook the fritters
When you are ready to eat, preheat your oven to 200°C/Fan 180°C/Gas Mark 6. Heat the oil for deep-frying in a deep-fryer or other suitable deep, heavy pan to 180°C. When it is hot, deep-fry the cuttlefish balls in batches for 2 minutes until crisp. Drain on kitchen paper and place on a tray in the oven for 1 minute.

To assemble and serve
While the cuttlefish balls are in the oven, tip the soup into a saucepan and reheat over a medium heat. Taste for seasoning again and adjust if necessary. Share the soup equally between 6 warmed soup plates and place 3 cuttlefish fritters in the centre of each. Drizzle some lemon and garlic oil around the soup and finish with a few wild garlic flowers if you have them. Serve at once.

The first decent lobsters of the year from the Port Isaac area are landed at this time of year. The weather can still be rough, so we don't always get them, but when they are available the quality is very good. You don't come across globe artichokes often and I'm not their biggest fan, but that's to do with their fiddly preparation; they are delicious to eat. As a young chef, I would be reprimanded if my artichokes weren't perfectly turned (trimmed) and white inside when you cut them, and that's stayed with me! There are many factors that influence discolouration, not least how long it is since the artichokes were harvested – something you have no control over unless you grow them yourself or know someone close by who does. Lemon juice helps to prevent discolouration, but if you use too much, it overpowers the delicate taste of the artichoke. This dish is good warm or cold. Personally, I prefer it hot, but I have served it cold for a big party before and everyone loved it.

LOBSTER, GLOBE ARTICHOKE, PEA AND MINT PURÉE

Serves 4 as a starter

2 live Cornish lobsters,
  600–700g each,
  placed in the freezer
  for 30 minutes
  before cooking
Cornish sea salt
  and freshly ground
  black pepper

For the herb mayonnaise
2 large egg yolks
2 teaspoons Dijon
  mustard
juice of ½ lemon
300ml light olive oil
2 tablespoons each
  parsley, chives and
  tarragon, chopped

For the pea and
mint purée
light olive oil
  for cooking
50g unsalted butter
1 small onion, peeled
  and finely chopped
2 garlic cloves, peeled
  and finely sliced
1kg peas in their pods,
  freshly podded
200ml vegetable stock
  (see page 288)
a large handful of
  mint leaves

For the globe artichoke
4 globe artichokes
juice of 1 lemon
1 small onion, peeled
  and sliced
2 garlic cloves, peeled
  and sliced
light olive oil
  for cooking

For the mint and
coriander dressing
3 anchovy fillets in
  oil, drained
25ml lime juice
50g coriander leaves
50g mint leaves
about 150ml olive oil

For the garnish
200g peas in their pods,
  freshly podded
herb leaves

First make the herb mayonnaise
Put the egg yolks, mustard and lemon juice into a bowl and whisk together for 10 seconds. Now slowly pour in the olive oil in a thin, steady stream, whisking continuously until it is all incorporated and you have a thick mayonnaise. Season with salt and pepper to taste, then add the chopped herbs and mix well. Cover and place in the fridge until needed.

To cook the lobsters
Bring a large pan of water (big enough to hold the lobsters) to the boil and add plenty of salt (the water really needs to be as salty as the sea to ensure that the flavour of the lobster isn't lost during cooking). Lower the heat so the water is at a steady simmer.

Take your lobsters from the freezer and place them on a board. Insert the tip of a strong, sharp knife firmly into the cross on the back of each lobster's head. (The lobster will be killed instantly, although it may continue to move a little; this is normal.)

Carefully pull the lobster tail away from the head and remove the claws too. Add the claws to the pan of simmering water and cook for 2 minutes, then add the tails to the pan and cook for another 3 minutes. Immediately remove all the lobster from the pan and leave until cool enough to handle.

To prepare the lobsters for serving
Using a sharp knife, cut the lobster tails in half lengthways and remove the dark intestinal thread that runs the length of the tail. At this stage the lobster should be still raw in the middle. Crack the claws and extract the meat, keeping it intact as far as possible. Trim the tail and claw meat and cut into neat pieces; save the trimmings. (Save the shells for stock.)

Gather all of the lobster trimmings on a board and chop them, then place in a bowl with 1 tablespoon of the herb mayonnaise and mix well. Cover and refrigerate until needed. Place all the lobster pieces on a tray and drizzle with a little olive oil. Set aside, ready to be grilled.

...continued on page 28

To make the pea and mint purée
Heat a large pan and add a drizzle of olive oil. When it is hot, add the butter and onion and sweat for 1 minute. Add the garlic and cook for another minute, then toss in the peas. Cook for a further minute and season with salt and pepper. Pour in the vegetable stock and cook until the peas are soft, about 8 minutes.

Add the mint, then transfer the contents of the pan to a blender and blitz until smooth. Scrape the pea and mint purée into a bowl and set it over a larger bowl of iced water to cool quickly and help keep the vivid colour. When cold, cover and place in the fridge until needed.

To prepare and cook the artichokes
Fill a pan, large enough to hold the artichokes after trimming, with water. Add the lemon juice and a good pinch of salt. Trim the artichokes, removing the base and inedible leaves, then add to the pan, with the onion, garlic and 2 tablespoons olive oil. Bring to a simmer and cook the artichokes until soft in the centre, anywhere from 20–40 minutes, depending on age. Remove from the heat and leave the artichokes to cool in the liquor. Refrigerate until ready to finish the dish.

Before serving, using a spoon, gouge out the hairy, inedible choke from the centre of each artichoke, then trim to neaten if required.

For the mint and coriander dressing
Place all the ingredients in a blender and blitz thoroughly for 2–3 minutes until emulsified and smooth. Season with a little salt to taste. Cover and refrigerate until needed.

To prepare the garnish
Add the peas to a pan of boiling salted water and blanch for a few minutes until just tender. Drain and refresh in ice-cold water. Drain the peas well and toss them with a little of the coriander and mint dressing.

To prepare for serving
Preheat your grill to low. Heat a generous splash of olive oil in a frying pan. When hot, add the artichoke hearts and fry briefly, turning them carefully, so they take on some colour. In the meantime, grill the lobster pieces for 1–2 minutes until just cooked. Gently heat up the pea and mint purée in a pan.

To assemble and serve
Spoon the lobster mayonnaise into the artichoke hearts. Spoon the mint and pea purée onto 4 warmed plates, dividing it evenly.

Place an artichoke heart on each portion of purée and arrange the cooked lobster on top. Finish with the fresh peas, some mint and coriander dressing and a few herb leaves.

FISH AND SEAFOOD
A chef's challenge

Fish and seafood may be a popular choice for diners, but the number of people who cook it fresh, at home, is still relatively small. And for those who do, the 'go-to' dishes most often involve cod, salmon or tuna, which isn't even fished around Britain's shores. As a child, it was no different for me. The fish we ate was cod – usually in the form of fish fingers or in batter with chips! – so how did I come to specialise in fish and seafood cookery?

My first job as a young chef was in London, with the late Peter Kromberg at the Intercontinental Hotel on Hyde Park Corner. It was here, working with chefs from all over the world, that I began to appreciate the wealth of fish and seafood species available and the variety of different ways you could prepare and cook them. It fuelled my imagination and gave me a desire to learn more.

In the mid 90s, while I was still working in London, Rick Stein hit the television screens with his programmes on seafood cookery. I realised that if I could work with Rick I could learn so much about cooking fish and seafood in the UK, so I applied for a job at The Seafood Restaurant in Padstow. Luckily, I got it! My first year in the kitchen was spent endlessly prepping fish, which at the time I found tedious, but I now know it was the best training I could have had!

At The Seafood Restaurant, I was mentored by then Head Chef Paul Ripley. Paul's wealth of knowledge and Rick's enthusiasm for all things food in general was inspirational. I also talked to local fishermen, as I was keen to find out how they handled the fish and seafood before it arrived in our kitchen, and learn about the fishing industry in general.

It was at Padstow that I first became aware of the need for sustainability – something that is crucial to my ethos now. And I became increasingly focussed on seasonality, which continues to be an important element in my cooking.

When asked why I have chosen to cook fish and seafood exclusively, I say it's because it presents a lot of challenges, which I find exciting and stimulating. It's never dull!

We tend to forget that the fish caught in the seas are wild animals, swimming in different locations, in different conditions and eating slightly different things. The physical condition of a fish depends on how much swimming it has done, the quality of water it has lived in and the type and quality of food it has consumed. Each piece of fish will therefore be a little different, and will need to be assessed individually and prepared and cooked accordingly. That's no mean feat when the result must be perfect every time!

Sustainability is vital for the future, so I use fish which is caught in the waters around Cornwall from small day boats, employing sustainable techniques. This is a challenge as many of our fishermen go out alone and, if the weather is bad, it can be too dangerous for them to do so. During the winter months, supplies can be scarce so we preserve fish, such as herring, in our kitchens to put on the menu when the need arises.

Coaxing customers to eat different species of fish is another challenge. Some are willing to experiment, but many are cautious of eating things they've never had before, or that have given them a bad experience in the past. The challenge is to find different ways to serve the fish that will entice them to try it. For instance, many of those who say they don't like oysters will eat them when they are shucked, deep-fried and presented as crispy oysters, because of the change of appearance and texture.

It's surprising how many people come along saying they're not keen on fish, but change their minds after dining at our restaurants. Of course, the fact that all of our fish and seafood is as fresh as it could be is a major factor.

With all these challenges to face each day, I find that cooking fish and seafood is always exciting and rewarding. I can honestly say that no two services are ever the same!

With most of my dishes, Mother Nature does the hard work for me. All I have to do is respect the ingredients, bring them together and cook them with care and passion. To my mind, there is a reason why this dish works so well. Plaice, as a fish, loves to smash mussels from the rocks using its hard mouth. So, naturally, the earthy sweetness of plaice pairs well with sweet and slightly bitter mussels. I picture samphire growing on the edge of the estuary nearby, too. Maybe that is just in my imagination but I'd like to think this is how it plays out!

PLAICE WITH MUSSELS AND SAMPHIRE

Serves 4 as a
main course

2 plaice, about 1kg
    each, filleted
    and trimmed
olive oil for cooking
Cornish sea salt
    and freshly ground
    black pepper

For the mussels
1kg live mussels,
    cleaned and
    de-bearded
1 shallot, peeled and
    chopped
1 garlic clove, peeled
    and chopped
1 bay leaf
200ml white wine
100g plain flour
2 large eggs, beaten
200g panko
    breadcrumbs
sunflower oil for
    deep-frying

For the mustard oil
200ml light olive oil
2 tablespoons English
    mustard powder

For the sauce
2 large egg yolks
30ml white
    wine vinegar
1 teaspoon English
    mustard
a pinch of saffron
    strands
300ml light olive oil
saved mussel cooking
    liquor (see recipe)

For the garnish
2 leeks, trimmed and
    well washed
200g samphire, washed
    and picked of any
    woody bits
sea aster, if available,
    or flat-leaf parsley

First make the mustard oil (a day ahead)
Whisk the olive oil and mustard powder together in a bowl to combine. Pour into a container, cover and leave to stand for 24 hours. Decant the oil into a bottle, leaving the sediment behind. It is now ready to use.

To prepare the plaice for grilling
Preheat your grill to high. Lightly oil the grill tray and sprinkle with salt. Lay the plaice fillets on the tray, skin side down, and sprinkle with salt, then turn over, so the skin is on top. Make sure they are not touching or they'll stick together as they cook.

To prepare the mussels
Place a large saucepan (one with a tight-fitting lid) over a medium-high heat. When hot, add the mussels, shallot, garlic, bay leaf and wine. Put the lid on and steam the mussels for 3 minutes or until they have opened. Tip into a colander over a bowl to catch the liquor (for the sauce). When the shells are cool enough handle, pick out the meat and place in a bowl. Discard the shells and any unopened mussels. Leave to cool, then place in the fridge unless using straight away.

To make the sauce
Put the egg yolks, wine vinegar, mustard and saffron into a bowl and whisk together for 30 seconds. Slowly, in a steady stream, add the oil whisking constantly until it is all incorporated. Add enough of the reserved mussel cooking liquor to thin the mayonnaise to a sauce consistency. Season with salt and pepper to taste. Transfer to a pan.

To breadcrumb the mussels
Have the flour, eggs and breadcrumbs ready in separate bowls. One by one, pass the mussels through the flour, then the eggs and finally the panko crumbs to coat. Set aside on a tray.

To prepare for serving
Preheat your grill to the highest setting. Heat the oil for deep-frying in a deep-fat fryer or other suitable pan to 180°C. Gently warm the sauce over a low heat; don't let it boil.

For the leek and samphire garnish
Bring a pan of salted water to the boil, add the leeks and simmer for 4 minutes, then remove with a slotted spoon. Add the samphire to the water and simmer for 1 minute; drain. Slice the leeks on an angle into 1cm pieces.

To cook the fish and serve
Place the tray of fish fillets under the grill and cook for 3 minutes; they will overcook easily, so watch carefully. At the same time, deep-fry the mussels in the hot oil for 2 minutes until crisp. Drain on kitchen paper and season with salt and pepper.

Spoon the sauce onto warmed plates and arrange 2 plaice fillets on top. Add the leeks and samphire and finish with the breaded mussels, sea aster and a drizzle of mustard oil.

So often sidelined by Mr Dover, the lemon sole is sadly neglected and misunderstood, but not by me. It is tasty and delicate, needing only the lightest of cooking – a few minutes and it's ready. To show its qualities to the full, I'm cooking the fish two ways here: grilled and deep-fried. Grilled lemon sole is pure and simple, while the fried fish is juicy and crisp. The green sauce mayo is addictive … you have been warned!

LEMON SOLE AND SALSIFY WITH GREEN MAYONNAISE

Serves 4 as a main course

2 lemon sole, 700–800g each, scaled, filleted and trimmed
olive oil for cooking
100g gluten-free self-raising flour
100ml soda water
oil for deep-frying
Cornish sea salt and freshly ground black pepper

For the green mayonnaise
1 shallot, peeled and finely chopped
1 garlic clove, peeled and finely chopped
2 anchovy fillets in oil, drained and chopped
2 teaspoons capers, drained and chopped
1 teaspoon English mustard
2 large egg yolks
finely grated zest and juice of 1 lemon
2 tablespoons chopped parsley
2 tablespoons chopped mint
2 tablespoons chopped rocket leaves
1 tablespoon chopped basil
300ml light olive oil

For the salsify
400g salsify
juice of ½ lemon
50g unsalted butter
1 garlic clove, peeled and crushed
3 sprigs of thyme

For the herb butter
100g unsalted butter
2 tablespoons mixed chopped herbs including parsley, chives, tarragon and chervil
a few drops of lemon juice

First make the green mayonnaise
Put the shallot, garlic, anchovies, capers and mustard into a food processor and blitz for 30 seconds. Add the egg yolks, lemon zest and juice and blitz again for 30 seconds. Add all the chopped herbs and blend briefly. Now with the motor running on a low speed, slowly add the olive oil in a thin, steady stream through the feeder tube until the mixture is emulsified and thick. Taste the mayonnaise and season with salt. Transfer to a container, cover and refrigerate until required.

To prepare the salsify
Peel the salsify and cut into 5–7cm lengths, immersing them in a bowl of cold water with the lemon juice added as you do so to prevent discolouration. Transfer the salsify to a pan and pour on enough of the lemon water to cover. Add the butter, garlic, thyme and a good pinch of salt. Bring to a simmer and cook for 10–15 minutes, until the salsify is tender. Remove with a slotted spoon and allow to cool.

To prepare the lemon sole for cooking
Preheat your grill to the highest setting. Oil the grill tray and season it with salt. Lay the 4 brown-skinned lemon sole fillets on the tray, skin side down, and sprinkle with salt, then turn the fillets over, so the brown skin is uppermost.

Remove the white skin from the other 4 fish fillets. In a bowl, mix the flour with the soda water to make a smooth, light batter and season with salt. Heat the oil for deep-frying in a deep-fryer or other suitable deep, heavy pan to 180°C.

For the herb butter
Just before cooking the fish, warm the butter in a pan and add the herbs and lemon juice. Season with salt to taste. Keep warm.

To finish the salsify
Heat a frying pan over a medium heat and add a drizzle of oil. When hot, add the salsify and fry, turning, for a minute or so, until golden and lightly caramelised. Keep warm.

To cook the fish
Dip the skinned fish fillets into the batter to coat them all over, then carefully transfer to the hot oil and deep-fry for 2 minutes. At the same time, place the tray of fish fillets under the grill and cook for 2–3 minutes, depending on thickness.

As soon as the fried fillets are ready, remove them from the oil and drain on kitchen paper, then sprinkle with salt and pepper. When the grilled fillets are cooked, remove them from the tray and carefully peel off the skin. Season with a little salt.

To serve
Place a grilled lemon sole fillet on each warmed plate and arrange the salsify alongside. Spoon over the herb butter sauce and top with a deep-fried lemon sole fillet. Finish with a generous spoonful of green mayonnaise and serve at once.

I love profiteroles! Some of my fondest childhood memories are of stuffing my face with them when my parents had parties at home, or when we would go to the local Beefeater. I admit they are not exactly helping my waistline, but I can't resist them.

This recipe is fantastic. We top the choux buns with a shortbread crumble mix that cooks to a lovely crunchy topping. The mousse filling is more like a bavarois, a classic enriched set custard, to which we add a hint of orange and malt. The chocolate sauce, served warm over the top of the buns, is just naughty … there's no other way to describe it.

MALTED ORANGE PROFITEROLES AND BITTER CHOCOLATE SAUCE

Serves 6

For the crumble topping
125g unsalted butter, softened
150g demerara sugar
150g plain flour

For the choux pastry
160g plain flour
125ml water
125ml whole milk
125g unsalted butter
4g sea salt
4g caster sugar
250g beaten eggs (about 5 large eggs)
egg wash (1 medium egg, beaten with 1 tablespoon milk)

For the malted orange filling
2 sheets of bronze leaf gelatine
5 large egg yolks
120g caster sugar
50g Horlicks (malted milk drink powder)
400ml double cream
finely grated zest of 1 large orange
260g cream cheese

For the chocolate sauce
225ml double cream
50ml water
50ml Cointreau
100g caster sugar
190g dark chocolate (70% cocoa solids), chopped into small pieces

To finish
1 orange, for zesting

To make the crumble topping
Put the butter and demerara sugar into a stand mixer fitted with the paddle attachment and mix on a medium speed until light and well combined. Add the flour and mix on a low speed until fully incorporated. Turn the mixture out onto a floured surface and roll out to the thickness of a £1 coin. Lift the sheet of dough onto a tray and freeze for an hour or so (to make it easier to handle once cut). When frozen, cut out discs, using a 3cm plain cutter. Place the discs on a tray in the freezer until you are ready to cook the choux buns.

To make the choux pastry
Sift the flour onto a piece of baking parchment. Put the water, milk, butter, salt and sugar into a medium saucepan and bring to the boil over a medium heat. When the butter has melted and the liquid is boiling, add the flour all at once and stir well to combine. Turn the heat down low and cook out the dough for 10 minutes, stirring occasionally. Remove the pan from the heat and beat thoroughly for about 2 minutes until it comes away from the sides of the pan.

Gradually beat the beaten eggs into the choux mix; ensure each addition is fully incorporated before adding the next. When it is all incorporated and the mixture is smooth and shiny, transfer it to a large piping bag fitted with a 1cm plain nozzle.

To shape the choux buns
Pipe small mounds of the choux pastry onto a tray, 3cm across and 2cm high, leaving space in between for them to expand. Brush the choux mounds with egg wash. Place the tray in the freezer until the buns are completely frozen. (You can then transfer them to a suitable container and keep them in the freezer until ready to cook.)

To bake the choux buns
Preheat the oven to 195°C/Fan 175°C/Gas Mark 5–6. Line a baking tray with a non-stick baking mat or silicone paper. Lay a shortbread crumble disc on top of each choux bun and bake for 30 minutes until golden brown. When you remove the tray from the oven, make a small hole on the underside of each choux bun to allow the steam to escape. Place the buns on a wire rack and leave to cool. Store them in an airtight container until needed.

For the malted orange filling
Soak the gelatine in a shallow dish of ice-cold water to soften. Put the egg yolks, sugar and Horlicks into a stand mixer fitted with the whisk attachment and whisk together until very pale and fluffy. In a saucepan, bring the cream and orange zest to

…continued on page 38

a simmer. Squeeze out the excess water from the gelatine then add it to the whisked egg mixture as you pour on the hot cream, whisking constantly to dissolve the gelatine. When the mixture is fully combined, place in the fridge to cool and set for about 2 hours. At this point, take your cream cheese out of the fridge and set aside to soften.

Once the base mousse is set, whisk in the cream cheese and then transfer the mixture to a piping bag fitted with a small plain nozzle, ready to pipe before serving (refrigerate if preparing ahead).

To make the chocolate sauce
Put the cream, water and Cointreau into a pan and add the sugar. Heat slowly to dissolve the sugar and then bring to a simmer. Take off the heat, give the mixture a good whisk and add the chocolate. Whisk until melted and smooth. Keep the sauce warm if you are serving it straight away or pour into a container, leave to cool and then refrigerate (ready to reheat before serving).

To assemble and serve
Pipe the mousse into the choux buns through the hole in the base of each. Place 4 filled profiteroles on each serving plate and pour over some hot chocolate sauce. Grate over a little orange zest and serve straight away.

When it comes to fruit in spring there isn't much about in Cornwall or, in fact, anywhere in the UK, so I resort to tropical climes to create my desserts at this time of the year. This lime tart is wonderfully zingy and the roasted banana ice cream goes perfectly. On those all-too-frequent, dull, rainy, spring days, it brings a ray of sunshine.

LIME TART, MERINGUE AND ROASTED BANANA ICE CREAM

For the sweet pastry
200g unsalted
 butter, diced
180g icing sugar, sifted
1 large egg
140g egg yolks (roughly
 6 large yolks)
500g plain flour, plus
 extra to dust

For the lime filling
600ml double cream
finely grated zest of
 2 limes
200ml lime juice
8 large eggs
200g caster sugar

**For the roasted banana
ice cream**
6 medium bananas
600ml whole milk
200ml double cream
8 large egg yolks
150g demerara sugar
2 vanilla pods, split
 lengthways and seeds
 scraped out

For the crisp meringue
2 medium egg whites
100g caster sugar
1 teaspoon cornflour

For the Italian meringue
240g caster sugar
100g liquid glucose
40ml water
4 large egg whites

To finish
icing sugar to sprinkle
finely grated lime zest

To make the pastry
Using a stand mixer or electric hand mixer, cream the butter and icing sugar together in a bowl until pale and fluffy. Lightly beat the egg and egg yolks together, then gradually beat into the creamed mixture. Add the flour and stop mixing as soon as a dough is formed.

Tip the dough onto a lightly floured surface and knead briefly until smooth. Divide in half, shape each piece into a ball and flatten to a disc. Wrap both pastry discs in cling film. Place one in the fridge to rest for at least 30 minutes; freeze the other to make a tart for another day.

For the roasted banana ice cream
Preheat your oven to 220°C/Fan 200°C/Gas Mark 7. Roast the bananas in their skins for 1 hour. When cool enough to handle, peel the bananas; you need 300g roasted banana flesh. Put this flesh into a food processor with the milk and cream and blitz until the mixture is well combined, then transfer to a saucepan and bring to a simmer.

Meanwhile, in a large bowl, whisk the egg yolks, sugar and vanilla seeds together until light and fluffy. Pour on the hot banana mixture, whisking constantly until smooth.

Stand the bowl over a larger bowl of ice to cool the mixture quickly, then pour into an ice-cream machine. Churn until frozen and then transfer to a suitable container and place in the freezer until ready to serve.

To shape and bake the tart case
Roll the chilled pastry out on a floured surface to the thickness of a £1 coin and use to line a loose-based 25cm round tart tin, pressing it firmly into the edges of the tin and making sure there are no holes or cracks. Leave a little excess pastry extending above the rim. Prick the bottom of the pastry case with a fork several times.

Line the tart case with a scrunched-up piece of greaseproof paper and add a layer of baking beans. Place in the fridge to rest for 20 minutes. Meanwhile, preheat your oven to 200°C/Fan 180°C/Gas Mark 6.

Bake the pastry case in the oven for 15 minutes, then remove the baking beans and paper and return the tart case to the oven for 5 minutes until golden and cooked.

Take the tart case out of the oven and brush the inside well with egg wash. Return to the oven for 2 minutes to set the egg wash. Place the tart case on a wire rack to cool; do not remove it from the tin at this stage. Lower the oven setting to 130°C/Fan 110°C/Gas Mark 1.

To make the lime filling
Pour the cream into a saucepan, add the lime zest and juice and bring to a simmer over a medium heat. In the meantime, whisk the eggs and

...continued on page 42

sugar together in a bowl. Pour on the hot cream mixture and whisk to combine. Pass the mixture through a fine sieve into a large jug and allow to cool.

To bake the tart

Once the filling has cooled, stand the tart tin on a baking sheet in the oven and carefully pour the custard mixture into the pastry case. Bake for 25–30 minutes until the custard is set with a slight wobble in the middle. Remove from the oven and allow to cool. Trim off the excess pastry, crumble a little of it and reserve for serving.

For the crisp meringue

Heat your oven to 130°C/Fan 110°C/ Gas Mark 1 and line a baking sheet with a non-stick silicone mat or baking parchment. Wipe your stand mixer bowl (or other bowl) with kitchen paper dipped in vinegar to remove any trace of grease. Using a stand mixer or electric hand whisk, beat the egg whites with one-third of the sugar to soft peaks. Add another third of the sugar and whisk for 2 minutes, then add the remaining sugar and whisk for 30 seconds. Using a large metal spoon, carefully fold in the cornflour.

Spoon the meringue onto the lined baking sheet and spread out evenly, using a cranked palette knife. Bake in the oven for 1 hour until crisp. Transfer to a wire rack to cool. Once the meringue is cool, break it up into pieces and keep in an airtight container until needed.

To make the Italian meringue

Put the sugar, liquid glucose and water into a heavy-based saucepan and bring to a simmer. Let the sugar syrup bubble steadily until it registers 120°C on a sugar thermometer. Meanwhile, wipe your stand mixer bowl with kitchen paper dipped in vinegar to remove any trace of grease. When the sugar syrup reaches about 115°C, whisk the egg whites in the mixer bowl on a medium speed until soft peaks form, but don't overmix.

When the sugar syrup is at 120°C, pour it in a steady stream onto the egg whites with the mixer on full speed. Turn the speed to low and continue to mix until the meringue is cooled. Transfer to a piping bag and refrigerate until needed.

To finish the tart

Sprinkle the icing sugar over the surface of the tart and caramelise evenly, using a cook's blowtorch. Sprinkle with lime zest and then, using a hot, sharp knife, cut the tart into 10 slices.

To serve

Place a slice of lime tart on each plate and pipe a dome of Italian meringue alongside. Place some crisp meringue pieces on top of the dome. Create a small pile of reserved pastry crumbs on the plate and place a neat spoonful of roasted banana ice cream on top. (The crumbs will stop the ice cream sliding on the plate.) Serve at once.

As a child, my favourite biscuit was a custard cream and it still is to this day, so when we set about making this recipe the expectation was high. It took a few attempts, but we got there in the end and I'm really happy with the final result … I have eaten enough of them to know!

SHORTBREAD CUSTARD CREAMS

For the shortbread
250g unsalted butter
80g caster sugar, plus
  extra to dust
330g plain flour
1 tablespoon cornflour
a pinch of fine sea salt

For the custard filling
150g icing sugar
15g custard powder
75g unsalted butter

To make the shortbread
Beat the butter and sugar together in a food processor until pale and fluffy. Add the flour, cornflour and salt and mix on a low speed until the mixture comes together and forms a dough. Wrap in cling film and leave to rest at cool room temperature for 1 hour.

Roll out the shortbread on a floured surface to a 1cm thickness. Lift onto a tray and place in the fridge to rest for 30 minutes. Meanwhile, preheat the oven to 180°C/Fan 160°C/Gas Mark 4 and line a baking sheet with a non-stick silicone mat or baking parchment.

Using a 3cm plain cutter, cut the shortbread into discs and place on the prepared baking sheet. Bake for 16–18 minutes until golden. Remove the shortbread biscuits from the oven and sprinkle with extra caster sugar.

Transfer the shortbread rounds to a wire rack and leave to cool, then store in an airtight container until needed.

To prepare the custard filling
Cream all the ingredients together until light, fluffy and incorporated. Transfer to a piping bag and keep in a cool place until you are ready to serve the biscuits.

To assemble the custard creams
Pipe some custard filling onto the centre of a shortbread disc and sandwich together with another disc. Repeat with the rest of the shortbreads. Serve the custard creams at room temperature.

Late Spring

THE LOCATION
Port Isaac

Port Isaac, on the north Cornish coast, is a tiny village with a huge history, most of it linked to the sea. It is not a destination you pass through on a journey elsewhere, you need to make a special detour to get here, but it's worth the effort!

In modern times, its popularity first as a picturesque and quaint coastal holiday destination, and more recently as the fictional Port Wenn in the *Doc Martin* TV series has meant that it has become one of the most visited places in Cornwall.

The 'old village' in the area around the harbour contains around ninety houses listed for their architectural and historical importance. Many date from the eighteenth and nineteenth centuries and were fishermen's cottages but there are also chapels, a school and fish cellars. Most buildings are whitewashed or cladded in granite slate and sit on steep, narrow, winding streets such as the fantastically named Squeezy Belly Alley. However, many of them today are holiday lets. In fact, the population of Port Isaac swells in the summer months almost threefold.

Once a busy harbour where ships had docked since the Middle Ages, to carry stone, coal, timber, salt, pottery and the famous slate from nearby Delabole, it quietened down after the Industrial Revolution with the introduction of larger ships that couldn't gain entrance to the narrow harbour. Finally, the introduction of better transport links by rail and road at the beginning of the twentieth century meant an end to Port Isaac's role as a trade port.

However, the fishing industry, which was first registered in 1340, has been vibrant throughout history and remains an important feature of the village. Port Isaac boasts a small fishing fleet, its fishermen focussing on a catch of crab and lobster which are attracted to the sheltering rocks around its coastline. Port Isaac harbour is, in fact, one of the very few safe places to moor along an otherwise rough and hostile coast.

The people of Port Isaac are a tight-knit community, many having links with its fishing heritage. Nowadays, as well as fishing, many of the locals are employed in the tourism business and they are well accustomed to the change that takes place in the village during the summer months. In addition, there are a number of artists working in the village, often depicting aspects of the sea and coastline in their work.

One reminder of Port Isaac's fishing heritage is the local singing group, The Fishermen's Friends, which has gained national recognition for its renditions of traditional Cornish songs and sea shanties. The members of the group are all linked to fishing in some way. Port Isaac also boasts an RNLI station, which has been in operation for around 100 years, the current D-class inshore lifeboat being launched on missions around the north Cornwall coastline.

The area surrounding Port Isaac is one of lush, green fields, many visible on the steep hills surrounding the centre of the village. Designated as an Area of Outstanding Natural Beauty and recognised as having a heritage coastline, it is a haven for walkers and those wanting to 'get away from it all'.

Restaurant Nathan Outlaw sits on the cliff above the harbour with panoramic views across both the bay and the surrounding fields. The setting is magical. While dining in the restaurant, it is often possible to watch the fishermen out on their boats, bringing in the catch that will soon be cooked and presented to diners. What better place to have a fish and seafood restaurant?

In late spring the fisherman in Port Isaac catch great crab. In particular, we get good-sized male cock crabs and spider crabs. I like to serve them freshly cooked and picked as a nibble, so customers can fully appreciate their quality. Something so simple is pure joy for me. The scones have a hint of fennel seed and cheese, and the crab meat is bonded with mayonnaise. Finished with a touch of lemon, peppery, freshly sliced radishes and pea shoots, they are dressed to impress.

CRAB SCONES

Makes 10–15 canapés

1 large live brown
  crab, about 1kg,
  placed in the freezer
  for 30 minutes
  before cooking
Cornish sea salt
  and freshly ground
  black pepper

For the mayonnaise
2 large egg yolks
1 tablespoon brown
  crab meat (from the
  crab above)
juice of 1 lemon
300ml light olive oil

For the scones
225g self-raising flour,
  plus extra to dust
4g sea salt
55g unsalted butter, cut
  into small cubes, plus
  extra for greasing
25g mature Cheddar
  cheese, freshly grated
4g fennel seeds
150ml whole milk, plus
  extra for brushing

To garnish
1 lemon, peeled (all pith
  removed), segmented
  and sliced
3–4 radishes, thinly
  sliced
a few pea shoots

To cook and prepare the crab

Bring a large pan of water (big enough to hold the crab fully submerged) to the boil. Season the water generously with salt, to make it as salty as sea water. Once it comes to a rolling boil, lower the crab into the water and cook for 14 minutes.

Carefully lift the crab out of the pan, place on a tray and leave until cool enough to handle. Remove all the legs and claws from the cooked crab, by twisting them away from the body. Now, holding the crab in both hands, use your thumbs to push the body up and out of the hard, top shell or carapace. Remove and discard the dead man's fingers, stomach sac and hard membranes from the body shell.

Using a spoon, remove the brown crab meat from the carapace and place it in a bowl.

Cut the body in half, using a sharp knife, to reveal the little channels of white crab meat. Use a crab pick or the handle of a spoon to pick out all the crab meat from these crevices and put it into a separate bowl.

Using a heavy knife, break the claws with one hard tap if possible and pick out the white meat, prising out the cartilage from the middle of the claw. Do the same with the legs to extract the meat. Once you have extracted all the white meat, with clean hands, pick through it to search for any shell or cartilage. Refrigerate if preparing ahead or just set aside while you make the mayonnaise. (To me, crab is always best eaten freshly prepared.)

For the mayonnaise

Place the egg yolks, brown crab meat and lemon juice in a bowl and whisk to combine. Slowly add the olive oil in a thin, steady stream, whisking constantly until it is all incorporated. Season with salt and pepper to taste. Add enough of the mayonnaise to the white crab meat to combine.

To make the scones

Using a stand mixer fitted with the paddle attachment, mix the flour, salt, butter, cheese and fennel seeds together. With the mixer on a low speed, slowly add the milk and mix until the ingredients come together as a dough; do not overwork. Transfer to a lightly floured surface and gently roll out the dough to a 3cm thickness.

Line a baking tray with baking parchment. Using a 5cm plain cutter, stamp out rounds from the dough and place on the lined tray; don't twist the cutter or you'll get misshaped scones. Brush the scones with milk and place in the fridge to rest for 30 minutes.

Meanwhile, preheat your oven to 220°C/Fan 200°C/Gas Mark 7. Bake the scones for 12 minutes until they are golden and sound hollow when tapped on the bottom. Transfer them a wire rack and leave to cool.

To assemble and serve

Once cooled, slice the scones in half and spoon on the white crab, then some of the brown crab. Top with a few slices of lemon segment, sliced radishes and pea shoots. Just before serving, add a twist of black pepper and a few flakes of sea salt.

Gilt head bream is my favourite fish to eat raw. It tastes almost buttery and the texture is wonderfully soft. I like to slice it thinly, but not so finely that your taste buds can't grasp the amazing flavour. The dressing makes good use of the pea pods that you'd usually throw away. When juiced, the flavourful pods make a great base for a dressing for raw fish, especially bream. If you can't find bream, then you can prepare the same dish with bass, brill or scallops.

RAW WILD GILT HEAD BREAM WITH PEA AND MINT

Serves 6 as a starter

2 wild gilt head bream,
about 750g each,
filleted, pin-boned
and skinned
Cornish sea salt

For the mint oil
100g mint leaves
300ml light
rapeseed oil

For the pea dressing
700g peas in their pods,
freshly podded, pods
well washed and saved
½ cucumber, peeled and
roughly chopped
20ml agrodolce vinegar

To garnish
200g full-fat Greek-
style yoghurt
a handful of blanched
freshly podded peas
dill leaves

First prepare the mint oil
If possible, do this a day ahead. Bring a pan of salted water to a simmer and have a bowl of iced water ready. When the water is simmering, add the mint and blanch for 20 seconds. Immediately scoop out the mint and plunge it straight into the iced water to cool quickly. Drain and squeeze out excess water. Put the mint into a blender with the rapeseed oil and blitz for 2 minutes. Transfer to a container, cover and refrigerate for at least 3–4 hours, ideally overnight.

To prepare the bream
Simply trim off anything that doesn't look nice and slice the fish fillets evenly, laying the slices straight onto serving plates or into shallow bowls (about 10 each). Cover and place in the fridge.

For the pea dressing
Put the clean pea pods and cucumber into a blender and blitz thoroughly for 2 minutes.

Line a fine sieve with damp muslin and set over a bowl. Strain the pea pod juice through the muslin and squeeze out all the juice into the bowl. Set aside (or place in the fridge if you're not serving straight away).

To finish the dressing
Measure 6 tablespoons pea juice into a bowl and add the agrodolce vinegar with a pinch of salt. Stir to combine, then add 4 tablespoons mint oil and mix well. Taste to check the seasoning and set aside.

To finish and serve
Stir the yoghurt in a bowl until smooth then spoon into a piping bag fitted with a 1cm nozzle.

Spoon the pea and mint dressing equally between the slices of fish and scatter over the fresh peas. Pipe 4 or 5 little blobs of yoghurt on each portion (don't overdo it) and top each with a dill leaf. Serve at cool room temperature, not fridge-cold.

In the late spring the fishermen in Port Isaac throw out their cuttlefish traps. Over the past few years they have been very successful at it, which is fortunate for me as I adore cuttlefish. In my opinion, it is better than its mate Mr Squid. Here, the cuttlefish is cooked two ways: slow-braised, which in turn produces an amazing sauce, and pan-fried, which takes just 10 seconds. The idea for this dish came to me when I was out fishing and saw a lobster pot pulled up, with both lobsters and cuttlefish inside. As they were attracted to the same bait, I thought perhaps they might taste good together. Well, I can confirm that they do! I wouldn't say this is an easy dish to cook, but it's definitely worth the effort.

LOBSTER AND CUTTLEFISH WITH RED PEPPER SAUCE

Serves 6 as a starter

For the braised cuttlefish
1kg cuttlefish, cleaned
light olive oil for cooking
1 white onion, peeled
    and finely diced
2 garlic cloves, peeled
    and chopped
2 flamed red peppers
    in brine, deseeded
    and chopped
1 tablespoon thyme
    leaves
500ml cider
3 plum tomatoes, halved
500ml water
1 tablespoon chopped
    parsley
Cornish sea salt
    and freshly ground
    black pepper

For the lobster
3 live Cornish lobsters,
    600–700g each,
    placed in the freezer
    for 30 minutes
    before cooking

For the red pepper dice
1 large red pepper

For the fried cuttlefish
200g cuttlefish, cleaned
light olive oil for cooking

For the smoked paprika oil
3 teaspoons smoked
    paprika
250ml light
    rapeseed oil

To garnish
sea aster, if available,
    or flat-leaf parsley

First make the smoked paprika oil (a day ahead)
Sprinkle the smoked paprika into a dry frying pan and toast over a medium heat for 1–2 minutes until it releases its aroma; don't let it burn. Pour the oil into the frying pan and immediately remove from the heat. Give it a good stir and then pour into a jug. Leave to infuse and settle for 24 hours. Decant into a container and seal. The oil will keep in the fridge for up to 3 months.

For the braised cuttlefish
Cut the cuttlefish into 2cm slices and pat dry. Heat a large saucepan over a high heat and add a drizzle of olive oil. When it is hot, add the onion, garlic, red peppers and thyme and cook for 2 minutes. Pour in the cider, add the tomatoes and bring to the boil. Let it bubble over a medium heat until reduced by half. Pour in the 500ml water and bring to the boil.

Heat a frying pan over a high heat and add a drizzle of olive oil. When the oil is hot, fry the cuttlefish in batches, to avoid overcrowding the pan. Cook each cuttlefish batch for 2–3 minutes, season with salt and pepper, then transfer to a colander to drain.

Now add the cuttlefish to the cooking liquor and bring to a simmer. Cook gently for 1½–2 hours, until tender. When the cuttlefish is tender, drain off the cooking liquor into another pan and reduce it over a medium heat to a sauce-like consistency. Chop the cuttlefish into smaller pieces and add them back to the reduced sauce. Keep warm until ready to serve, or allow to cool if you are preparing ahead.

To cook the lobsters
Bring a large pan of water (big enough to hold the lobsters) to the boil and add plenty of salt (the water really needs to be as salty as the sea to ensure that the flavour of the lobster isn't lost during cooking). Lower the heat so the water is at a steady simmer.

Take your lobsters from the freezer and place them on a board. Insert the tip of a strong, sharp knife firmly into the cross on the back of each lobster's head. (This will kill it instantly, although it may still move a little.)

Carefully pull the lobster tail away from the head; remove the claws too. Add the claws to the simmering water and cook for 2 minutes, then

...continued on page 56

add the tails to the pan and cook
for another 3 minutes. Immediately
remove all the lobster from the pan
and leave until cool enough to handle.

For the red pepper dice
While the lobster is cooling down,
spear the red pepper on a fork and
scorch over a gas flame, turning until
blackened all over. (If you don't have
a gas hob, blacken under a grill on its
highest setting.) Put the pepper into
a small bowl, cover with cling film
and leave for 10 minutes to allow the
steam to loosen the skin.

Scrape away the skin from the pepper
with a small knife; don't rinse it or
it will lose flavour. Halve the pepper
and remove the core and seeds. Cut
the flesh into 1cm dice. Set aside.

To prepare the lobsters for serving
Using the heel of a knife, crack the
point where the claws meet the
knuckles and remove the meat from
the shell. Crack open the claws and
extract the meat. Hold the tail firmly
with both hands and crack it flat.
Placing your hands either side of the
lobster, pull it apart. Cut through
the centre of the tail at an angle to
remove the dark intestinal tract.
Trim all the tail and claw meat into
neat pieces and keep to one side until
ready to serve. If you're not serving

the lobster straight away, refrigerate.
(Save the shells for stock.)

For the fried cuttlefish
Slice the cuttlefish as thinly as
possible into strips and season with
salt and pepper. Place in a bowl and
toss together with a generous splash
of olive oil.

To prepare for serving
Preheat the grill to low. Oil the
lobster pieces and season with salt
and pepper. Pop under the grill to
warm through.

Meanwhile, gently heat up the
cuttlefish stew and add the chopped
parsley and two-thirds of the
red pepper dice (save the rest for
garnishing the dish).

Heat a large frying pan over a high
heat until hot, then add a drizzle of
oil. When it is hot, carefully add the
raw cuttlefish strips and cook for
10 seconds, then immediately remove
from the pan and drain.

To assemble and serve
Share the braised cuttlefish among
6 warmed plates and top with the
fried cuttlefish and warm lobster.
Finish with sea aster (or parsley),
a few pepper dice and a drizzle of
smoked paprika oil.

I sometimes think that the salmon we get now is too dull to serve at the restaurant and, let's face it, it can be. Wild salmon was given to us by the food gods, but unfortunately, we've abused it and we are now paying the price. We do have local salmon swimming nearby in the Camel Estuary, but fishing them is forbidden, so I buy good-quality farmed salmon instead. So how do we make it taste amazing? Cure it, of course… This dish is actually very simple. It calls for the finest quality ingredients, great seasoning and balance, that's it. Give it a go!

CURED SALMON, SEAWEED SALAD CREAM AND CUCUMBER RELISH

Serves 6

To cure the salmon
800g very fresh, wild
  or organic farmed
  salmon, trimmed
  and skinned
100g sea salt
100g soft brown sugar
150ml dry white wine

For the seaweed salad cream
2 large egg yolks
2 tablespoons dried
  seaweed powder (or
  flakes blitzed to a
  powder in a blender)
2 teaspoons English
  mustard
2 teaspoons caster
  sugar
2 tablespoons
  lemon juice
200ml light olive oil
100ml double cream
Cornish sea salt
  and freshly ground
  black pepper

For the cucumber relish
1 large cucumber
½ green chilli, deseeded
  and finely chopped
1 small shallot, peeled
  and finely chopped
1 garlic clove, peeled
  and finely chopped
50ml cider vinegar
50g soft brown sugar
1 teaspoon fennel seeds

To garnish
dill leaves

To cure the salmon
Lay the fish on a tray and sprinkle evenly with the salt and brown sugar. Turn the fish over in the cure a few times to ensure it is coated all over. Drizzle the white wine evenly over the fish, then wrap the whole tray in cling film and place in the fridge to cure for 6 hours.

When the salmon curing time is up, wash off the cure under cold water and then pat the fish dry. Wrap the fish tightly in fresh cling film and place back in the fridge for 3 hours to firm up.

To make the seaweed salad cream
Whisk the egg yolks, dried seaweed, mustard, sugar and lemon juice together in a bowl for 1 minute, then gradually whisk in the olive oil, a little at a time, until fully incorporated. To finish, slowly whisk in the cream and season with salt and pepper to taste. Put the salad cream into a piping bag and keep in the fridge until required.

To make the cucumber relish
Grate the cucumber into a sieve and then squeeze the cucumber flesh with your hands to remove as much liquid as you can. Put the cucumber into a clean bowl and add the chilli, shallot and garlic.

Heat the cider vinegar, brown sugar and fennel seeds in a pan over a medium heat until the sugar has dissolved, then pour the mixture over the cucumber. Mix together well and season with salt and pepper to taste. Leave to cool. Once the relish has cooled, it's ready to serve.

To assemble and serve
Unwrap the cured salmon and cut it into even, thin slices. Lay neatly on individual serving plates. Pipe a little blob of salad cream on each salmon slice and top with a dill leaf. Place a small pile of cucumber relish on each slice too. Serve at cool room temperature, but not fridge-cold. If you have any cured salmon left over, it freezes beautifully.

I love asparagus. It is the only vegetable that has had its own spot on the menu, although we did serve it with a clam dressing. In this dish, the asparagus goes perfectly with the sweetness from the scallops. As you'd expect, we only use top-quality scallops that are hand-dived rather than dredged, which damages the sea bed.

I'm not a big fan of those gigantic scallops that you can get, as they are inclined to overcook on the outside before the centre is done. I prefer to use medium-sized scallops for dishes cooked in this way, saving the large ones for slicing and curing in raw dishes.

The hazelnut butter is an old faithful of mine. It's been used to top many different fishes. Here, the hazelnut flavour is great with the other components, especially the smoked hollandaise sauce.

SCALLOPS, ASPARAGUS, SAMPHIRE AND SMOKED BUTTER HOLLANDAISE

Serves 4 as
a main course

12 live medium
scallops, removed
from the shell
and cleaned
light olive oil for cooking
Cornish sea salt
and freshly ground
black pepper

For the hazelnut butter
150g blanched
whole hazelnuts
1 tablespoon
caster sugar
100g unsalted butter,
at room temperature
2 tablespoons chopped
flat-leaf parsley
2 tablespoons
chopped chives

**For the smoked butter
hollandaise**
250g smoked butter
3 large egg yolks
juice of ½ lemon, or
to taste
cayenne pepper,
to taste

For the garnish
20 asparagus spears,
trimmed
100g samphire, washed
and picked

First make the hazelnut butter
Toast the hazelnuts in a dry frying pan for a minute or two until golden all over, then sprinkle with the sugar and allow them to colour. Transfer the nuts to a food processor and blitz until finely ground. Tip the nuts onto a plate and leave to cool slightly.

While the hazelnuts are still slightly warm, mix them with the butter and chopped herbs and season with salt and pepper to taste.

Spoon the hazelnut butter onto a sheet of greaseproof paper and form into a long sausage shape. Place another sheet of greaseproof paper on top and roll to form a more even log. Wrap in the paper, then chill in the freezer for an hour or so to firm up. (You will have more hazelnut butter than you need, but it can be kept in the freezer to use on another day.)

For the garnish
Bring a pan of salted water to the boil. Add the asparagus and blanch for 2 minutes, then remove and refresh in ice-cold water. Add the samphire to the boiling water and blanch for 10 seconds, then drain and refresh in the ice-cold water. Drain both vegetables and set aside.

To prepare for serving
Preheat your oven to 220°C/Fan 200°C/Gas Mark 7 and oil a baking tray. Slice 12 rounds of hazelnut butter, the thickness of a £1 coin, and set aside.

For the smoked butter hollandaise
Melt the smoked butter in a pan over a medium heat until it begins to bubble, then remove from the heat and leave to cool until tepid.

Meanwhile, put the egg yolks and lemon juice into a heatproof bowl over a pan of simmering water, making sure the base of the bowl isn't in contact with the water. Whisk the mixture until it thickens enough to leave a ribbon trail when you lift the beaters from the bowl. Remove the bowl from the pan.

Now slowly add the tepid butter, whisking constantly until it is all incorporated. Season the hollandaise with the cayenne and salt to taste. Add a little more lemon juice if you think it needs it. Keep warm while you finish the other components.

...continued on page 62

To cook the scallops

Heat a large non-stick frying pan over a medium-high heat. Add a drizzle of olive oil to the pan and season the scallops with salt. When the oil is hot, carefully lay the scallops in the pan, placing the side of the scallop down that would have been against the flat shell. Cook the scallops for 1½–2 minutes until golden on the underside.

Immediately remove the scallops from the pan and transfer to the oiled baking tray, coloured surface uppermost. Lay a slice of hazelnut butter on each scallop and place the tray in the oven. Cook the scallops for 2–3 minutes, depending on their size.

To finish the garnish

As you put the scallops in the oven, lay the asparagus and samphire on a baking tray, drizzle with oil and season with salt and pepper. Warm through in the oven for a few minutes.

To serve

Arrange the asparagus on 4 warmed plates and spoon on some warm hollandaise. Arrange the scallops on the plates, scatter over the samphire and serve straight away.

JAX BUSE
Our asparagus supplier

Asparagus is one of life's great pleasures. It is only available for a very short time, which is probably what makes it so special. Occasionally you might come across some growing wild on a remote Cornish cliff, but our supply comes from local grower Jax Buse of St Enodoc Asparagus. Jax starts harvesting her crop in April, and continues for just six weeks. Although this fine vegetable is grown all over the world, there is nothing quite like the flavour of British asparagus.

Revered for centuries, asparagus was used by the ancient Egyptians for medicinal purposes and presented as a gift for the gods. In ancient Rome, Emperor Augustus is said to have built a fleet of ships to transport the prized vegetable around the Roman Empire. The ancient Greeks loved it too.

In sixteenth century Britain, asparagus was known affectionately as 'sparrow's grass', the actual name 'asparagus' being derived from the Persian word for 'a shoot'. In a sixteenth century Arabian book of love, the vegetable is even heralded for its aphrodisiac properties!

Today, we value asparagus for its exquisite flavour and texture. It is also highly nutritious, providing a rich source of vitamins A, B1, C and K, and useful amounts of potassium, calcium and folic acid. In addition, asparagus is a natural diuretic and a good source of fibre. All these qualities packed into the wonderful little shoots!

Jax has been growing asparagus in Cornwall since 1991. Having a dairy farm, she found a need to diversify and began growing asparagus on ground in Trebetherick near Daymer Bay, where the soil and aspect lend themselves perfectly to the crop. Asparagus is very labour intensive. New plants take three years to mature and be ready to harvest, and the spears have to be cut by hand, which partly explains the cost of the vegetable and its luxury status.

After harvesting, the remains of the plants are left to grow into a 'forest of green', almost two metres tall. This dies down in the autumn, allowing the crowns to recover and fortify ready for the next crop. Jax now provides many of our local chefs with their annual supply, and has supplied our restaurants in Cornwall for several years.

Jax's crop couldn't be more local to Restaurant Nathan Outlaw. It is grown just five miles up the road, coming into the kitchen within a couple of hours of being cut, so the flavour and goodness are well preserved … we are so fortunate!

Jax's main aim is to grow a high-quality crop with intense flavour, and she does this admirably. Her small team shuns the use of poly-tunnels to bring on the crop, instead allowing it to grow naturally in its own time. The mild Cornish climate is ideal for this and the sea winds leave salty deposits on the land, which enhance the flavour of the asparagus as it grows. The natural shelter afforded by Brae Hill, and the warm spring breezes mean that Jax's crop is often ready to harvest several weeks before the asparagus grown naturally in other parts of the country.

So how should you choose asparagus? British asparagus should be a lovely delicate green. Look for tightly furled, firm tips and long, straight stems. The cut ends should look fresh rather than dried or shrivelled, as this suggests some of the sweetness and vitamin and mineral content will have been lost.

To prepare asparagus, simply bend along the lower end of the stem until it snaps off then rinse the spears and use as required, taking care not to overcook.

Delicious!

There is nothing wrong with battered haddock and chips, but if you haven't yet tasted grilled haddock you are really missing out. A fillet of haddock taken from a medium to large fish, seasoned simply with salt and pepper and grilled to perfection, has an amazing flavour.

This is a lovely seasonal dish. Young, tender broad beans are both added to a chowder sauce and served as a purée on the side. New potatoes are baked, then stuffed with smoked haddock mixed with the scooped-out potato, cheese and herbs, and baked again. The grilled haddock fillets sit atop the chowder sauce, all finished with parsley oil.

HADDOCK, BROAD BEANS AND SMOKED HADDOCK POTATOES

First prepare the parsley oil

If possible, do this a day ahead. Bring a pan of salted water to a simmer and have a bowl of iced water ready. Add the parsley to the simmering water and blanch for 20 seconds. Scoop out the parsley and plunge into the iced water to cool fast. Drain and squeeze out excess water. Put the parsley into a blender with the rapeseed oil and blitz for 2 minutes. Transfer to a container, cover and refrigerate for at least 3–4 hours, ideally overnight.

For the smoked haddock new potatoes

Preheat your oven to 220°C/Fan 200°C/Gas Mark 7. Put the potatoes on a baking tray and bake for 1 hour. When cool enough to handle, halve the potatoes and scoop out the flesh into a bowl, keeping the skins intact. Leave to cool until barely warm. Dice the smoked haddock and add it to the potato flesh with the cheese and parsley. Mix well and season with salt and pepper. Spoon the mixture back into the potato skins and place in a baking dish. Bake the potatoes for 30 minutes until crispy.

To make the broad bean purée

Bring a pan of salted water to the boil and have a bowl of ice-cold water ready. Add the broad beans to the boiling water and cook for 3 minutes. Drain and plunge into the cold water to cool quickly and keep their colour. Drain well. Tip the broad beans into a food processor and add the cream cheese, yoghurt and lime juice. Blitz for 3 minutes, then taste for seasoning and adjust with salt and pepper if needed. Spoon into a container. Keep the purée in the fridge, ready to reheat and serve.

To make the chowder sauce

Heat a saucepan over a medium heat then add a drizzle of olive oil and the butter. When the butter is melted and bubbling, add the shallot, leek, celery, garlic, thyme and bay leaf. Cook, stirring, for 3 minutes, to soften but not colour. Add the cider vinegar and simmer until reduced totally. Add the cider and fish stock and cook until reduced by half. Add the cream and potato and cook until the potato is tender. Remove and set aside.

To cook the haddock

Preheat the grill and oil the fish and grill tray. Season the fish well with salt and pepper. Grill skin side up, without turning, for 4–5 minutes. Leave to rest on the tray.

To assemble and serve

While the fish is grilling, reheat the broad bean purée. Heat up the sauce in a pan, then add the broad beans and parsley and heat for 30 seconds. Share the sauce among 4 warmed plates. Place 2 potato halves and a grilled haddock fillet on each plate. Add a generous spoonful of broad bean purée and finish with a drizzle of parsley oil. Serve at once.

Serves 4 as a main course

4 haddock fillets, about 200g each, trimmed and pin-boned
light olive oil for cooking
Cornish sea salt and freshly ground black pepper

For the potatoes
4 large new potatoes
150g smoked haddock fillet, skinned
20g Cheddar cheese, grated
1 tablespoon chopped parsley

For the broad bean purée
300g freshly podded young broad beans
100g full-fat cream cheese
100g full-fat Greek-style yoghurt
juice of 1 lime

For the chowder sauce
olive oil for cooking
50g unsalted butter
1 banana shallot, peeled and diced
1 leek, washed, trimmed and finely sliced
2 celery sticks, diced
2 garlic cloves, peeled and finely chopped
2 sprigs of thyme
1 bay leaf
50ml cider vinegar
100ml cider
200ml fish stock (see page 288)
200ml double cream
1 large potato, peeled and cut into 1cm dice
100g freshly podded young broad beans, cooked and skinned
1 tablespoon chopped flat-leaf parsley

For the parsley oil
100g flat-leaf parsley leaves
300ml light rapeseed oil

I like to put this style of dish on the menu in late spring, because it has a foothold in the summer and makes me excited for what's to come. Young courgettes, which become available now, are wonderful made into a purée with fennel and basil. The flavours are great together and go beautifully with the red mullet. Butterflying is my favourite way to prepare red mullet – it looks so impressive on the plate. The squid salad is lovely on its own, but when eaten together with the red mullet it's something else. Squid cooked this way – simply blanched in garlicky water and tossed in a dressing – is delicious, and it will keep in the dressing for 2–3 days in the fridge. This really is late spring on a plate!

RED MULLET, SQUID SALAD, COURGETTE AND FENNEL

First prepare the squid salad

Slice the squid into strips and set aside. In a saucepan, bring about 1 litre water to a simmer and season well with salt. Add the crushed garlic and simmer for 5 minutes. Meanwhile, pour the cider vinegar and olive oil into a bowl and add the sliced red onion and fennel.

Drop the squid into the simmering water and blanch for 10 seconds. Immediately drain and add to the onion and fennel mixture. Toss well to coat the squid and vegetables in the dressing. If preparing ahead, cover and place in the fridge, but bring back to room temperature before serving.

For the courgette and fennel purée

Heat a medium saucepan (that has a tight-fitting lid) over a medium heat and add a drizzle of olive oil and the butter. When the butter is melted and bubbling, add the onion and fennel and cook for 3 minutes without colouring. Add the courgettes and garlic and continue to cook until the courgettes start to collapse and release their liquid. Put the lid on the pan, turn the heat down low and cook the vegetables slowly for 10 minutes.

Season with salt and pepper and add the basil leaves. Transfer the contents of the pan to a blender and blitz for 3 minutes. Pour the purée

into a bowl and set over a larger bowl of iced water to cool quickly, stirring occasionally as it cools. Once the purée is cold, cover and refrigerate until needed.

For the roasted courgettes

Preheat your oven to 220°C/Fan 200°C/Gas Mark 7. Heat a large ovenproof frying pan over a medium-high heat and add a drizzle of olive oil. When the oil is hot, add the courgettes carefully, cut side down. Cook for 2–3 minutes until the underside is golden and lightly caramelised. Turn the courgettes over, season with salt and then transfer the pan to the oven. Bake for 8 minutes until the courgettes are tender right through (when tested with a knife). Slice the courgettes on an angle and place in a warmed dish. Keep warm until ready to serve.

To prepare for serving

Slice the 6 basil leaves and toss them through the squid salad. Season with salt and pepper to taste and leave to come to room temperature.

Gently warm the courgette and fennel purée in a pan over a low heat, then taste to check the seasoning and adjust as necessary.

...continued on page 70

Serves 4 as a main course

4 red mullet, about 400g each, scaled, gutted and butterfly filleted
light olive oil for cooking
Cornish sea salt and freshly ground black pepper

For the squid salad
2 medium squid, about 150g each
2 garlic cloves, peeled and crushed
50ml cider vinegar
100ml olive oil
1 red onion, peeled and finely sliced
1 fennel bulb, trimmed and finely sliced on a mandoline
6 basil leaves

For the courgette and fennel purée
light olive oil for cooking
30g unsalted butter
1 white onion, peeled and finely diced
1 fennel bulb, trimmed and finely sliced
2 medium courgettes, trimmed and finely sliced
2 garlic cloves, peeled and finely chopped
a bunch of basil, leaves picked

For the roasted courgettes
light olive oil for cooking
2 medium courgettes, halved lengthways

To cook the red mullet
Preheat your grill to medium-high and oil a grill tray large enough to hold all 4 butterflied red mullet. Oil the fish and season them all over with salt and pepper. Lay the fish skin side up on the grill tray and grill for 4 minutes. Try to get some nice colour and blistering of the skin (this not only looks good, it gives the skin a great flavour). Leave the fish to rest on the tray for 2 minutes; save any juices that collect in the grill tray.

To assemble and serve
Carefully place a butterflied red mullet on each of 4 warmed plates and add a generous spoonful of courgette and fennel purée. Using a slotted spoon, share the squid salad among the plates and top with the roasted courgette pieces. Add the cooking juices from the fish to the dressing left in the squid salad bowl. Trickle some of this dressing onto each plate and serve immediately.

At the end of spring, if we are lucky, we start to get some really good cherries from Spain, Greece and other warmer European countries, ahead of the short UK summer season. I really do like a good cherry. Classic flavour combinations like chocolate and cherry are always popular with our customers and this chocolate tart has been with me for a while now. I've tweaked it a bit over time, but I think this recipe is really great! The slightly salted pistachio ice cream, which has an almost savoury edge, is the perfect foil for the rich chocolate tart.

CHOCOLATE TART, CHERRIES, PISTACHIO ICE CREAM AND TUILES

Serves 10

For the chocolate pastry
150g unsalted butter
80g icing sugar
4 large egg yolks
1 tablespoon
  whole milk
175g plain flour
40g cocoa powder

For the chocolate filling
200ml whole milk
300ml double cream
2 large eggs
2 tablespoons
  caster sugar
410g dark chocolate
  (70% cocoa solids),
  chopped into
  small pieces

**For the pistachio
ice cream**
450ml whole milk
400ml double cream
150ml kirsch
8 large egg yolks
150g honey
100g roasted and salted
  pistachio nuts,
  shelled and blitzed
  in a blender to grind
  (but not too finely)

For the cherry compote
100g caster sugar
200ml water
400g fresh cherries,
  pitted

For the cherry jam
225g frozen dark
  cherry purée
190g caster sugar
5g pectin
5g tartaric acid

For the pistachio tuiles
125g unsalted butter
150g caster sugar
50g liquid glucose
40ml whole milk
15g cocoa powder
150g roasted and salted
  pistachio nuts, shelled
  and roughly chopped

For the pistachio ice cream
Pour the milk, cream and kirsch into a pan and bring to a simmer over a medium heat. Meanwhile, whisk the egg yolks and honey together in a bowl. Pour on the hot creamy milk, whisking as you do so. Place the bowl over a larger bowl of ice and stir the mixture as it cools. Transfer to an ice-cream machine and churn until almost set. Add the blitzed pistachios and continue to churn until frozen. Transfer the ice cream to a suitable container and place in the freezer.

To make the chocolate pastry
Using a stand mixer or electric hand mixer, cream the butter and icing sugar together in a bowl until pale and fluffy. Lightly beat the egg yolks in a separate bowl, then gradually beat them into the creamed mixture, along with the milk. Add the flour and cocoa together and stop mixing as soon as a dough is formed.

Tip the dough onto a lightly floured surface and knead briefly until smooth. Shape into a ball, flatten slightly and wrap in cling film. Chill in the fridge for at least 30 minutes.

For the cherry compote
Put the sugar and water in a medium pan and dissolve over a medium heat. Add the pitted cherries to the sugar syrup and simmer for 5 minutes. Remove from the heat and leave to cool. Reserve the cherries in the syrup until ready to serve.

For the cherry jam
Put the cherry purée and 180g of the sugar into a heavy-based pan and bring to the boil. Mix the pectin with the remaining 10g sugar, stir into the boiling mixture and cook until the temperature registers 106°C on a cook's thermometer. Whisk in the tartaric acid. Pour the mixture onto a tray and leave to cool. Blitz the cooled mixture in a blender until smooth, then transfer to a disposable piping bag and refrigerate until serving.

To shape and bake the pastry case
Roll the chilled pastry out on a lightly floured surface to the thickness of a £1 coin and use to line a rectangular tart tin, 25 x 10cm and 3cm deep (or, you could use an 18cm round tart tin, 3cm deep). Press the pastry firmly into the edges of the tin and make sure there are no holes or cracks. Trim off the excess pastry, crumble a little of it and reserve for serving. Put the tart case in the fridge to rest for 20 minutes. Preheat your oven to 200°C/Fan 180°C/Gas Mark 6.

Prick the base of the pastry case with a fork several times and line it with a scrunched-up piece of greaseproof paper and a layer of baking beans. Bake the pastry case for 15 minutes, then remove the paper and beans and return the tart case to the oven for a

...continued on page 74

further 5 minutes to cook the base. Place on a wire rack to cool; do not remove the tart case from the tin.

To make the chocolate filling

Lower the oven setting to 180°C/Fan 160°C/Gas Mark 4. Pour the milk and cream into a saucepan and bring to a simmer over a medium heat. Meanwhile, whisk the eggs and sugar together in a bowl. Add the chocolate, pour on the hot creamy milk and whisk to combine, until the chocolate is melted and the mixture is smooth.

To bake the tart

Pour the filling into the pastry case and bake in the oven for 20 minutes, until the filling is set. Allow the tart to cool before slicing. Lower the oven temperature to 170°C/Fan 150°C/ Gas Mark 3 (for the tuiles).

For the pistachio tuiles

Put the butter, sugar, liquid glucose and milk into a pan and heat slowly to melt the butter and dissolve the sugar, then bring to the boil. Cook until the mixture registers 110°C on a cook's thermometer. Add the cocoa and mix well, then incorporate the chopped pistachios. Transfer to a container, cover and chill for an hour.

Line a baking sheet with a non-stick silicone baking mat. Once the tuile mixture has firmed up, shape it into a log on a sheet of baking parchment, wrapping it in the paper to help roll it. Unwrap and slice thinly into 5mm slices. Lay on the prepared baking sheet and bake for 10 minutes until the mixture stops bubbling, but don't let the nuts colour too much. Slide the non-stick mat off the baking sheet onto a work surface. Leave the tuiles to cool and firm up, then carefully lift them off. Break into pieces to serve.

To assemble and serve

Using a sharp knife, cut the tart into slices and place a slice on each plate. Place a generous spoonful of cherry compote on the plate. Pipe a blob of cherry jam on top of each tart slice. Create a small pile of reserved chocolate pastry crumbs alongside and place a neat spoonful of pistachio ice cream on top. (The crumbs will stop the ice cream sliding.) Finish with a pistachio tuile or two.

Anyone who knows me well, knows that I'm a little obsessed with trifle. To me, it's the ultimate pudding. In a good trifle, the layers are pure joy. This sponge base has a delightful soft texture and a touch of sweetness from its swirl of rhubarb jam. The rhubarb and orange jelly gives a fresh fruitiness with a hint of acidity to cut the richness of the luscious, thick and creamy custard. Topped with whipped vanilla cream, tangy, sweet rhubarb and a sprinkling of toasted almonds, who can resist?

RHUBARB AND ORANGE TRIFLE

Serves 6

For the rhubarb jam
500g rhubarb, cut into
  2–3cm slices
50g unsalted butter
150g caster sugar
50g ginger beer

For the sponge
3 large eggs, plus
  3 large egg whites
15g caster sugar
100g icing sugar
100g ground almonds
30g plain flour
30g butter, melted

For the rhubarb and orange jelly
5 sheets of bronze
  leaf gelatine
400ml freshly squeezed
  orange juice
100ml water
300g caster sugar
400g rhubarb, cut into
  6cm pieces

For the custard
400ml whole milk
200ml double cream
8 large egg yolks
80g caster sugar
1 heaped tablespoon
  cornflour

For the whipped cream
400ml double cream
1 vanilla pod, split
  lengthways and seeds
  scraped out
60g icing sugar, sifted

To finish
80g flaked almonds,
  toasted

To make the rhubarb jam
Put the rhubarb into a pan with the butter, sugar and ginger beer. Cover and cook over a medium heat for about 10 minutes until the rhubarb is completely soft, then remove the lid. Cook until the liquor is reduced and syrupy. Allow to cool slightly, then blitz in a food processor until smooth. Transfer the rhubarb jam to a container and leave to cool.

To make the sponge
Preheat your oven to 220°C/Fan 200°C/Gas Mark 7. Lightly grease a 30 x 20cm Swiss roll tin and line with baking parchment.

Using an electric hand whisk, whisk the 3 egg whites in a very clean bowl to stiff peaks. Whisk in the caster sugar, a teaspoonful at a time, until it is all incorporated and the meringue is glossy. Cover the bowl with cling film and put to one side.

Using a stand mixer, whisk the icing sugar, ground almonds and whole eggs together for 4 minutes, until doubled in volume. Remove the bowl from the stand. Using a large metal spoon, carefully fold in the flour. Now gently and gradually fold in the meringue, a quarter at a time. Pour in the melted butter and fold through the mixture until incorporated.

Tip the mixture into the Swiss roll tin and gently level with a palette knife. Bake for 6 minutes, or until the sponge is pale golden brown and springy to the touch. Lay a sheet of

baking parchment on a wire rack and turn the sponge out onto it. Peel off the lining paper from the sponge and leave to cool.

To form the Swiss roll
Once cooled, spread the sponge with the rhubarb jam. With a long side facing you, roll up the sponge to enclose the jam and make a Swiss roll. Slice into rounds, about 4cm thick. Place a sponge round in each trifle serving glass.

To make the rhubarb and orange jelly
Soak the leaf gelatine in a shallow dish of ice-cold water to soften. Put the orange juice, water and sugar in a pan (big enough to take the rhubarb) and heat gently to dissolve the sugar. Add the rhubarb, bring slowly to a simmer and cook gently for 4 minutes until it is tender but still holding its shape. Lift the rhubarb out of the pan with a slotted spoon and set aside on a plate; cover and leave to cool.

Pour the juice from the pan into a measuring jug. You need 500ml to make the jelly, so pour this amount back into the pan. Bring to just below simmering and remove from the heat. Immediately squeeze out the excess water from the gelatine, then add it to the hot juice and whisk until fully dissolved. Leave to cool.

...continued on page 78

Once cooled, pour the fruit juice over the sponge in the glasses and place in the fridge to set for at least an hour.

To make the custard
Pour the milk and cream into a heavy-based pan and slowly bring to the boil. In the meantime, whisk the egg yolks and sugar together in a large bowl and then whisk in the cornflour. As the creamy milk comes to the boil, pour it onto the egg mixture, whisking as you do so. Pour the custard back into the cleaned pan and cook, stirring continuously, over a medium heat until it thickens; do not allow to boil.

Pass the custard through a sieve into a bowl and cover the surface with cling film to prevent a skin forming. Leave the custard to cool completely.

When the custard is cold, take the trifle glasses from the fridge and pour the custard on top of the jelly. Return the trifles to the fridge to set the custard.

For the whipped cream
When the custard is set, pour the cream into a medium-large bowl and add the vanilla seeds and icing sugar. Whisk until soft peaks form.

To finish and serve the trifles
Take the trifles from the fridge and spoon or pipe the cream on top of the custard. Drain the rhubarb pieces, pat dry and arrange on top of the cream. Scatter over the toasted flaked almonds to serve.

These little ice cream sandwiches are a great finish to a meal. The raspberries we get at the restaurant have such an amazing flavour that I never want to discard any. Even the older and ugly ones (which happen to be much tastier anyway) get blitzed up and put into the freezer to make a purée for these beauties. The base recipe also works well with blackberries, blueberries and strawberries.

Makes about 20 (petit four sized)

RASPBERRY ICE CREAM SANDWICH

For the raspberry ice cream
300g raspberries, puréed and sieved, or 280g frozen raspberry purée
400ml double cream
5 large egg yolks
120g caster sugar
260g cream cheese, at room temperature

For the brandy snaps
70g unsalted butter
140g caster sugar
70g honey
70g plain flour

For the raspberry ice cream
Pour the raspberry purée into a saucepan and bring to a simmer over a medium heat. Cook until reduced to a quarter of the original volume. Pour in the cream, stir to combine and bring back to a simmer. Meanwhile, whisk the egg yolks and sugar together in a bowl until pale and fluffy. Pour on the hot raspberry cream, whisking as you do. Leave to cool, then refrigerate for 30 minutes or so to chill.

Line a 30 x 15cm freezerproof tray with a double layer of cling film (or use a silicone tray of rectangular moulds). Put the cream cheese into a bowl and whisk in the cold raspberry mixture. Pour the mixture into the lined tray (or moulds) and level with a palette knife. Freeze until firm. (Once frozen, the ice cream will keep well in the freezer for up to 2 weeks.)

To make the brandy snaps
Preheat the oven to 190°C/Fan 170°C/Gas Mark 5 and line a baking tray with baking parchment. Melt the butter, sugar and honey together in a pan over a medium heat. Remove from the heat, add the flour and mix well. Pour the mixture into a bowl and leave to cool.

Lay a sheet of baking parchment on your work surface and spoon the cooled brandy snap mixture onto the middle of it. Lay another sheet of parchment on top. Using a rolling pin, roll out the mixture thinly and evenly between the sheets of parchment, then lift off the top parchment and invert the mixture onto the lined tray. Peel off the paper that is now on top.

Put the tray into the oven and cook for 10 minutes, or until the brandy snap sheet starts to turn golden and bubble. Remove the tray from the oven and leave to stand for 2 minutes.

Now, with a large knife, mark your required biscuit shapes. (If you've used moulds for the ice cream, the biscuits will need to be the same size.) Leave the brandy snap to cool. Once cooled, the biscuit should snap where marked.

To assemble and serve
If you've frozen the ice cream in a tray, turn out onto a board and cut to the size of your brandy snaps. Sandwich the raspberry ice cream bars together with the brandy snaps. Serve straight away, while the ice cream is still frozen!

Early Summer

In early summer we usually start to see large catches of mackerel. It's my favourite fish so I'm always pleased to welcome the fisherman. The combination of mackerel and gooseberry is a classic and these nibbles are seriously tasty, with the rich smokiness of the mackerel working well with the zingy gooseberry pickle. We cure and smoke the mackerel ourselves, which is a lovely thing to do if you have time. This recipe makes plenty of fritters, but trust me, that won't be an issue!

SMOKED MACKEREL FRITTERS AND **GOOSEBERRY PICKLE**

Makes 20 fritters

For the smoked mackerel
2 large mackerel,
   gutted and filleted
100g fine sea salt
75g caster sugar
oak chips for smoking

For the fritter mix
light olive oil
   for cooking
1 small leek (white and
   pale green part only),
   thoroughly washed
   and finely sliced
1 banana shallot,
   peeled and finely
   chopped
2 garlic cloves, peeled
   and finely chopped
2 large baking potatoes
finely grated zest of
   1 lemon
2 tablespoons chopped
   flat-leaf parsley
Cornish sea salt
   and freshly ground
   black pepper

For the coating
100g plain white flour
2 eggs, beaten
150g panko
   breadcrumbs

For the gooseberry pickle
1kg gooseberries,
   topped and tailed
2 banana shallots,
   peeled and finely
   chopped
250ml cider vinegar
150ml dry cider
260g golden
   caster sugar
1 teaspoon fennel seeds
2 bay leaves
2 sprigs of thyme,
   leaves picked
2 teaspoons sea salt
2 cooking apples,
   peeled, cored
   and grated

To finish
dried seaweed powder
flat-leaf parsley

To cure the mackerel
Lay the mackerel fillets on a large tray. In a bowl, mix the salt and sugar together well. Sprinkle evenly over the fillets and turn them a few times to ensure they are evenly coated. Place in the fridge to cure for 1 hour.

To make the gooseberry pickle
While the mackerel is curing, put all the ingredients for the pickle, except the apples, into a large heavy-based saucepan and bring to a simmer. Cook gently until the gooseberries are soft, about 10 minutes. Drain the gooseberries in a sieve over another pan to save the liquor. Place the pan over a medium heat and reduce until the liquor becomes syrupy. Add the grated apples and continue to cook until the liquor turns syrupy again. Add the cooked gooseberries to the pan and cook for another 10 minutes. Season with salt and pepper to taste. Allow the pickle to cool and refrigerate until needed.

To cook the potatoes for the fritter mix
Preheat your oven to 200°C/Fan 180°C/Gas Mark 6 and bake the potatoes for 1 hour until cooked.

To smoke the mackerel
Wash off the cure and pat the fillets dry. Set up your smoker with the oak chips to hot smoke and get it smoking well (or you can cold smoke the fish, then grill it). Place the fish on the smoking rack and smoke for 10 minutes or until cooked. Remove from the smoker and leave to cool,

then peel off the skin. Flake the fish into a bowl, cover and refrigerate.

To prepare the fritter mix
Heat a frying pan over a medium heat then add a drizzle of olive oil. When it is hot, add the leek, shallot and garlic. Cook, stirring, for a few minutes, to soften the vegetables until they become translucent. Take off the heat and allow to cool.

Cut the baked potatoes in half and scoop out the flesh. Pass it through a potato ricer into a large bowl or mash smoothly, using a hand masher. Add the sweated veg, lemon zest, chopped parsley and smoked mackerel. Mix together well, seasoning with salt and pepper to taste. Shape the mixture into balls, the size of a golf ball, rolling them neatly. Place on a tray and allow to cool then refrigerate for at least 30 minutes to firm up.

To deep-fry the smoked mackerel balls
Have the flour, beaten eggs and panko breadcrumbs ready in three separate bowls. Heat the oil for deep-frying in a deep-fat fryer to 180°C. Pass the balls through the flour, then the egg and finally the breadcrumbs to coat. Deep-fry in the hot oil in batches for 3 minutes until crispy. Drain on kitchen paper and season with salt and seaweed powder.

To serve
Serve the mackerel fritters hot, with the gooseberry pickle on the side and parsley sprigs to garnish.

I have been cooking fish for a while now, so it takes something special to get me really excited, but when large wild gilt head bream turn up in our waters, I'm so, so excited.

These fish are seriously special and have a fantastic texture and flavour. At their best, the flesh is firm to touch, yet as soft as butter when you eat it. All you need to do is sprinkle slices of the fish with sea salt and dress them with the tomato dressing below. If you come across large, wild gilt head bream, buy them at any cost!

RAW GILT HEAD BREAM, TOMATO WATER AND SAMPHIRE

Serves 4 as a starter

1kg very fresh gilt head bream, about 1kg, scaled, filleted, pin-boned and skinned
Cornish sea salt and freshly ground black pepper

For the dressing
6 very ripe, juicy plum tomatoes (or similar)
1 medium-hot red chilli, deseeded and chopped
1 garlic clove, peeled and sliced
3 tablespoons extra virgin olive oil

For the salad cream
2 large egg yolks
4 teaspoons creamed horseradish
1 teaspoon caster sugar
2 tablespoons lemon juice
300ml light olive oil
50ml double cream

For the garnish
a couple of handfuls of samphire, picked and washed
6 small ripe tomatoes, skinned and deseeded

First make the tomato dressing
Put the tomatoes, chilli and garlic into a food processor with some salt and pepper and pulse 4 times. Place a muslin-lined sieve over a bowl and tip the contents of the food processor into it. Place in the fridge and allow the juice to drip naturally from the blitzed tomatoes, for up to 6 hours.

To make the salad cream
Put the egg yolks, horseradish, sugar and lemon juice into a bowl and whisk together for 1 minute. Gradually add the olive oil, drop by drop to begin with and then in a steady stream, whisking constantly, until it is all incorporated. Finally, whisk in the cream and season with salt and pepper to taste. Transfer to a disposable piping bag and refrigerate until needed.

For the garnish
Bring a small pan of water to the boil and add the samphire. Blanch for 10 seconds then drain and refresh in a bowl of ice-cold water. Drain the samphire well.

Halve and deseed the small tomatoes, then cut the flesh into petal shapes; set aside.

To finish the dressing
Take the tomato juice from the fridge and measure out 5 tablespoons into another bowl. Add the extra virgin olive oil and whisk to combine. Taste the dressing and season with a little sea salt if you wish.

To prepare the fish
Trim away any bits of the fish that look tough and sinewy. Now slice the fillets across, at a slight angle towards the tail end, laying the slices directly onto 4 serving plates.

To finish the dish
Pipe a small dot of salad cream on each slice of fish and arrange the tomato petals and samphire on top. Finish with the tomato dressing, spooning it all over the fish and samphire. Serve immediately.

CORNWALL
A food lover's paradise

As a child, I loved our family holidays in Cornwall – camping in the dunes just outside Hayle near St Ives was bliss. Back then, I used to dream of living in Cornwall. That dream became a reality when I moved to Padstow to work with Rick Stein. At the time, I didn't know why Cornwall was such a magnet for chefs and foodies, but now I appreciate the features that make it such an amazing place to live and work.

Situated at the furthest south-western tip of mainland Britain, Cornwall boasts the most southerly point at The Lizard and the most westerly at Land's End. Bounded on three sides by sea, it is a long, narrow peninsular with a coastline of almost 300 miles, Rugged and steep to the north with dramatic scenery, yet gentle to the south with pretty villages and traditional coastal resorts, it has been popular with holidaymakers for many years.

For centuries, the Cornish way of life has been entwined with the sea and it still is today in many communities, through fishing and, more recently, hospitality. Inland, lush, green pastures provide grazing for cattle and sheep, giving us milk and meat of the finest quality. Bodmin Moor is home to cattle, sheep and ponies, and its mysterious landscape is a haven for walkers by day and stargazers at night.

Generally, Cornwall is milder than the rest of the UK and the land rarely freezes. This means that crops such as new potatoes, strawberries and asparagus come to harvest slightly earlier than elsewhere in the country. It is also wetter than many other areas, because of its proximity to the Atlantic Ocean, hence the lush pastures.

The seas around the Cornish coast are home to an abundance of fish species, affording conditions that are cold enough for the likes of cod but warm enough for the occasional sunfish, gilt head bream and triggerfish, too.

Cornwall's heritage of fishing and farming, along with tin mining, are what its communities have been built on. A rich and varied history has made Cornwall unique in many ways. In bygone years, smugglers and wreckers would lure unsuspecting ship's captains onto the rocks to wreck the ship so they could help themselves to the cargo. The booty was often fine foods and drinks being transported from the Continent and further afield. No wonder Cornish folk developed a taste for fine foods!

Cornwall has its own language, which is still used by some and can be seen on various road signs and in the names of many villages. Local people are proud of their heritage and you will often see the Cornish flag flying.

Not everything is steeped in the past, there is forward thinking, too. Cornwall was the place where transatlantic phone cables and internet first entered the UK, and the Goonhilly telecommunications station continuously relays signals and data from its satellites in space. Soon, the county could also become the site for the first commercial space launch pad.

Foodwise, Cornwall is probably best known for its pasties. Family recipes are jealously guarded but they're traditionally filled with beef, swede, potato and onion. Deliciously rich, thick clotted cream is another speciality, but Cornish food is about so much more these days. In recent years, there has been an upsurge of artisan producers in Cornwall, most of them using ingredients local to the area. All manner of excellent cheeses are produced, home-grown meats are turned into Cornish salamis and sausages, and locally made jams and chutneys can be found at every Farmers' Market. In addition, Cornish sea salt is produced on the south coast, seaweeds are farmed all around the coastline and even tea is being grown at the Tregothnan Estate.

With everything Cornwall has to offer, not least the finest fish and seafood, there is no better venue for Restaurant Nathan Outlaw … and nowhere else I'd rather be. It's perfect!

This isn't the traditional salt cod that you buy, it's my lighter version. I salt cod to draw out the excess water it often has, which firms up the flesh and improves its structure. Blitzing fennel seeds into the salt gives a lovely aniseed flavour that works well with the dish.

Lobster scampi is a bit of a play on words too. Scampi is the familiar name for langoustines or Dublin Bay prawns – typically crumbed and served with chips in a basket as pub food. I enjoy scampi and chips, so I decided to mimic the scampi with some of our finest Cornish lobster – slicing it into pieces the size of scampi and deep-frying them in batter. We sometimes get lobsters that are either too big to be served alone or have a claw missing – both are ideal for a dish like this. The sauce is a take on my signature Porthilly crab sauce, using lobster instead of crab and ramped up with some aniseedy fennel.

Serves 4 as a starter

For the salt cod
600g thick cod fillet, pin-boned and skinned
100g sea salt
4 teaspoons fennel seeds

For the lobster sauce
olive oil for cooking
150g unsalted butter, diced
1 fennel bulb, trimmed and roughly chopped
1 tomato, halved and grilled
1 litre lobster stock (see page 290)
1.5 litres fish stock (see page 288)
a pinch of saffron strands
Cornish sea salt and freshly ground black pepper

For the mayonnaise
2 egg yolks
2 teaspoons Dijon mustard
juice of ½ lemon
300ml light olive oil

For the lobster cocktail and scampi
1 live Cornish lobster, about 600g, placed in the freezer for 30 minutes before cooking
2 teaspoons chopped dill
100g gluten-free self-raising flour
120ml soda water, chilled
sunflower oil for deep-frying
smoked paprika to dust

To serve
4 portions of tenderstem broccoli

SALT COD, LOBSTER SCAMPI AND **LOBSTER SAUCE**

To salt the cod
Put the salt and fennel seeds into a spice blender or small food processor and blitz for 2 minutes. Tip the fennel salt into a container (that will take the cod). Add the cod and turn to coat all over. Place in the fridge for 1 hour. Wash the salt off the fish thoroughly and then pat dry. Wrap the cod fillet tightly in cling film and leave in the fridge for 3 hours to firm up.

To prepare the lobster sauce
Heat a large pan over a medium-high heat and add a drizzle of olive oil and the butter. When the butter is melted and bubbling, add the fennel and tomato. Cook for 5 minutes. Pour in the stocks, add the saffron and bring to the boil. Simmer for about 1 hour to reduce to a sauce consistency. Tip the contents of the pan into a blender and blitz until smooth, then pass the sauce through a sieve if required. Taste for seasoning, adding salt and pepper as required. Set aside.

For the mayonnaise
Put the egg yolks, mustard and lemon juice into a bowl and whisk together for 10 seconds, then slowly pour in the olive oil, whisking constantly until fully incorporated. Season with salt and pepper to taste. Cover and refrigerate until needed.

To cook the lobster
Bring a large pan of water (that will hold the lobster) to the boil and add plenty of salt (the water needs to be as salty as the sea to ensure that the flavour of the lobster isn't lost during cooking). Lower the heat so the water is at a steady simmer.

Take your lobster from the freezer and place it on a board. Insert the tip of a strong, sharp knife firmly into the cross on the back of the lobster's head. (The lobster will be killed instantly, although it may continue to move a little; this is normal.)

Carefully pull the lobster tail away from the head and remove the claws too. Add the claws to the pan of simmering water and cook them for 2 minutes, then add the tail to the pan and cook for another 2 minutes. Immediately remove all the lobster from the pan and leave until cool enough to handle.

To prepare the lobster for serving
Using a sharp knife, cut the lobster tail in half lengthways and remove the dark intestinal thread that runs

...continued on page 92

the length of the tail. At this stage
the lobster should be still partially
raw. Trim the tail and cut it into
12 pieces (3 per portion). Place these
on a tray in the fridge, ready to be
dipped in batter.

To make the lobster cocktail

Crack the claws and extract the
meat. (Save the shells for stock.) Chop
the claw and knuckle meat and place
in a bowl. Add about 2 tablespoons
of the mayonnaise and stir gently to
bind the lobster. Mix in the chopped
dill and season with salt and pepper
to taste. Cover and place in the fridge
until needed.

To prepare the lobster scampi

Line a tray with kitchen paper
ready to drain the scampi. Mix the
flour and soda water together in a
bowl to make a smooth batter and
season with salt. Heat the oil for
deep-frying in a deep-fryer or other
suitable deep, heavy pan to 180°C.
(You need to cook the fish and the
scampi at the same time.)

To cook the fish

Unwrap the salt cod and cut it into
4 equal portions. Heat a non-stick
frying pan over a medium heat and
add a drizzle of olive oil. When the
oil is hot, carefully place the fish
in the pan, presentation side down
(the side where the bone would
have been, not the skin side). Cook
gently for 3 minutes until golden,
then turn the fish over and take the
pan off the heat. The fish will finish
cooking in the residual heat of the
pan. While the fish is cooking, add
the tenderstem broccoli to a pan of
boiling salted water and cook for
3 minutes. Drain and keep warm.

To deep-fry the scampi

Dip the lobster tail pieces into the
batter to coat all over, then add to
the hot oil and deep-fry for 2 minutes
until golden and crisp. Drain on the
lined tray, season with salt and dust
with smoked paprika.

Heat the lobster sauce and pour some
onto each of 4 warmed plates. Place
a cod portion on each plate with a pile
of lobster cocktail next to it. Finish
with the lobster scampi, broccoli and
a drizzle of olive oil. Serve at once.

This dish is a real 'crowd pleaser'. The hand-dived scallops we get are amazing and taste so good simply pan-fried with a little salt. It takes a bit of time to prepare the braised fennel and broad beans, but they are worth it. You may find you have more fennel condiment than you need here but it is incredibly more-ish, so it won't be wasted, I promise!

Serves 4 as a starter

SCALLOPS, BRAISED FENNEL AND BROAD BEANS

12 live medium
  scallops, removed
  from the shell
  and cleaned
olive oil for cooking
Cornish sea salt
  and freshly ground
  black pepper

For the fennel condiment
200ml light olive oil
1 fennel bulb, trimmed
  and finely sliced
1 large egg yolk
3 tablespoons
  cider vinegar
50g Pernod

For the braised fennel
1 large fennel
  bulb, trimmed
1 garlic clove, peeled
  and crushed
1 teaspoon coriander
  seeds
1 teaspoon fennel seeds
a sprig of thyme
1 bay leaf
4 tablespoons olive oil

For the dressing
6 tablespoons olive oil
1 fennel bulb, trimmed
  and finely diced
1 small shallot, peeled
  and finely diced
finely grated zest and
  juice of 1 lime
1 teaspoon Pernod

To garnish
4 tablespoons freshly
  podded broad beans
2 teaspoons chopped
  fennel herb
deep-fried sea purslane
  (optional)
olive oil to drizzle

To make the fennel condiment
Heat a large pan (one with a tight-fitting lid) over a medium heat. When it's hot, add a generous drizzle of olive oil, then the fennel. Sweat gently for 2 minutes without colouring, then barely cover with water. Put the lid on and cook until the fennel is soft, about 25 minutes, adding a little more water if needed. Remove the lid and cook until the liquor has almost totally reduced. Transfer to a blender and blend until smooth. Allow to cool.

Weigh 125g of the cooked fennel and place in a food processor with the egg yolk, cider vinegar and Pernod. Blitz to combine, then add the rest of the olive oil in a slow, steady stream through the feeder tube, blending until fully incorporated. Season with salt to taste. Transfer to a bowl and leave to cool, then cover and place in the fridge unless using straight away.

To braise the fennel
Place the fennel bulb in a pan and add the garlic, coriander and fennel seeds, thyme, bay leaf and olive oil. Top up with water to just cover the fennel and add a pinch of salt. Bring to a simmer and cook gently until the fennel is tender, about 15 minutes. Leave to cool in the cooking liquor, then cut the fennel into quarters.

To make the dressing
Heat the olive oil in a pan over a low heat, add the fennel and shallot and cook gently for 10 minutes or until soft. Add the lime zest and juice and the Pernod, then take off the heat. Season with salt and leave to cool.

To cook the broad beans for the garnish
Bring a pan of salted water to the boil, add the broad beans and cook for 2 minutes. Immediately transfer the beans to a bowl of ice-cold water to cool quickly. Drain, then slip the broad beans out of their dull outer skins. Refrigerate until needed.

To cook the scallops
Take the scallops out of the fridge 20 minutes before cooking to bring them to room temperature. Place a large non-stick frying pan over a medium-high heat. When it's hot, add a drizzle of olive oil, then the braised fennel quarters. Colour until golden on all sides, then remove and cut each fennel quarter into 3 pieces. Wipe out the pan and place it back on the heat.

Season the scallops lightly with salt. When the pan is hot, carefully lay them in the pan, placing the side of the scallop down that would have been against the flat shell. Cook for 2–3 minutes until the scallops turn golden. Flip them over and remove the pan from the heat. The scallops will finish cooking in the residual heat of the pan.

To assemble and serve
Warm the dressing, add the broad beans and fennel herb and season with salt and pepper. Spoon a few tablespoons of fennel condiment onto each warmed plate. Add 3 pieces of fennel and the dressed broad beans. Place 3 scallops on each plate and spoon on 1 tablespoon of the dressing. Finish with the sea purslane, if using, and a drizzle of olive oil.

The smell of this dish when it's cooking is something else! The pan-frying of the fish along with the roasting kohlrabi in garlic and lemon oil fills the kitchen with a wonderful aroma. It's a dish that often surprises customers, because they are not quite sure what they will get. Attractive, aromatic and different, it doesn't disappoint.

GURNARD WITH KOHLRABI AND SAFFRON AÏOLI

Serves 4 as a starter

2 gurnard, about 500g
  each, gutted, scaled,
  filleted and pin-boned
Cornish sea salt
  and freshly ground
  black pepper

For the pickled kohlrabi
1 large kohlrabi
150ml olive oil
50ml white
  wine vinegar
1 banana shallot,
  peeled and finely
  chopped
a small pinch of
  saffron strands

For the pan-roasted
kohlrabi
1 large kohlrabi
30g unsalted butter
1 garlic clove, peeled
  and crushed
2 sprigs of thyme

For the saffron aïoli
1 large garlic bulb, split
  into individual cloves
  (unpeeled)
150ml olive oil, plus
  extra to drizzle
500g floury potatoes,
  peeled (300g
  cooked weight)
a small pinch of
  saffron strands
2 egg yolks
50ml white wine
  vinegar

For the lemon and
garlic oil
1 garlic clove, peeled
finely grated zest of
  1 lemon
200ml olive oil

First make the lemon and garlic oil
Put the garlic, lemon zest and olive oil into a small food processor or blender and blitz for 2 minutes. Pour into a container, cover and leave to settle for 24 hours. Decant the oil into a bottle and keep in the fridge.

For the pickled kohlrabi
Peel the kohlrabi and slice very finely, using a mandoline. Lay the slices in a dish. Put the olive oil, wine vinegar and shallot into a saucepan with the saffron and a pinch of salt and bring to a simmer over a medium heat Pour the simmering liquid over the kohlrabi, making sure the slices are submerged. Cover with cling film and let cool. Refrigerate until needed.

To make the saffron aïoli
Preheat your oven to 220°C/Fan 200°C/Gas Mark 7. Take a square of foil and scrunch up the sides. Put all the garlic cloves inside, sprinkle with salt and drizzle with olive oil. Seal the foil into a bag, place on an oven tray and roast for 30 minutes. Meanwhile, add the potatoes and saffron to a pan of cold salted water, bring to the boil and cook until soft. Drain and leave to dry in the colander for 5 minutes. Leave the garlic to cool slightly, then peel and put into a food processor with the potatoes and egg yolks. Blend to combine, then add the olive oil in a steady stream through the feeder tube. When it is emulsified, add the wine vinegar and a little salt. Blend for 1 minute, then taste and adjust the seasoning. Spoon into a bowl and cover with cling film. Refrigerate unless serving at once.

For the pan-roasted kohlrabi
Peel the kohlrabi, cut into 8 slices and trim to roughly the same size. Place in a pan, cover with water and add the butter, garlic, thyme and a pinch of salt. Bring to a simmer and cook until the kohlrabi is just tender, about 10 minutes. Remove from the pan and leave to cool on a tray.

When you are ready to serve, place a frying pan over a medium-high heat. When it is hot, add a drizzle of lemon and garlic oil, then the 8 kohlrabi pieces. Colour until golden all over, turning as necessary; keep warm.

To cook the fish
Heat a frying pan over a medium heat. Oil the gurnard fillets with the lemon and garlic oil and season them with salt and pepper. Lay the fillets skin side down in the hot pan and cook for 2 minutes until the fish starts to turn golden and become crisp at the edges. Flip the fish over, turn the heat down and cook for another 2 minutes, until cooked.

To assemble and serve
Remove 16 slices of pickled kohlrabi from the pickling liquor and drain them. Spoon about 1 tablespoon saffron aïoli onto each warmed plate. Lay a slice of pickled kohlrabi and 2 pieces of roasted kohlrabi next to the aïoli. Top with a cooked gurnard fillet. Arrange a few more pickled kohlrabi slices decoratively on top and trickle these with a little of the kohlrabi pickling liquor. Finish with a drizzle of the lemon and garlic oil. Serve immediately.

Triggerfish is a fish like no other. With skin like armour plating and teeth that are razor sharp, it's the bully of the fish world. These aggressive creatures have even been known to attack divers who come too close. That said, they are very, very tasty. I would say they compare to the flavour of bream, with the texture of John Dory.

Even if you don't prepare this dish, make the ketchup. It's great with simple grilled fish or breaded and deep-fried fish. It also keeps well in the fridge and can be frozen, but it's unlikely to get as far as the freezer, because you will have eaten it all!

TRIGGERFISH, AUBERGINE PURÉE, SARDINE AND TOMATO KETCHUP, TOMATO AND OLIVE DRESSING

Serves 4 as a
main course

2 triggerfish, gutted,
    filleted and skinned
olive oil for cooking
Cornish sea salt
    and freshly ground
    black pepper

For the aubergine purée
2 aubergines
100g smoked almonds
juice of 1 lemon
1 garlic clove, peeled
    and finely chopped
2 tablespoons extra
    virgin olive oil
1 teaspoon sesame oil

**For the sardine and
tomato ketchup**
olive oil for cooking
1 red onion, peeled and
    chopped
3 garlic cloves, peeled
    and sliced
2 teaspoons chopped
    thyme leaves
2 bay leaves
1.5kg very ripe
    tomatoes, roughly
    chopped
a small tin top-
    quality sardines
    in tomato sauce
50g soft dark
    brown sugar
50ml red wine vinegar
1 cinnamon stick

**For the tomato and
olive dressing**
8 tablespoons extra
    virgin olive oil
1 teaspoon fennel seeds
1 teaspoon chopped
    rosemary
2 salted anchovies,
    finely chopped
2 ripe plum tomatoes,
    skinned, deseeded
    and diced
12 black olives, stoned
    and sliced
1 tablespoon capers
2 tablespoons cider
    vinegar
2 teaspoons shredded
    coriander leaves

First make the ketchup
Heat a large saucepan over a medium heat and add a drizzle of olive oil. When it is hot, add the onion, garlic, thyme and bay leaves. Allow to sweat for 2 minutes, then add the tomatoes and cook for 5 minutes until they start to collapse. Add the sardines, sugar, wine vinegar and cinnamon and cook over a low heat for about 25 minutes until well reduced. Discard the cinnamon and bay leaves.

Using a blender, blitz the mixture until smooth, then pass through a sieve into a bowl. Allow the ketchup to cool, then cover and refrigerate (for up to a week) if you are not using it straight away.

To prepare the aubergine purée
Heat your grill to its highest setting. Pierce the skins of the aubergines in a few places and place them on a tray under the grill. Grill, turning them every few minutes until they are soft and almost collapsing, and the skins are blackened. Allow the aubergines to cool for a minute or so, then cut them in half lengthways and scoop out the cooked flesh.

Blitz the aubergine flesh with the smoked almonds, lemon juice and garlic in a food processor, then add the olive and sesame oils with some salt and pepper and blend until smooth.

Transfer the aubergine purée to a bowl and allow it to cool. Cover and refrigerate if you are not using it straight away.

To get the fish ready for cooking
Take the fish out of the fridge about 30 minutes before cooking to bring it to room temperature.

For the tomato and olive dressing
In a pan over a low heat, warm the extra virgin olive oil with the fennel seeds, rosemary and anchovies. Keep warm while you cook the fish.

To cook the fish
Heat a large non-stick frying pan over a medium heat. When it is hot, add a good drizzle of olive oil. Season the fish fillets with salt and carefully place them in the pan. Cook steadily for 3 minutes on each side.

To finish and serve
While the fish is cooking, add the tomatoes, olives, capers, cider vinegar and a little salt to the dressing.

Season the fish fillets with some pepper and place on 4 warmed plates. Place a spoonful each of the ketchup and aubergine purée alongside. Stir the shredded coriander through the tomato and olive dressing and spoon it on top of the fish and around the plates. Serve immediately.

Bass is a particular favourite with our customers and, like most of my dishes these days, I don't really like to do much to it because the quality of the fish that I get is so good. Here it is simply cooked on a griddle and served with baked courgettes, olive oil mash, hazelnut butter and a zingy English mustard dressing. You could drop the mash and serve some new potatoes instead if you like.

GRIDDLED BASS, OLIVE OIL MASH, BAKED COURGETTE AND HAZELNUTS WITH MUSTARD DRESSING

Serves 4 as a main course

4 bass portions, about 140g each, scaled and pin-boned
4 tablespoons olive oil
2 sprigs of thyme, leaves picked
1 garlic clove, peeled and finely chopped
Cornish sea salt and freshly ground black pepper

For the mustard dressing
1 banana shallot, peeled and finely chopped
1 garlic clove, peeled and finely chopped
2 teaspoons English mustard
1 egg yolk
4 teaspoons cider vinegar
300ml light olive oil

For the olive oil mash
800g medium-large potatoes, washed
200ml whole milk
100ml double cream
100ml extra virgin olive oil
3 tablespoons curly parsley leaves, chopped (optional)

For the courgettes
3 small courgettes (ideally a mix of green and yellow)
150g blanched hazelnuts
1 tablespoon caster sugar
100g unsalted butter, at room temperature
2 tablespoons chopped curly parsley
2 tablespoons chopped chives
olive oil for brushing

To finish
extra virgin olive oil

To marinate the bass
Place the bass portions in a bowl. Using a small food processor, blitz the olive oil, thyme leaves and garlic with some salt and pepper. Add this marinade to the fish and turn to coat. Cover and leave to marinate in the fridge for a few hours.

For the mustard dressing
Put the shallot, garlic, mustard, egg yolk and cider vinegar into a bowl. Whisk together for 30 seconds and then add the olive oil, drop by drop to begin with and then in a steady stream, whisking constantly, until it is all incorporated. Season with salt and pepper to taste. Set aside.

For the olive oil mash
Preheat your oven to 220°C/Fan 200°C/Gas Mark 7. Put the potatoes on an oven tray, sprinkle with salt and bake for 1 hour. Remove from the oven (leaving it on for the courgettes). Heat the milk, cream and olive oil together in a pan until simmering. Working quickly, halve the potatoes and scoop out the flesh into a bowl. Pass the cooked potato through a potato ricer into another bowl, or mash with a hand masher. Mix in the hot liquid, a ladleful at a time, until you have the consistency you like. Season with salt and pepper and mix in the parsley, if using. Keep warm.

For the courgettes
Toast the hazelnuts in a hot, dry small frying pan until golden all over. Sprinkle with the sugar and cook until the sugar starts to caramelise on the nuts. While still hot, tip the nuts into a food processor and blitz until ground. Let cool slightly, then mix with the butter, chopped herbs and salt and pepper to taste.

To bake the courgettes
Halve the courgettes lengthways and oil and season them. Place on a large oven tray and bake in the oven at 220°C/Fan 200°C/Gas Mark 7 for 15 minutes. Remove from the oven (leaving it on) and dot each courgette half with 1 teaspoon hazelnut butter. Set aside while you cook the fish.

To cook the fish
Heat a large griddle pan over a high heat. Lift the bass portions out of the bowl and scrape off any excess marinade. Carefully place the fish skin side down on the hot griddle pan and cook for 2 minutes until the skin starts to char and go crisp. Turn the fish over and cook on the flesh side for 1 minute. Lay the fish on the tray with the courgettes and place in the oven for 3 minutes.

To finish and serve
While the fish and courgettes are in the oven, warm the mash. Spoon it equally onto 4 warmed plates and add 3 courgette halves to each plate. Top with a portion of bass and place a spoonful of the dressing alongside. Finish with a trickle of extra virgin olive oil. Serve immediately.

THE MENU
A taste of the seasons

At Restaurant Nathan Outlaw, our menu is always dictated by what is available on the day, whether that be the seafood or accompanying vegetables. Quality is the key and nothing goes into dishes unless it's at its very best. My ethos of serving only seasonal produce is sometimes challenging, but it is the only way to ensure ingredients are at their optimum. For this reason, the menu at Restaurant Nathan Outlaw has never been a lengthy affair. I simply wouldn't be able to source enough locally produced, top-quality seasonal ingredients. Instead, I've chosen to offer a tasting menu, serving customers a variety of fish and seafood, together with vegetables that are always the very best available to us. This is also the reason why dishes tend to change often; it's all about not accepting a compromise to the quality of each item on the plate.

In the past, I have offered customers a choice of tasting menus, running two side by side. I also tried a tasting menu with twelve to fourteen different courses. Ten years of experimenting has taught me that honing things down to one tasting menu of six to eight courses, is the way to go. Serving too many courses becomes overly complicated and we have to factor in the length of time it takes to prepare each dish, and the time the customer has to sit down to eat them. The current expectation is that it will take diners up to three hours to enjoy our menu, and not many people would want to sit for longer than that!

Before dinner, customers are offered 'nibbles'. These are small bites, designed to interest and excite the palate, in anticipation of what is to come. They are ideal to enjoy with pre-dinner drinks.

Our menus always follow the same pattern, even though dishes are constantly changing. Each menu begins with a duo of cold dishes, of either raw or cured seafood. A light start, they are designed to show off the quality of the seafood, which is laid bare and cannot hide behind anything else on the plate.

It sets down the intention of what is to come. The third course is always shellfish, typically crab or lobster, caught locally, of course. The dishes are light but with slightly more richness than the previous ones.

The next course is designed to surprise the customer, as the fish is cooked in a way that is unexpected. For example, the menu might state 'salt cod' but it won't be traditional salt cod that they have encountered before. Next comes the main course. Here, diners can expect a dish showcasing a prime, seasonal fish like turbot or Dover sole. The sauce will be richer, but without overpowering the flavour of the fish.

To conclude the meal, there is dessert. It is always something fairly substantial, designed to delight the diner, by the way it is presented and the flavours it offers. I like to think it rounds off the meal perfectly, complementing the rest of the dishes on the menu it follows.

Each dish has a wine especially chosen to serve with it. The 'match' is always tasted by our front-of-house team and chefs. This allows members of staff to be able to experience the pairing, so they will have first-hand knowledge with which to answer any questions from customers. Dishes never go onto the menu until wines have been selected to accompany them.

We do have a number of dishes that return to the menu every so often, either as a request from customers or because I feel it's the right time to do so. However, they never return in exactly the same guise. We take the opportunity to improve or simplify the dish in the kitchen, often as a result of feedback from customers who have experienced it before. This means that although the dishes are 'returning', we tweak them, so the menu constantly evolves.

In my view, offering one tasting menu showcases the very best seafood and means that customers don't have to make choices. They can just sit back, relax and enjoy the whole experience!

I was so excited when we first came up with this dish and I still am today. It is everything you want from a dessert: fruity with strawberries, crisp with pastry, rich and creamy with elderflower custard and refreshing from the sorbet. Classic flavours and great textures sing together. The sorbet, in particular, is exceptionally good, especially when strawberries are at their best.

STRAWBERRIES, ELDERFLOWER CUSTARD AND STRAWBERRY CHAMPAGNE SORBET

Serves 6

For the rough puff pastry
500g plain flour, plus
  extra to dust
10g fine sea salt
500g ice-cold butter,
  cut into 1cm dice
250ml ice-cold water
200g icing sugar,
  to dust

**For the elderflower
and lemon custard**
300ml double cream
100ml elderflower
  cordial
4 large eggs
100g caster sugar
50ml lemon juice

**For the strawberry
champagne sorbet**
500g strawberries,
  hulled and halved
500ml champagne
100g liquid glucose
100g caster sugar

**For the elderflower and
strawberry syrup**
100g strawberries,
  hulled
100ml elderflower
  cordial
200g liquid glucose

For the strawberries
20 strawberries, hulled
  and halved

To make the rough puff pastry
Put the flour, salt and butter into a bowl and rub in the butter using your fingertips, until the pieces are roughly half the size. Add the water and mix to a dough. On a floured surface, roll the dough out to a neat rectangle, about 50 x 20cm. Fold the top third down, then the bottom third up over the top. Wrap in cling film and rest in the fridge for 30 minutes. Give the dough a quarter-turn, then roll out and fold as before, twice more. Now dust your work surface with icing sugar and roll out the pastry to the thickness of a £1 coin. Dust the pastry heavily with icing sugar and roll up, like a big sausage. Wrap in cling film and chill in the freezer.

To bake the pastry
Preheat your oven to 200°C/Fan 180°C/Gas Mark 6. Line a baking sheet with a non-stick baking mat or silicone paper. Unwrap the pastry roll and cut into 6 slices, the thickness of a £1 coin. Lay these on the baking sheet. (Freeze the rest of the pastry roll for another day.) Bake the pastry discs for 8–10 minutes until crisp and golden. Carefully transfer to a wire rack to cool. Keep in an airtight container until ready to serve.

To make the custard
Pour the cream and elderflower cordial into a pan and bring to the boil over a medium heat. Meanwhile, whisk the eggs and sugar together in a large bowl. Pour on the hot cream mix, whisking as you do so, then add the lemon juice. Pour into a thermomix set at 90°C and cook on full speed for 5 minutes. Or cook, stirring over a low heat, until the custard reaches 90°C. Immediately pour into 6 serving dishes. Let cool slightly and then place in the fridge to set; this will take 2 hours.

For the strawberry champagne sorbet
Put all the ingredients into a pan and bring to a simmer over a medium heat. Cook for 15 minutes. Take off the heat and blitz the mixture with a hand blender, then pass through a sieve into a jug and leave to cool. Once cooled, churn in an ice-cream machine until firm, then transfer the sorbet to a suitable container and freeze until ready to serve.

To make the syrup
Put the strawberries, elderflower cordial and glucose into a pan, bring to a simmer and cook for 10 minutes. Remove from the heat and leave to cool, then pass the syrup through a sieve into a jug. Set aside for serving.

To finish the dish
Put the fresh strawberries into a bowl, add some of the syrup and toss carefully to dress. Remove the elderflower custards from the fridge and arrange the strawberries equally on top of them. Spoon a neat scoop of strawberry sorbet on top of each pile of strawberries and finish with a puff pastry disc. Serve immediately.

As a child, 'Arctic Roll' was my 'special occasion' ice-cream dessert of choice and raspberries were a rare treat because they were expensive, so this dish has a huge nostalgic buzz for me. Raspberries also happen to be my Dad's favourite and he now grows the tastiest ones I've ever eaten on his allotment!

ARCTIC ROLL, RASPBERRY SORBET AND SUGARED ALMONDS

First make the mascarpone filling

Soak the leaf gelatine in a shallow dish of ice-cold water to soften. Pour the cream and lemon juice into a pan and bring to a simmer over a medium heat. Meanwhile, whisk the eggs and sugar together in a large bowl. Pour on the hot cream mixture, whisking as you do so, and continue to whisk for 30 seconds. Immediately squeeze the excess water from the gelatine, then whisk into the hot custard until fully dissolved. Pass the custard mixture through a sieve into a clean bowl and leave to cool.

Once cold, place the custard mix in the fridge to thicken for about 2 hours then whisk in the mascarpone. Spoon the mixture into a disposable piping bag and refrigerate.

For the raspberry jam

Put the raspberries, lemon juice and all but 30g of the sugar into a pan and place over a low heat. When the raspberries start to release their juice and break down, increase the heat a little. Mix the pectin with the remaining 30g sugar. When the liquid in the pan looks syrupy, add the pectin mix and whisk in well. Cook until the temperature registers 105°C on a sugar thermometer, then pour onto a tray and leave to cool.

Once cold, blitz to a purée, using a blender, then pass through a sieve to remove the seeds. Put the jam into a disposable paper piping bag and place in the fridge until ready to serve.

To prepare the raspberry sorbet

Put the raspberries, water, framboise liqueur, sugar and glucose into a pan and bring to a simmer. Cook gently for 5 minutes, then remove from the heat and blitz with a hand blender. Pass through a sieve into a bowl to remove the seeds and leave to cool. Once cooled, churn in an ice-cream machine until firm, then transfer the sorbet to a suitable container and freeze until ready to serve.

To make the sponge

Preheat your oven to 220°C/Fan 200°C/Gas Mark 7 and line a 33 x 23cm Swiss roll tin with non-stick silicone paper or baking parchment. Put the 3 egg whites into a very clean bowl and whisk to a foam. Add the caster sugar and whisk until the meringue is holding firm peaks. In a separate bowl, whisk the whole eggs and icing sugar together, using a hand whisk, until the mixture is light and doubled in volume. Gently fold in the ground almonds, flour and lemon zest until evenly combined and then fold in the meringue. Finally fold in the melted butter.

Spoon the mixture into the prepared tin and gently level with a palette knife. Bake for 5–7 minutes until golden and springy to the touch. Lay a sheet of baking parchment on a clean surface and sprinkle with sugar.

...continued on page 110

Serves 6

For the sponge
3 large eggs, plus an extra 3 egg whites
15g caster sugar, plus extra to sprinkle
100g icing sugar
100g ground almonds
30g plain flour, sifted
finely grated zest of 1 lemon
30g butter, melted and cooled

For the mascarpone filling
2 sheets of bronze leaf gelatine
300ml double cream
50ml lemon juice
4 large eggs
100g caster sugar
300g mascarpone, left at room temperature for 1 hour to soften

For the raspberry jam
300g raspberries
juice of ½ lemon
240g caster sugar
4g pectin

For the raspberry sorbet
250g raspberries
200ml water
50ml framboise liqueur
100g soft light brown sugar
100g liquid glucose

For the sugared almonds
100g skinned whole almonds
100g light soft brown sugar
40ml water

To finish
30 raspberries

When the sponge is cooked, invert it out of the tin onto the sugared baking parchment. Lift the sponge on the paper onto a wire rack and leave to cool, keeping it covered with the lining paper.

To assemble the arctic roll
Remove the lining paper and trim the sponge to a neat rectangle. Lay a sheet of cling film on a clean surface and place the sponge on top. Spread with a generous layer of raspberry jam. Cut a large hole in the piping bag to the diameter you want your filling to be in your arctic roll. Pipe the mascarpone filling along the jam-covered sponge. Carefully roll the sponge around the filling, making sure you do not overlap the edges at the join (trim if necessary). Wrap the sponge in the cling film and place in the freezer. Freeze until solid; this will take about 3 hours.

To prepare the sugared almonds
Preheat your oven to 200°C/Fan 180°C/Gas Mark 4. Scatter the almonds on a baking tray and toast in the oven for 10 minutes until golden. Meanwhile, put the sugar and water in a heavy-based pan and dissolve over a medium heat. Continue to heat the syrup until it is pale golden, then remove from the heat and immediately add the almonds, stirring continuously, until the sugar crystallises around them. Spoon the sugared almonds onto a tray to cool, breaking up any that have clustered together. Once cooled, store them in an airtight container.

To serve
Cut the sponge roll into 6 equal slices and place on individual plates. Pipe a few dollops of raspberry jam on top of each slice and arrange halved and whole raspberries on the plates and on each slice. Scatter 5 or 6 sugared almonds on each serving and finish with a neat scoop of raspberry sorbet. Trickle over a little more raspberry jam and serve at once.

I have been serving these chocolates since I opened my first restaurant in 2003. They are very simple to make, but many of the best things in life are simple – take it from me! You can make a big batch and freeze them; in fact we serve these truffles straight from the freezer. When they get to room temperature they become very soft … you have been warned.

Makes about 50

100g dark chocolate,
  chopped into
  small pieces
500g milk chocolate,
  chopped into
  small pieces
125ml double cream
70ml brandy
60g unsalted butter

For the coating
100g dark chocolate,
  chopped into
  small pieces
70g cocoa powder
70g caster sugar

CHOCOLATE AND BRANDY TRUFFLES

Line a 30 x 20cm Swiss roll tin with a couple of layers of cling film.

Put the dark and milk chocolate into a heatproof bowl and pour on the cream. Place over a pan of gently simmering water, making sure the base of the bowl is not touching the water. Leave until melted.

Add the brandy and butter to the melted mixture, remove the bowl from the heat and whisk the mixture until it is fully emulsified.

Pour the chocolate mixture into the prepared Swiss roll tin and place in the fridge to set for 2 hours.

For the coating
Melt the chocolate in a heatproof bowl over a pan of simmering water (as above). Mix the cocoa powder and sugar together in a large bowl.

To finish the truffles
Turn the chilled truffle mixture out onto a board, peel away the cling film then cut into 2cm squares.

Spread some melted chocolate onto the palm of one hand. One at a time, coat each truffle square in melted chocolate then place in the cocoa mix and turn to coat. Once all of the truffle squares are coated, freeze them in a suitable container in the excess cocoa mixture.

To serve, take the truffles from the freezer, knock off the excess cocoa mix and arrange on a plate.

Late Summer

I love a cheeky vol au vent, even if it is reminiscent of 70s party food. Those little pastry cases are ideal vessels for savoury treats, like lobster cocktail. The perfect finger food, they're a great way to serve fresh crab, too. In fact you can stick pretty much anything in a vol au vent!

LOBSTER VOL AU VENTS

Makes 15

1 live Cornish lobster, about 600g, placed in the freezer for 30 minutes before cooking
Cornish sea salt and freshly ground black pepper

For the pastry cases
500g plain flour, plus extra to dust
10g fine sea salt
500g ice-cold butter, cut into 1cm dice
250ml ice-cold water
egg wash (1 medium egg, beaten with 1 tablespoon milk)

For the mayonnaise
1 egg yolk
2 teaspoons Dijon mustard
juice of ½ lemon
250ml light olive oil
2 teaspoons chopped fennel herb

For the garnish
1 lemon, peel and pith removed, segmented and cut into small pieces
fennel herb (plus pollen, if available)

To make the rough puff pastry

Put the flour, salt and butter into a bowl and rub in the butter using your fingertips, until the pieces are roughly half the size. Add the water and mix to a dough. On a floured surface, roll the dough out to a neat rectangle, about 50 x 20cm. Fold the top third down, then the bottom third up over the top. Wrap in cling film and rest in the fridge for 30 minutes. Give the dough a quarter-turn, then roll out and fold as before, twice more. Wrap the pastry and rest in the fridge for 30 minutes before rolling out.

To shape and bake the vol au vent cases

Preheat your oven to 220°C/Fan 200°C/Gas Mark 7. Line a baking sheet with baking parchment. Dust your work surface with flour and roll out the pastry to the thickness of a £1 coin. Using a 5.5cm fluted cutter, cut out 30 discs. Place 15 of the discs on the prepared baking sheet. Using a 3.5cm plain cutter, cut a hole in the middle of the other discs.

Brush the pastry rounds on the baking sheet with egg wash and top with the other pastry discs. Bake for 12 minutes until crisp and golden. Carefully transfer the pastry cases to a wire rack to cool, then gently prise out the centres. Keep in an airtight container unless using straight away.

To cook the lobster

Bring a large pan of water (big enough to hold the lobster) to the boil and add plenty of salt (the water really needs to be as salty as the sea to ensure that the flavour of the lobster isn't lost during cooking). Lower the heat so the water is at a steady simmer.

Take your lobster from the freezer and place it on a board. Insert the tip of a strong, sharp knife firmly into the cross on the back of the lobster's head. (The lobster will be killed instantly, although it may continue to move a little; this is normal.)

Carefully pull the lobster tail away from the head and remove the claws. Add the claws to the simmering water and cook for 3 minutes, then add the tail to the pan and cook for another 3 minutes. Immediately remove all the lobster from the pan and leave until cool enough to handle.

To make the mayonnaise

Whisk the egg yolk, mustard and lemon juice together in a bowl for 1 minute. Slowly whisk in the olive oil until it is all incorporated. Season with salt and pepper to taste. Cover and refrigerate until needed.

To prepare the lobster cocktail

Using a sharp knife, cut the lobster tail in half lengthways and remove the dark intestinal thread that runs the length of the tail. Discard the shell. Crack the claws and extract the meat. Chop the claw and knuckle meat and place in a bowl. Add about 2 tablespoons of the mayonnaise and stir gently to bind the lobster. Mix in the chopped fennel herb and season with salt and pepper to taste. Cover and keep in the fridge, taking it out 30 minutes before serving.

To finish and serve

Fill the vol au vent cases with the lobster cocktail and finish with a few pieces of lemon and snippets of fennel herb, with some pollen if you happen to have some. Serve immediately.

Red mullet and red pepper is a classic flavour combination that works brilliantly. Red mullet is unique – it even smells quite different from other fish when it's cooking. Within the species there are many different varieties. Personally, I like to cook red mullet in the 500g to 1kg range – I find the texture of smaller ones disappointing, as they are a bit too thin.

The red pepper pickle can be made well in advance and is great as a side for cheese too, especially a young goat's cheese. The hint of smoked paprika in the mayonnaise brings the whole dish together beautifully. I like to make my pastry by hand, but the choice is yours.

RED MULLET AND RED PEPPER TART WITH SMOKED PAPRIKA

Serves 4 as a starter

2 red mullet, 600g
    each, scaled, gutted,
    filleted, pin-boned
    and trimmed
olive oil to drizzle
Cornish sea salt
    and freshly ground
    black pepper

For the thyme pastry
250g plain flour, plus
    extra to dust
1 teaspoon fine sea salt
2 teaspoons chopped
    thyme leaves
150g unsalted
    butter, diced
1 egg yolk, beaten with
    1 tablespoon milk

For the red pepper pickle
1 red onion, peeled and
    finely sliced
1 garlic clove, peeled
    and finely chopped
4 tablespoons red
    wine vinegar
1 red pepper, halved,
    cored, deseeded and
    thinly sliced
2 tablespoons dark
    brown sugar
2 teaspoons chopped
    thyme

**For the smoked
paprika oil**
400ml light olive oil
4 teaspoons smoked
    paprika
½ teaspoon sea salt

**For the smoked paprika
mayonnaise**
1 egg yolk
2 teaspoons English
    mustard
3 teaspoons red
    wine vinegar
250ml smoked paprika
    oil (from above)

To garnish
wild sea aster or sea
    purslane leaves, or
    blanched samphire

Prepare the paprika oil a day ahead
In a bowl, whisk together the olive oil, smoked paprika and salt. Cover and leave to infuse overnight.

To make the thyme pastry
Put the flour, salt, thyme and butter into a bowl and rub in the butter, using your fingertips, until the mixture resembles fine breadcrumbs. Add the beaten egg and milk and mix carefully until the mixture comes together as a dough; don't overwork it. Flatten the dough to a disc and wrap in cling film. Leave to rest in the fridge for 2 hours.

To shape and bake the tart cases
Roll out the pastry on a lightly floured surface. Using a small plate as a guide, cut out 4 circles, 14cm in diameter. Use to line four 10cm tart tins, carefully moulding the pastry into the tins. Trim away the overhanging pastry. Line each pastry case with a piece of greaseproof paper and add a layer of baking beans (I use dried beans or lentils). Place in the fridge to rest for 30 minutes.

Preheat your oven to 200°C/Fan 180°C/Gas Mark 6. Place the tart tins on a baking sheet and bake for 20 minutes. Lift out the paper and baking beans and brush the pastry with egg wash. Bake for a further 5 minutes until the pastry is cooked and golden brown. Transfer the tart cases to a wire rack and leave to cool.

To make the red pepper pickle
Put the red onion, garlic and wine vinegar in a pan over a medium heat and cook gently until the vinegar has reduced totally. Meanwhile, place a frying pan over a medium heat and add a drizzle of paprika oil. When it is hot, add the red pepper and cook, stirring occasionally, for 5 minutes until softened. Add the sugar, thyme and some salt and pepper and cook for another 2 minutes, then add the red onion mixture. Stir together, take off the heat and set aside.

To make the mayonnaise
Whisk the egg yolk, mustard and wine vinegar together in a bowl. Slowly add the smoked paprika oil in a steady stream whisking constantly until you have a thick mayonnaise. Season with salt to taste. Cover and refrigerate until required.

To cook the fish
Preheat your grill to high. Oil the fish fillets and season with salt. Lay them skin side up on the grill tray and grill for 3 minutes until the skin starts to blister and almost char.

To assemble and serve
While the fish is grilling, warm the red pepper pickle and share among the 4 pastry cases. Place on warmed plates and top each with a grilled fish fillet. Finish with a dollop of smoked paprika mayonnaise and the garnish. Serve immediately.

This dish looks very simple, but it's not quite as straightforward as it appears to be. Fresh mackerel fillets are cured, grilled and whizzed into a dish of utter yumminess. Cucumber is juiced and used to make the cure as well as a delicious jelly, which brings balance to the dish with its fresh zingyness. For optimum flavour, serve at room temperature, when the jelly will be barely holding, not fridge-cold.

CURED MACKEREL WITH CUCUMBER JELLY

Serves 4 as a starter

2 mackerel, gutted,
  filleted, pin-boned
  and trimmed
Cornish sea salt

For the cure
100g fine sea salt
75g caster sugar
½ large cucumber,
  roughly chopped
10g dill, leaves picked
  and chopped

For the cucumber jelly
1 large cucumber,
  chopped
100ml apple juice
50ml cider vinegar
3 sheets of bronze
  leaf gelatine

For the cured
mackerel pâté
olive oil for grilling
3 cured mackerel fillets
  (from above)
100g full-fat Greek
  yoghurt
100g full-fat cream
  cheese
juice of 1 lemon
1 tablespoon creamed
  horseradish

For the sourdough crisps
1 small sourdough loaf,
  thinly sliced
olive oil to drizzle

For the cucumber garnish
1 cucumber, halved
  and deseeded
2 teaspoons
  chopped dill
juice of ½ lemon
1 tablespoon light
  olive oil

For the cure
Put the salt, sugar, cucumber and dill into a blender and blitz until smooth. Lay the mackerel fillets on a tray, pour on the cure and turn the fillets to ensure they are coated all over. Cover the tray with cling film. Place in the fridge to cure for 1 hour. Wash off the cure with cold water and then pat the mackerel fillets dry with kitchen paper.

To prepare the cucumber jelly
Put the cucumber, apple juice, cider vinegar and a pinch of salt into a juicer or food blender and blitz until smooth. Pass through a muslin-lined sieve into a jug then measure 300ml and pour into a bowl. Soak the leaf gelatine in a shallow dish of ice-cold water to soften. Heat 3 tablespoons of the blitzed juice gently in a pan. When the gelatine is soft, squeeze out all the excess water, then add it to the warmed juice and stir to dissolve. Add to the rest of the blitzed juice in the bowl and mix well. Set aside, while you make the pâté.

To make the cured mackerel pâté
Preheat your grill to high. Oil 3 of the cured mackerel fillets and place, skin side up on the grill tray. Grill for about 3 minutes until just cooked. Leave to cool, then peel off the skin and flake the fish.

Place the flaked fish, yoghurt, cream cheese, lemon juice and horseradish in a food processor. Blitz for 1 minute, scraping down the sides once or twice. Taste and season with salt if needed.

Spoon 2 tablespoons of mackerel pâté into each of 4 shallow serving bowls. Gently tap the bottom of the bowls to level the pâté. Place in the fridge for 30 minutes.

To assemble the dish
Slice the remaining cured mackerel fillet thinly, using a sharp knife. Share the slices equally between the 4 bowls, laying them neatly on top of the pâté and gently pressing each slice in slightly.

Spoon 3 tablespoons cucumber jelly onto each pâté, making sure the fish slices and pâté are covered. Carefully place the dishes back in the fridge and leave to set for 2 hours.

To make the sourdough crisps
Preheat your oven to 190°C/ Fan 170°C/Gas Mark 5. Lay the sourdough slices on an oven tray, drizzle with olive oil and season with salt. Bake for 8–10 minutes until golden and crisp. Transfer to a wire rack to cool.

For the cucumber garnish
Slice the cucumber into fine ribbons, using a mandoline or vegetable peeler, and place in a bowl. Toss with the chopped dill, lemon juice, olive oil and a little salt.

To serve
Take the plates out of the fridge about 30 minutes before serving, to take the chill off the dish. Finish with the cucumber garnish and serve the sourdough crackers on the side.

I love this plate of sunshine and late summer colours. Everyone seems to like their squid crispy, but I would urge you to try it this way: simmered for seconds in salty water and then immersed in a tasty dressing to cool and marinate. It makes the squid tender and really delicious. The dish works best with medium-sized squid – small squid are too insubstantial and big squid are best reserved for slow-cooking. I like to make squid fritters, like the Spanish croquettes, to finish the dish. We also bake a squid ink brioche to use for the crumb coating, though you can use ordinary breadcrumbs if you haven't the time to do so.

MARINATED SQUID WITH INK AND TARRAGON DRESSING

Serves 4 as a starter

For the squid ink brioche
125g white bread flour
5g fresh yeast
12g caster sugar
15g squid ink
2 medium eggs
1 teaspoon sea salt
60g unsalted butter,
  in pieces, softened

For the squid croquettes
300g squid, cleaned,
  bodies and fins
  left whole
light olive oil for cooking
1 red onion, peeled
  and halved
2 garlic cloves, peeled
  and crushed
1 red pepper, halved,
  cored, deseeded and
  cut into chunks
2 teaspoons smoked
  paprika
200ml red wine
300ml fish stock (see
  page 288)
150g unsalted butter
120g plain flour, plus
  extra for coating
2 large eggs, beaten
100g squid ink brioche
  crumbs (from above)
sunflower oil for
  deep-frying
Cornish sea salt
  and freshly ground
  black pepper

For the marinated squid
400g squid, cleaned,
  body cut into rings,
  fins scored
2 garlic cloves, peeled
  and crushed
½ teaspoon sea salt
75ml white wine
  vinegar
150ml extra virgin
  olive oil
1 tablespoon chopped
  tarragon

To make the squid ink brioche
Put the flour, yeast, sugar, squid ink and eggs into an electric mixer fitted with a dough hook and mix on a medium speed for 6 minutes. Add the salt and then slowly add the butter, a little at a time, continuing to mix until fully incorporated. Remove the bowl from the machine and cover with a damp, clean cloth. Leave the dough to rise in a warm place for 1 hour.

On a floured surface, knock back the risen dough and shape into a loaf. Place in a greased 500g loaf tin, cover with a damp cloth and leave to prove in a warm place for 1 hour.

Preheat your oven to 220°C/Fan 200°C/Gas Mark 7. Bake the brioche loaf for 20 minutes or until the loaf sounds hollow when you turn it out and tap it on the underside. Place on a wire rack to cool.

To cook the squid for the croquettes
Season the cleaned whole squid with salt and pepper. Heat a large frying pan with a drizzle of olive oil, then add the squid and cook for 2 minutes, turning occasionally. Add the red onion, garlic, red pepper and smoked paprika and cook for 2 minutes. Pour in the red wine and fish stock, bring to a simmer and cook gently for 1 hour.

Drain the cooked squid and vegetables in a colander over a pan. Strain the liquor and measure 120ml of it for the dressing; set aside.

Heat a pan over a medium heat and add the butter. When it is melted and starting to bubble, add the flour and cook, stirring for 2 minutes. Now add the rest of the reserved cooking liquor, a ladleful at a time, until you have a thick sauce consistency, stirring constantly to keep it smooth. Lower the heat and simmer for 20 minutes, stirring often. Chop the cooked squid and pass the cooked veg through a potato ricer. Add it all to the sauce and season with salt and pepper to taste. Tip onto a tray lined with greaseproof paper and allow to cool, then refrigerate for at least 2 hours to firm up.

To marinate the squid
Bring a pan of water to the boil, add the garlic and salt and simmer for 5 minutes. Meanwhile, to make the dressing whisk the wine vinegar and extra virgin olive oil together in a large bowl and place in the fridge. Add the squid to the simmering water and cook for 20 seconds. Immediately drain off the water and add the squid to the dressing. Toss

...continued on page 124

...ingredients continued on page 124

to combine and season with salt and pepper to taste. Allow to cool, turning the squid a few times in the dressing. Once cooled, the marinated squid is fine kept in the fridge for a few days.

For the squid ink brioche crumbs
Warm your oven to 110°C/Fan 100°C, Gas Mark ¼. Cut the cooled brioche into cubes and place on a tray in the oven until dry. Blitz in a blender to crumbs and keep in an airtight container until ready to use.

To prepare the carrots and beets
Put the carrots, butter, garlic, thyme and bay leaf into a pan and cover with water. Season with salt and bring to a simmer. Cook for 6 minutes or until the carrots are cooked, but still have a bite. Remove from the pan and place on a tray to cool. Add the wine vinegar to the liquor in the pan. Slice the beetroot on a mandoline or using a vegetable peeler and lay on another tray. Bring the liquor to the boil and pour over the beetroot, making sure it is covered. Leave to cool.

To make the dressing
Put the squid braising liquor, squid ink and wine vinegar into a bowl and whisk to combine. Gradually whisk in the olive oil and season with a little salt if required. Set aside.

To prepare the squid croquettes
Using a spoon, divide and shape the squid mixture into balls, each weighing 50g. Have the beaten eggs ready in one bowl, the flour in another and the brioche crumbs on a tray. Pass the squid balls through the flour, then the egg and finally the crumbs to coat. Set aside until you are ready to fry them.

To prepare for serving
Heat the oil for deep-frying the squid croquettes in a deep-fryer or other suitable deep, heavy pan to 180°C.

In a frying pan, heat a drizzle of olive oil over a medium heat. When hot, add the carrots cut side down and colour, turning, for 2–3 minutes until lightly caramelised all over. Drain the beetroot of its liquor and dry on kitchen paper.

When the oil for deep-frying is ready, carefully add the squid balls and fry for 2–3 minutes until crisp. Drain on kitchen paper and season with salt.

To finish the dish
Toss the chopped tarragon through the marinated squid. Share the marinated squid and the carrots among 4 warmed plates. Lay 3 or 4 slices of beetroot on top. Whisk the dressing well and spoon it over the marinated squid and vegetables. Place a squid croquette on top of each portion, finish with a few tarragon leaves and serve immediately.

For the carrots and beets
8 small carrots, peeled and halved lengthways
50g unsalted butter
1 garlic clove, peeled and crushed
a sprig of thyme
1 bay leaf
50ml red wine vinegar
2 small beetroot, peeled
Cornish sea salt

For the dressing
120ml squid braising liquor (from above)
1 tablespoon squid ink
40ml red wine vinegar
240ml olive oil
Cornish sea salt

For the garnish
tarragon leaves

OUR WINE LIST

It goes without saying that the wines we offer at Restaurant Nathan Outlaw must be compatible with the food we serve. It is also our intention to offer honest value for money.

Since 2007, I have worked with Damon Little, our Beverages Manager/Sommelier, to build an eclectic wine list that excites customers without being intimidating in any way. We offer both standard favourites and more unusual wines so that everyone can find something to enjoy.

Unlike many other restaurants of our standard, the wine list is organised by wine style rather than country of origin. Each section is then arranged according to price, allowing customers to choose a wine that suits their pocket too. The wine that is always on our list acting as a 'house wine' is Grolleau Gris, a dry, floral, flinty choice, ideal with seafood.

Another unusual feature of our wine list is that we offer a wide range of wines by the glass. The use of a coravin means that we can access and serve premium wines without opening the bottle. With a selection of around sixty diverse wines by the glass to choose from, there should be something for everyone!

Some would consider our wine list to be quite small, but this is a conscious decision. In the same way that we want to know the story of the food we offer, the traceability of the wine is important. We make a point of building relationships with our wine producers, often selecting smaller vineyards where only a few hundred bottles may be produced each year. This suits us as we can develop a more personal relationship with our winemakers.

Damon and his wife, Stephi (who is also our Maître D), spend most of their winter break visiting vineyards, seeking out new and exciting wines to bring back to the restaurant. This means not only can we offer something different to our customers, but also that Damon gains first-hand knowledge of how the wines are produced. In turn, he passes this information onto our front-of-house staff and those customers who have an interest in wines. Our front-of-house staff take part in regular training, often having wine tastings at the restaurant to sample new wines and see how they pair with certain dishes. Suppliers often visit to meet and discuss their wines too.

In addition to our constantly evolving, 'basic list', some wines appear as 'guest wines', according to what is on the menu. This keeps the list interesting, especially for those who dine with us regularly. As well as the traditional wine areas, we currently have wines on our list from Hungary, Uruguay, Brazil, Canada, Austria, Tenerife, Switzerland and China. However, the most popular at present is a Japanese sparkling wine that beautifully pairs with our raw seafood dishes.

In recent years, wine pairing has gained popularity and guests often choose this option rather than selecting one bottle for their meal. So, with each course, they can savour a different wine that is perfectly matched with the dish. Customers must put their trust in Damon's expertise if they go this route, but their overall meal experience is enhanced, I can promise.

There is also a cocktail list, mostly wine based, offering both traditional drinks like Kir Royale and our own inventions such as Kir Cornwall, a light, refreshing cocktail made with Cornish sparkling wine and Cornish cassis.

We are proud to have Cornish wines from several local vineyards on our wine list. Cornwall is on the same latitude as northern Germany in terms of viticulture and our slatey soil means that cool climate wines can be made here successfully. Owing to climate change, viticulture is moving northwards, allowing Cornish winemakers to produce sparkling wine that can compete with champagne.

So, we are in the enviable position of having a truly international wine list and the prospect of more local wines to enjoy in the future too.

I really rate the species of bream we get – wild gilt head, red couch's and black bream – but the wild gilt head is my favourite. All three fish have very sharp teeth that nibble mussels off rocks or steal bits of bait out of lobster pots; they even graze on seaweed. This dish is one of my old faithfuls, revisited. The orange and rosemary butter is also great with grilled lobster and scallops in the shell. The potato dumplings are basically Italian potato gnocchi, but rolled differently and pan-fried to crisp the outside. Feel free to flavour them with different herbs.

BREAM WITH CAULIFLOWER, FENNEL AND POTATO DUMPLINGS

Serves 4 as a main course

1 wild gilt head bream, 1kg, or 2 fish, each 500–600g, gutted, scaled, filleted, pin-boned and trimmed
olive oil for cooking
2–4 sprigs of rosemary
Cornish sea salt and freshly ground black pepper

For the dumplings
1 potato, 300g, baked until tender, peeled
1 egg yolk
1½ tablespoons freshly grated Parmesan
65g '00' flour (pasta flour), sifted
2 teaspoons extra virgin olive oil
1 tablespoon fennel herb, chopped
1 tablespoon flat-leaf parsley, chopped
light olive oil for cooking

For the orange and rosemary butter
200g unsalted butter, softened
1 small shallot, peeled and finely chopped
1 garlic clove, peeled and finely chopped
finely grated zest of 1 orange
2 tablespoons orange juice
1 teaspoon rosemary leaves, finely chopped

For the fennel and cauliflower
1 fennel bulb, trimmed and quartered lengthways
100ml water
1 small white cauliflower, trimmed
1 small purple cauliflower, trimmed
olive oil for cooking

To garnish
fennel herb

To make the dumplings
Pass the cooked potato through a potato ricer or drum sieve into a bowl. Add the egg yolk and Parmesan and fold together lightly; do not overwork. Fold in the flour, extra virgin olive oil, herbs and some salt and pepper.

Bring a large pan of salted water to the boil and add a drizzle of olive oil. Have ready a bowl of ice-cold water. Turn the potato dough out onto a floured surface and shape into small balls, the size of marbles. Blanch them in the boiling water, in batches if necessary, until they float to the surface, about 2 minutes. Transfer to the ice-cold water to cool quickly. Once cooled, remove from the water and dry on a clean tea towel. Unless using straight away, gently toss the dumplings in olive oil and keep in a covered container in the fridge.

For the orange and rosemary butter
Mix all the ingredients together in a bowl, using a spatula, and season with salt and pepper.

To cook the fennel and cauliflower
Preheat your oven to 200°C/Fan 180°C/Gas Mark 6. Place the fennel in an ovenproof dish with the water and 40g of the orange and rosemary butter. Bake for 30 minutes until tender, adding more water if needed. Remove and keep warm until ready to serve. Keep the oven on for the fish. Bring a pan of salted water to the boil. Cut both of the cauliflowers into 2cm-thick slices and blanch in the boiling water for 4 minutes. Remove and place on a tray to cool.

To bring the dish together
Heat a non-stick ovenproof frying pan and add a drizzle of olive oil. Add the dumplings and fry for 3 minutes or until lightly golden brown all over. Place in a warmed dish; keep warm. Wipe out the pan and add some more oil. When it is hot, add the cauliflower slices and cook on both sides until golden. Remove and place on the tray with the dumplings to keep warm.

Wipe out the pan, heat again and add a drizzle of olive oil. Season the bream portions with salt and place in the hot pan, skin side down. Lay the rosemary sprigs on top. Cook gently for 2 minutes until the fish starts to turn golden at the edges. Transfer the pan to the oven to cook the fish for another 3 minutes.

To assemble and serve
While the fish is cooking, heat up the fennel, cauliflower and dumplings in the oven if necessary. Warm the orange and rosemary butter. When the bream is ready, take the pan from the oven, flip the fish over and leave to finish cooking in the residual heat of the pan. Share the fennel and cauliflower among 4 warmed plates and add a few dumplings to each. Spoon over the orange and rosemary butter. Top with the bream and finish with a few sprigs of fennel herb.

Monkfish is a fish that really benefits from some sort of marination or heavy seasoning, and it can handle robust flavours. It's also a fish that I choose to cook on the bone, if possible. In this dish I'm marinating the fish in yoghurt, with herbs and garlic. It tenderises the flesh and makes it so scrumptious. Towards the end of the summer we get really good local ceps, which I like to pan-roast and finish with freshly chopped parsley and garlic. This is a seriously tasty dish … you must try it!

MONKFISH WITH CEPS AND OXTAIL SAUCE

Serves 4 as a main course

2kg monkfish tail, trimmed with the bone remaining
Cornish sea salt and freshly ground black pepper

For the marinade
4 tablespoons full-fat Greek yoghurt
1 garlic clove, peeled and chopped
finely grated zest of 1 lemon
1 tablespoon chopped parsley

For the oxtail
1 oxtail, cut into 5cm sections
olive oil for cooking
1 red onion, peeled and halved
2 carrots, peeled and trimmed
4 garlic cloves, peeled
3 sprigs of thyme
2 bay leaves
500ml red wine
50ml red wine vinegar

For the cep ketchup
200ml double cream
20g dried ceps
olive oil for cooking
1 banana shallot, peeled and finely chopped
325g button mushrooms, sliced
fresh cep trimmings
juice of 1 lime

For the leeks
8 baby leeks, trimmed and washed well

For the ceps
4 large ceps, trimmed and halved, trimmings saved
olive oil for cooking
50g unsalted butter
1 garlic clove, peeled and finely chopped
1 tablespoon chopped parsley

To marinate the monkfish
In a large bowl, mix the yoghurt with the garlic, lemon, parsley and 1 teaspoon salt. Add the monkfish, turn to coat all over, cover and leave to marinate in the fridge for at least 6 hours, or up to 24 hours.

To cook the oxtail
Preheat your oven to 200°C/Fan 180°C/Gas Mark 6. Place the oxtail in a roasting tray and season it all over with salt and pepper. Roast in the oven for 1 hour.

Meanwhile, heat a large pan that is big enough to hold all the oxtail and vegetables over a medium heat. Add a drizzle of olive oil and when it's hot, toss in the red onion, carrots and whole garlic cloves. Cook for about 5 minutes until softened and coloured. Add the thyme, bay leaves, wine and wine vinegar to the pan and bring to the boil. Add the roasted oxtail pieces to the pan and pour on enough water to cover them and the vegetables. Bring to a simmer then skim off any fat that rises to the surface. Cook gently for 2 hours until the oxtail is tender and the meat can be pulled away from the bone easily. Strain the liquor into another pan and place the cooked oxtail and vegetables on a tray to cool.

Bring the cooking liquor back to a simmer and let it bubble to reduce until it has good body and plenty of flavour. When the oxtail is cool enough to handle, take it off the bone, keeping it in as large pieces as possible. Discard the vegetables and bones. Put the oxtail to one side, or refrigerate if you are not using it straight away.

For the cep ketchup
Heat the cream in a pan over a medium heat almost to a simmer, then add the dried ceps and remove from the heat. Put the lid on the pan and leave to infuse for 1 hour. Heat a large saucepan and add a little olive oil. Add the shallot and cook for 1 minute. Toss in the button mushrooms, along with any cep trimmings, and cook over a medium heat until they release their liquid and start to colour, about 15 minutes. Strain the cream from the dried ceps and pour it over the button mushrooms. Season with salt and pepper. Remove the pan from the heat and stir in the lime juice.

Tip the mushroom mixture into a blender and blitz until smooth. Spoon the ketchup into a container, cover the surface with greaseproof paper to stop a skin forming and leave to cool. Refrigerate until needed.

For the leeks
Bring a pan of salted water to the boil. Add the whole leeks and simmer for 4 minutes, until cooked through. Remove the leeks from the water, drain and place on a tray to cool.

...continued on page 132

To cook the ceps

Warm a frying pan (that can hold all the ceps in a single layer) over a medium heat. When the pan is hot, add a drizzle of olive oil followed by the ceps. Cook them for 3 minutes, turning occasionally, until roasted and golden. Add the butter, garlic and parsley to the pan and cook for 30 seconds.

To prepare for serving

Add the oxtail to the ceps and pour on the reduced cooking liquor. Bring to a simmer and then remove the pan from the heat. Taste and add salt and pepper if you think it is needed. Heat the cep ketchup in another small pan and keep warm.

To cook the fish

Preheat your grill to its highest setting. Wipe off the excess marinade from the monkfish then lay it on the grill tray and slide under the grill. Cook the monkfish for 4 minutes on each side and then set aside to rest in a warm spot.

To assemble and serve

While the fish is resting, place the leeks under the grill to heat up for a few minutes. Share the leeks and the ceps and oxtail in their sauce among 4 warmed plates. Give the monkfish another 1 minute on each side under the grill, then cut it into 4 portions and place on the plates. Add a generous spoonful of the warm cep ketchup and serve straight away.

The hake we get from Cornish boats is really amazing. It's a fragile fish that really benefits from being at its freshest, so we are fortunate to have it soon after it's landed. In the late summer, when sweetcorn is at its best, I make a purée from the raw kernels, which I grate and cook with roasted fish stock. It gives the dish a really interesting flavour and texture, and works so well with the pickled red onions. The red onion brings a needed hint of acidity to the whole dish, but the final thing you taste is the delicious creamy peppercorn sauce.

BAKED HAKE, CREAMED CORN, PICKLED RED ONIONS AND PEPPERCORN SAUCE

Serves 4 as a main course

4 hake steaks, 180g each
    (cut across the bone)
olive oil for cooking
Cornish sea salt
    and freshly ground
    black pepper

For the pickled red onions
2 red onions, peeled
    and halved crossways
50ml red wine
50ml red wine vinegar
50g caster sugar
50ml water

For the sweetcorn purée
2 corn-on-the-cobs
100ml fish stock (see
    page 288)
2 pinches of ground
    cumin
30g Parmesan, grated
juice of 1 lime

For the cabbage roll
1 small hispi cabbage
50g unsalted butter
olive oil for cooking
1 banana shallot,
    peeled and finely
    sliced

For the peppercorn sauce
olive oil for cooking
30g unsalted butter
1 banana shallot,
    peeled and finely diced
½ teaspoon cracked
    black pepper
1 teaspoon green
    peppercorns, chopped
1 teaspoon pink
    peppercorns, chopped
75ml bourbon whisky
500ml fish stock (see
    page 288)
150ml double cream
1 tablespoon chopped
    tarragon
1 tablespoon chopped
    flat-leaf parsley

To finish
olive oil to drizzle

For the pickled red onions
Preheat your oven to 200°C/Fan 180°C/Gas Mark 6. Place the red onion halves in a baking dish. Put the red wine, wine vinegar, sugar and water into a pan and heat to dissolve the sugar, then bring to the boil. Season with salt and pour the liquor over the onions. Cover the dish with foil and bake in the oven for 40 minutes or until the onions are tender. Leave to cool in the liquor.

To make the sweetcorn purée
Grate the kernels from the corn cobs, collecting all the juices as you do so. Put the grated corn and juices into a pan with the fish stock. Add the cumin and a pinch of salt and cook over a medium heat for 10 minutes, stirring continuously. Push the corn mixture through a drum sieve into a bowl, to get rid of the kernel skins. Put the sweetcorn purée into a pan with the Parmesan and lime juice and warm through. Taste the purée and add salt and pepper if you wish. Spoon into a container and leave to cool. Refrigerate until needed.

To prepare the cabbage roll
Bring a large pan of salted water to the boil. Have a bowl of ice-cold water ready. Remove the 12 outermost leaves from the cabbage, keeping them whole; shred the rest of the cabbage and set aside. Add the whole cabbage leaves to the boiling water and cook for 3 minutes until tender. Immediately remove and plunge into the ice-cold water to cool quickly. Drain the leaves and dry on a clean tea towel.

Heat the butter and a drizzle of olive oil in a pan over a medium heat. When the butter is bubbling, add the shallot and cook for 3 minutes until softened, but not coloured. Add the shredded cabbage and cook until it is soft, about 4 minutes. Season with salt and pepper and then tip the shredded cabbage onto a tray and leave to cool.

Lay a large double layer of cling film on a clean surface. Cut away the hard central stem part of the cooked outer cabbage leaves and lay half of the leaves in an overlapping line on the cling film. Spoon the shredded cabbage and shallot mixture on top, in an even line. Now lay the rest of the outer leaves, overlapping, on top of the shredded cabbage.

Wrap the cling film around the cabbage to form a sausage shape, then holding the ends of the cling film, roll the cabbage so it forms a tighter roll. Tie the ends of the cling film to hold the shape and then stab

...continued on page 136

the cling film with a pin to let the excess juice seep out. Put the cabbage roll on a tray in the fridge to cool fully and set the shape.

To make the peppercorn sauce

Heat a sauté pan over a medium heat and add a drizzle of olive oil and the butter. When the butter is melted and starts to bubble, add the shallot and cook for 3 minutes until softened but not coloured. Add the black, green and pink pepper, with the whisky. Set alight with a long match to burn off the alcohol, then when the flame dies down pour in the fish stock. Let it bubble to reduce until you have about 200ml liquor left. Pour in the cream and bring to a simmer. Allow the sauce to cook gently for 5 minutes and then season with salt to taste; keep warm.

To colour the cabbage and onions

Slice the cabbage roll into 4 rounds, remove the cling film and place on a tray lined with silicone paper. Heat a large frying pan over a medium-high heat and add a drizzle of olive oil. Place the red onion halves cut side down in the pan and cook for 3 minutes until well caramelised. Remove from the pan and lay on the tray with the cabbage rounds.

To cook the hake

Preheat your oven to 220°C/Fan 200°C/Gas Mark 7. Season the hake steaks with salt and pepper. Wipe out the frying pan used to finish the onions and heat it again, adding a drizzle of olive oil. Carefully place the fish in the pan and cook for 2 minutes on each side. Lift the fish steaks onto an oven tray. Place in the oven to finish cooking for 3–4 minutes, depending on thickness, placing the tray of cabbage rounds and red onion halves in the oven at the same time.

To assemble and serve

While the fish and vegetables are heating through, heat up the sweetcorn purée and peppercorn sauce. Stir the chopped tarragon and parsley into the sauce. Once the fish is cooked, take everything out of the oven and allow the fish to rest for 2 minutes.

Meanwhile, scoop out the centre of the onion halves to create a deep hollow. Pour the peppercorn sauce equally onto 4 warmed plates and add the cabbage rolls. Place the onion halves on the plates and fill with the corn purée. Carefully place a fish steak on each plate and finish with a drizzle of olive oil. Serve immediately.

RICHARD HORE
Our vegetable grower

Restaurant Nathan Outlaw is known for its fish and seafood menu, but vegetables are an important element of most of our dishes too, and their quality needs to match that of everything else on the plate. I spent years searching for a reliable supplier who could supply me with high-quality produce on a consistent basis, without success. Then I came across local grower Richard Hore, by pure chance – through a conversation between one of our chefs and Richard's son, Hartley.

Born in Cornwall, Richard is the owner of Restharrow Farm, a smallholding in Trebetherick, near Rock, just a few miles from the restaurant. Richard has been growing produce at the farm for the past twenty-six years. Initially, he grew just cauliflowers and leeks but, like so many other farmers, he found the need to diversify. Around fifteen years ago, he started to increase the variety of his crop, to include carrots, courgettes, cabbage and spinach.

Today, twenty acres of Richard's land are turned over to growing vegetables. His success is based on two things: firstly, the soil on his land is fine, rich and loamy – ideal for growing vegetables; secondly, he is passionate about what he does, seeing it as 'a way of life' rather than just a job. Although he cannot claim to be completely organic, Richard uses very few non-organic products on his land, balancing the need to eradicate pests and disease with the desire to grow a crop as naturally as he can.

Restharrow Farm is a family business, with Richard and his son, Hartley, working the land together. Although he is now in his seventies, Richard insists that he will continue working for as long as he 'wakes up in the morning and can get out of bed'. His love of what he does is obvious to anyone who talks to him, and his enthusiasm for life is infectious.

Richard grows only enough vegetables to supply his farm shop, our restaurants and one other shop in a nearby village. He could increase his productivity and make more money, but his priority is quality over quantity. It is this attitude and his wealth of experience, coupled with the careful nurturing of his crop, that enables Richard to grow such excellent produce.

When I first sampled a few of his vegetables, I was amazed at the flavour and quality. It was such a great find for me. Over the years, Richard and I have collaborated at length about growing and cooking produce. I'm always happy to listen to the advice of a man with such a huge depth of knowledge. Fortunately, Richard has been keen to grow whatever we need in the kitchen, adding a variety of things to his range for us including fennel, onions, kohlrabi, celeriac, chard, rhubarb, broad beans and runner beans. He now supplies all of our restaurants in Cornwall.

For me, cooking is about letting the ingredients speak for themselves, each dish having several levels of flavour to discover. It isn't just the main ingredients on the plate that matter. It is also about the quality of the onion in the stock, the carrot in the sauce or the cucumber that is juiced for the dressing. It's not about fads like micro-veg but about full-flavoured 'real' vegetables, without which elements of the dish would suffer.

Richard's vegetables have a quality and depth of flavour that is quite remarkable. This can be partly attributed to the variety, the soil and favourable climate, but I'm certain that it has a lot to do with the way Richard and Hartley care for their crops, tending to them personally every day. Mass-produced vegetables on vast farms don't get that treatment.

As Richard would say 'Proper job!'.

When blackberries are growing wild all around the restaurant and they are at their best I want to make the most of them. Here I serve them two ways: fresh and as an intensely flavoured jam – pairing them with a rich cinnamon mousse and a boozy cider apple sorbet. Delicious…

BLACKBERRY AND APPLE TART, CINNAMON MOUSSE AND CIDER SORBET

Serves 6

For the tart cases
1 packet of filo pastry
100g unsalted butter,
   melted
100g icing sugar
4 teaspoons ground
   cinnamon

For the cinnamon mousse
2 sheets of bronze
   leaf gelatine
400ml double cream
2 cinnamon sticks
5 egg yolks
120g caster sugar
260g cream cheese

For the blackberry jam
500g blackberries,
   hulled and halved
100ml dry cider
100g caster sugar
50g unsalted butter

For the cider apple sorbet
500g cooking apples,
   peeled, cored
   and chopped
500ml dry cider
100g liquid glucose
100g caster sugar

For the golden raisins
250ml dry cider
150g soft brown sugar
170g golden raisins

For the blackberry syrup
100g blackberries
100ml dry cider
200g liquid glucose

To finish
18 blackberries (as
   perfect as possible)

To prepare the cinnamon mousse
Soak the gelatine in a shallow dish of ice-cold water to soften. Put the cream and cinnamon sticks into a pan and bring to a simmer over a medium heat. Meanwhile, in a bowl, mix the egg yolks and sugar together until frothy. Pour the hot cream mixture onto the egg and sugar mixture, whisking as you do so. Immediately squeeze out the excess water from the gelatine then add to the hot mixture, whisking until melted and smooth. Leave to cool, then refrigerate until thickened. Remove the cinnamon sticks. Whisk the cream cheese into the mixture until smooth. Spoon into a piping bag and refrigerate until ready to serve.

To make the blackberry jam
Put the blackberries, cider, sugar and butter into a heavy-based pan over a medium heat and cook until the liquor is thick and syrupy, giving it a stir every now and then; this should take 25 minutes. Transfer the mixture to a blender and blitz until smooth. Place in a piping bag and refrigerate until ready to assemble.

For the cider apple sorbet
Place all the ingredients in a pan, bring to a simmer over a medium heat and cook for 15 minutes. Remove from the heat and blitz with a hand blender, then pass through a sieve into a jug. Leave to cool. Once cooled, churn the mixture in an ice-cream machine until firm, then transfer to a suitable container and freeze until ready to serve.

For the golden raisins
Heat the cider and brown sugar in a pan over a medium heat to dissolve the sugar. Bring to a simmer, add the raisins and cook for 5 minutes, then leave to cool. Once cold, refrigerate, unless using straight away.

To make the blackberry syrup
Put the blackberries, cider and liquid glucose into a pan and bring to a simmer. Cook for 10 minutes then set aside to cool. Once cooled, pass through a sieve into a bowl or jug.

To prepare the tart cases
Preheat your oven to 200°C/Fan 180°C/Gas Mark 6. Lay a sheet of filo on a work surface and brush with melted butter. Mix the icing sugar and cinnamon together and sift some over the buttered filo. Add another layer of filo, brush with butter and sift over some cinnamon sugar, then add another layer of filo. Using a 16cm plate as a guide and a sharp knife, cut out 6 circles. Use to line six 7cm mousse rings, placed on a baking tray. Bake for 14 minutes until golden and crisp, then transfer to a wire rack to cool. Keep the filo cases in a cool, dry place until ready to serve.

To assemble and serve
Pipe a little blackberry jam into the bottom of each tart case, then pipe in the cinnamon mousse. Top with the blackberries and a scattering of golden raisins. Drizzle some syrup around 6 plates and place the filo tarts in the middle. Add a neat scoop of cider apple sorbet and serve at once.

Blackcurrants have a short season and if you grow your own you need to be quick to pick them when they ripen before the birds get them! The fruit has a distinctive, tart flavour that needs to be carefully balanced – like any other acidic fruit. Blackcurrant is the star in this dessert – the other components balance its lovely tartness beautifully. We tend to buy as many blackcurrants as we can when they are in season and preserve them to see us through the autumn and sometimes into winter!

BLACKCURRANT PAVLOVA, BITTER LEMON SORBET, AND CLOTTED CREAM

Serves 6

For the pavlova
3 medium egg whites
150g caster sugar
1 vanilla pod, split lengthways and seeds scraped
2 teaspoons cornflour
2 teaspoons white wine vinegar

For the bitter lemon sorbet
2 unwaxed lemons
50g honey
50g caster sugar
50ml water
50ml lemon juice
250ml sweet wine

For the lemon curd
finely grated zest of 1 lemon
130ml lemon juice (about 3 lemons)
100g caster sugar
80g egg yolks (about 4 medium)
1 medium egg white
200g unsalted butter, chilled and diced

For the blackcurrant compote
400g blackcurrants
150g caster sugar
75ml water

For the lemon syrup
200ml liquid glucose
finely grated zest of 1 lemon
100ml lemon juice (about 2 lemons)
100g caster sugar

To finish
200g Cornish clotted cream

To make the meringue
Preheat your oven to 130°C/Fan 110°C/Gas Mark 1 and line a baking sheet with silicone paper or a non-stick baking mat. Wipe your stand mixer (or other large) bowl with kitchen paper dipped in vinegar to remove any grease. Using the stand mixer, whisk the egg whites with one-third of the sugar to form stiff peaks. Add another third of the sugar with the vanilla seeds and mix on high speed for 2 minutes. Add the rest of the sugar and whisk on a medium speed for 30 seconds. Sift in the cornflour and trickle in the wine vinegar, then fold in carefully, using a spatula.

To shape and bake the pavlovas
Spoon the meringue into a piping bag fitted with a large plain nozzle and pipe 6 mounds onto the prepared baking sheet. With the back of a spoon, make a hollow in the middle (that will hold 1 tablespoon compote). Bake in the oven for 1 hour.

For the bitter lemon sorbet
Place the whole lemons in a small saucepan. Pour on enough water to cover them and bring to the boil, then drain. Repeat this process three times. Cover the lemons with water for a fourth time, bring to a simmer and cook for 45 minutes until they are tender. Drain off the water and then blitz the lemons in a blender to a purée. Strain through a sieve to remove the pips.

Measure 50g of this lemon purée and put it into a saucepan with the honey, sugar, water, lemon juice and wine. (Any leftover lemon purée can be frozen.) Place the pan over a medium heat to dissolve the sugar and bring to a simmer. Cook for 2 minutes. Pass the mixture through a sieve into a bowl and leave to cool. Once cooled, churn the mixture in an ice-cream machine until firm, then transfer the sorbet to a suitable container and freeze until ready to serve.

To make the lemon curd
Put the lemon zest and juice, sugar, egg yolks and egg white into a heatproof bowl set over a pan of simmering water, making sure the base of the bowl is not in contact with the water, and whisk until the mixture thickens. Remove the bowl from the pan and whisk in the cold butter, a piece at a time, until it is fully incorporated.

Strain the lemon curd through a sieve into a bowl, cover and place in the fridge until set. For serving, spoon the lemon curd into a disposable paper piping bag.

...continued on page 146

For the blackcurrant compote

Put 200g of the blackcurrants into a bowl and set aside. Put the rest of the blackcurrants into a pan with the sugar and water, bring to a simmer and cook until they burst. Blitz to a purée using a blender, then pass through a sieve into a clean pan. Bring to the boil, pour over the rest of the blackcurrants and stir to combine. Leave the compote to cool.

To make the lemon syrup

Heat the liquid glucose, lemon zest, lemon juice and sugar in a pan over a medium heat to dissolve the sugar. Simmer for 3 minutes, then pour the syrup into a bowl and leave it to cool.

To assemble and serve

Drizzle some lemon syrup equally onto 6 cold plates. Boil a kettle of water (for warming the spoon for the clotted cream). Snip the end off the piping bag filled with the lemon curd and pipe a mound on each plate. Place a spoonful of compote next to the lemon curd.

Place a pavlova in the centre of each plate and fill the hollow with blackcurrant compote. Heat a spoon in boiling water and use it to take a neat scoop of clotted cream and place on each pavlova. Drizzle over a little more lemon syrup and finally place a neat spoonful of bitter lemon sorbet on each pavlova next to the clotted cream. Serve immediately.

We bake these biscuits at the restaurant, and serve them still warm from the oven with coffee and tea. They are like Italian amaretti, but taste so much more delicious freshly baked and eaten warm. Get the best ground almonds you can, and use the finest raspberries in season. The great thing about these biscuits is that they are both gluten-free and dairy-free. They are so good they don't need dairy. I can't quite believe I'm saying that but it's true!

ALMOND AND RASPBERRY BISCUITS

Makes 20

For the almond biscuit
3 large egg whites
270g caster sugar
270g ground almonds
25ml amaretto liqueur
a pinch of fine sea salt

For the topping
20 raspberries
icing sugar to dust

To make the biscuit dough
Using a stand mixer fitted with the paddle attachment, mix together the egg whites, sugar, ground almonds, amaretto liqueur and salt until evenly combined. Tip the mixture out onto a tray or container and place in the fridge to firm up for 1 hour.

To shape and bake the biscuits
Preheat your oven to 180°C/Fan 160°C/Gas Mark 4. Line a baking tray with a non-stick baking mat or silicone paper. Have a bowl of cold water to hand. Dip your hands into the water then take walnut-sized pieces of dough and roll them into small balls in the palm of your hand. Place on the lined baking tray.

Using your wet index finger, make a hole in the centre of each biscuit and pop a raspberry into it. Bake in the oven for 18 minutes, or until the biscuits are golden. Leave to cool on the baking sheet for a couple of minutes then transfer to a wire rack and dust with icing sugar. Serve the biscuits either warm or once they have cooled, if you can wait that long!

Early Autumn

As a child, when I was taken to parties with my parents, cheese straws were always on the table. For me, they were a benchmark of just how good the party was likely to be. My recipe includes roasted onions, mature Cheddar and smoked paprika for a deeply savoury flavour. Dangerously scrumptious, these cheese straws make a great start to a meal and that's why our customers begin with them in the restaurant.

ROAST ONION AND CHEDDAR STRAWS

Serves 4 as a canapé

4 tablespoons light
   olive oil
3 white onions, peeled
   and finely sliced
200g plain flour, plus
   extra to dust
½ teaspoon smoked
   paprika
100g unsalted butter
50g Cheddar cheese
   (I use Davidstow)
1 large egg yolk
Cornish sea salt
   and freshly ground
   black pepper

To roast the onions, heat the olive oil in a frying pan over a medium heat. Add the onions and cook for about 20–25 minutes until they are soft and golden brown. Season with salt and pepper and then transfer to a tray to cool down. Preheat your oven to 220°C/Fan 200°C/Gas Mark 7.

Once cooled, tip the roasted onions into a food processor and blitz for 10 seconds. Add the flour, smoked paprika, ½ teaspoon fine sea salt, 10 turns of black pepper (from a mill), the butter, cheese and egg yolk and pulse until the mixture comes together and forms a dough, taking care not to overwork it.

Tip the dough onto a lightly floured surface and bring it together with your hands, then roll out to a 1cm thickness. Cut into rectangles, about 8cm long and 3cm wide (or into other shapes of your choice).

Lay the pieces on a baking tray lined with baking parchment and bake in the oven for 8–10 minutes. Transfer to a wire rack to cool.

To enjoy the cheese straws at their best, serve them within a couple of hours of baking, with a glass of champagne or a cold beer.

We've been curing monkfish at the restaurant for a while now, because it's a great way of showcasing this fish's finest qualities. The texture of monkfish can vary with the spawning season. Often, you get lovely firm and juicy flesh, but sometimes it can be a bit soft and flabby. Curing solves this problem by removing excess water and firming up the flesh, while lending flavour at the same time. Throughout the year, we cure monkfish in various ways but this version, with its piquant ginger juice and fennel dressing, is my favourite. The yoghurt seems to bring the whole thing together perfectly.

CURED MONKFISH, FENNEL, GINGER AND YOGHURT

Serves 4 as a starter

600g monkfish fillet,
  trimmed of any sinew

For the cure
250g fine sea salt
250g caster sugar
200ml white wine

For the dressing
400g freshly peeled
  root ginger, chopped
6 tablespoons agrodolce
  vinegar
8 tablespoons light
  olive oil, plus a drizzle
  for cooking
1 banana shallot,
  peeled and finely diced
1 fennel bulb, outer
  layer and fronds
  removed, finely diced

To assemble
6 tablespoons thick
  Greek yoghurt
Cornish sea salt
  and freshly ground
  white pepper

To garnish
sea purslane
oil for deep-frying
  (optional)

To cure the monkfish
Lay the monkfish fillet on a tray. Sprinkle the salt and sugar evenly all over the flesh and massage in well. Pour over the wine, then cover the tray with cling film. Place in the fridge to cure for 3 hours, turning the monkfish in the cure mixture every hour.

Once the curing time is up, wash off the cure mix and pat the fish dry with kitchen paper. Lay a sheet of cling film on a work surface and place the monkfish on top. Roll the fish up tightly in the cling film to form a sausage and tie the ends to secure. Place in the freezer for 24 hours.

To make the dressing
Put the ginger and vinegar into a small blender and blitz finely, then transfer to a muslin-lined sieve set over a bowl and squeeze out as much juice as possible. Put 4 tablespoons of the ginger juice into a bowl, whisk in the 8 tablespoons olive oil and season with salt to taste. Set aside.

Heat a drizzle of olive oil in a small pan over a medium heat, then add the shallot and fennel and sweat for 3 minutes, stirring all the time to ensure the fennel doesn't colour. Tip onto a tray to cool.

Once the fennel and shallot mixture is cold, add 2 tablespoons to the ginger dressing.

To prepare for serving
An hour or so before you intend to serve the monkfish, remove it from the freezer. Leave at room temperature to start defrosting for 30 minutes.

Season the yoghurt with salt and white pepper to taste and spoon into a disposable piping bag. Place in the fridge until ready to serve.

To assemble and serve
Using a very sharp, or serrated, knife and a clean board, slice the cured monkfish as thinly as you can and lay the slices straight onto individual plates. Don't worry if the fish is still partially frozen, by the time you have sliced and plated it all it will have defrosted fully.

Dress each plate with the fennel and ginger dressing. Pipe small dots of yoghurt on top. Finish with sea purslane leaves (either fresh or deep-fried in oil heated to 180°C until crisp, then drained and cooled).

Serve the dressed monkfish cold, as soon as it is garnished.

This is probably one of the simplest dishes we serve in the restaurant and for sure it's one of the tastiest. When mackerel is at its best you really don't need to do much to it. Here we just season it with salt and pan-fry it skin side down, so it gets nice and crisp, then serve it hot with the mushroom cream and crispy pancetta at room temperature. It's a great favourite with our customers. It appears to be a rather unassuming dish with humble ingredients, but boy does it pack a punch!

MACKEREL, MUSHROOM CREAM AND **PANCETTA**

Serves 4 as a starter

2 large mackerel,
   gutted, filleted and
   pin-boned
olive oil for cooking
Cornish sea salt

For the mushroom cream
a little olive oil
   for cooking
1 white onion, peeled
   and finely chopped
350g button
   mushrooms, sliced
2 sheets of bronze
   leaf gelatine
200ml double cream
1 teaspoon ground
   coriander
juice of 1 lime

To serve
6 slices of pancetta
4 tablespoons
   vinaigrette (see
   page 290)

To prepare the mushroom cream
Heat a little olive oil in a large saucepan, add the onion and cook over a medium heat for 1 minute, without colouring. Add the sliced mushrooms and cook, stirring now and again until they release their liquid and start to colour and roast in the pan; this should take about 15 minutes.

Soak the leaf gelatine in a shallow dish of ice-cold water to soften.

Pour the cream onto the mushrooms and season with a little salt and the ground coriander. Bring to the boil and then remove from the heat and tip the mixture into a blender. Add the lime juice and blend until smooth. Pour back into the pan.

Bring the mushroom cream back to a simmer then remove from the heat. Immediately squeeze out the excess water from the gelatine, then add it to the hot mushroom cream and stir until fully dissolved. Taste and adjust the seasoning if necessary.

Spoon the mushroom cream evenly onto 4 serving plates and place them in the fridge for a couple of hours to allow the cream to set.

To crisp the pancetta
While the mushroom cream is setting, preheat your oven to 200°C/ Fan 180°C/Gas Mark 6 and line a baking tray with a non-stick baking mat or silicone paper.

Lay the pancetta slices on the tray and place another baking tray on top. Cook in the oven for 20 minutes, then remove the top tray and return the pancetta to the oven for 5 minutes or so, until crispy. Remove from the oven and allow to cool.

Once cool enough to handle, transfer the pancetta to a board and chop it with a large knife to fine crumbs. Drain on a tray lined with kitchen paper; keep warm.

To prepare for serving
About 20 minutes before you intend to cook the mackerel, take the plates out of the fridge and set them aside, to allow the mushroom cream to come to room temperature.

To cook the mackerel
Drizzle some olive oil into a large non-stick frying pan. Season the mackerel with salt and lay it skin side down in the pan. Place over a medium-high heat and cook the fish for 2–3 minutes until the edges of the skin start to turn golden.

Carefully turn the fish over, then take the pan off the heat and leave the mackerel for about 30 seconds, to finish cooking in the residual heat.

To assemble and serve
Sprinkle the crumbed pancetta equally over the mushroom cream servings and top each with a fillet of mackerel. Drizzle with a little vinaigrette and serve straight away.

'Here lies Nathan Outlaw who made Porthilly sauce' will probably be on my headstone, if I have one. The sauce has become a real talking point amongst our customers. I wasn't sure if I should reveal the recipe, but the way I look at it, sharing knowledge is how we all improve. That said, it isn't as easy as it seems. Firstly, the stocks need a lot of attention. The tomatoes must be ripe, but not *too* ripe or the flavour will dominate. And you can't just use any old fish, you need to source very fresh cod or turbot heads. Finally, the most important ingredient is the shore crabs (the ones you take kids crabbing for). They need to be live and clean. We get ours from Porthilly bay – hence the name. I use them not only because they are super tasty, but also to help keep the little crabs in check. To mussel and oyster farmers, shore crabs are pests, devouring everything they can get their claws into – including baby mussels and oysters. Porthilly is also where I buy my oysters and mussels so I like to think that I'm helping our suppliers, but there are thousands of shore crabs in the Camel Estuary. Hopefully, we are making a dent in the population.

Here I have paired the sauce with gurnard. I'd also like to see gurnard become more popular. A lot of fisherman still don't rate this ugly fish, which has often been used for bait. Well, I don't agree! I find a good gurnard has a fantastic balance of firmness, texture and oiliness. Simply pan-fried until the skin is crisp and served on Porthilly sauce with a little drizzle of good olive oil, it tastes fantastic. Oh, and it is also great for traditional deep-fried fish and chips!

Serves 4 as a starter

2 gurnard, 500–600g
  each, gutted, filleted
  and pin-boned
light olive oil for cooking
Cornish sea salt

For the sauce
4 ripe plum tomatoes
750ml shore crab stock
  (see page 290)
500ml fish stock (see
  page 288)
50g unsalted butter

To finish
extra virgin olive oil
  to drizzle

GURNARD WITH PORTHILLY SAUCE

To make the sauce
Preheat your grill to high. Place the tomatoes on the grill rack and grill, turning occasionally, until they are soft and the skins are blistered all over. Pour both stocks into a large saucepan and add the tomatoes and butter. Bring to the boil over a medium heat and then let it bubble to reduce down to about 400ml.

Tip the contents of the pan into a blender and blitz for 4 minutes until smooth. Keep the sauce warm (or allow to cool if making ahead and reheat to serve).

To cook the fish
Preheat your oven to 240°C/Fan 220°C/Gas Mark 9. Trim the edges of the gurnard fillets to neaten and season them with salt. Heat a large non-stick, ovenproof frying pan over a medium heat.

When the pan is hot, add a drizzle of olive oil and carefully lay the fish fillets, skin side down, in the pan. Cook for 2 minutes.

Now transfer the pan to the oven and cook for a further 2–3 minutes. Remove the frying pan from the oven; the fish should still look a little translucent on the top.

Carefully turn the fillets over and leave them to finish cooking in the residual heat for 30 seconds or so.

To assemble and serve
While the fish finishes cooking, give the sauce a good whisk and pour it equally into 4 warmed bowls. Using a palette knife, carefully lift each fish fillet from the pan and place on top of the sauce. Finish with a generous drizzle of extra virgin olive oil and serve straight away.

WING OF ST MAWES
Fish and seafood supplier

As a seafood chef, it's crucial to me to have a respected and trusted fish and seafood supplier, who I can rely on to send me the very best of everything at market each day. Rob Wing, of Wing of St Mawes, is just that. He was born and brought up on the south coast of Cornwall in St Mawes, where his parents had a small shop. After leaving school, Rob trained in Hotel and Catering at Cornwall Technical College, before working as a chef for a number of years. However, family circumstances meant a move from the kitchen back to help run the family shop. As with many businesses in Cornwall, without tourists, custom dwindled during the winter months. To sustain an income, Rob began fishing commercially and soon realised that there was a hole in the supply chain for Cornish fish and seafood across the UK.

His early experiences have helped Rob to build a very successful business over the last 35 years, selling 'Cornish Gold', as he calls it. He takes charge of around 10–15 tonnes of fish and seafood per week, from the waters around Cornwall, which he refers to as 'the M25 of the seas around the UK'. He also smokes great fish on site. Rob deals with fishermen from all around the southwest coast, drawing fish from the fleets at Newlyn, Looe, Brixham and Plymouth amongst others. In 2007, he started an online service, 'The Cornish Fishmonger' to satisfy the home cook's demand for very fresh fish. Customers around the UK can have the catch within 24 hours of it being taken from the sea. He describes it as 'traditional fishmongery with modern technology'.

Rob's passion for what he does is evident when you speak to him, and his knowledge is grounded in his catering background so he understands exactly what I want for my restaurants. He still finds walking into a wholesale fish market exciting, taking in the colours, the aromas and the surprise of what is on offer on any given day. If you ask him why he still does it, he simply says 'I love it!'.

Rob is fully committed to sustainability, which we both agree is the only way to guarantee a supply of fish in the future. Assuring the future of Wing of St. Mawes, Rob is training up his son Jack, who shares his passion for seafood. As for the fishermen, Rob says that the culture has changed and they now realise the necessity to protect what is there, to ensure supplies in the years ahead.

Over the last decade or so, Rob has seen a huge change in the requirements of his customers, both in the restaurant industry and in retail. Customers used to want just cod, haddock and plaice, but now they looking to try different species. He puts this down to people travelling and experiencing different species abroad. To Rob, this has been the saving grace of his industry and has also taught people to correctly value seafood. He says that if you think about it seafood is 'the last hunted, wild, bulk food', but also reminds us that as a wild creature which roams where it wants to 'if it's not there, you can't catch it!'.

Well respected, both by his customers and the fishing community, Rob is often called upon to advise and support causes linked to his business. As Chair of the Harbour Commission at Newlyn, he played a major role in the regeneration and revitalisation of the fishing port. He sees Newlyn as an important fishing port in England, not least because parts of the quay date back to Tudor times.

Rob has also recently become the Chair of the National Lobster Hatchery in Padstow. It's a nod to his commitment to sustainability and his desire to educate the public about the need to preserve our seafood stocks for future generations.

When asked for his advice on buying and cooking fish, Rob says to store it for as little time as possible, and keep it cold, on ice if you can. Overcooking fish is the biggest problem, he insists, and reminds us that all our UK fish can be eaten raw.

And Rob's final word? 'Always try something different'. I'd agree with that!

Over the past few years, steaming has become my favourite way to cook certain fish, including fillets of bass. The technique shows off the amazing texture of this lovely fish and allows you to enjoy its natural flavours. Chefs sometimes overdo it with seasoning, herbs and butter, overpowering the delicate flavours of the fish. I like to keep it simple.

Hollandaise was one of the first sauces I learnt to make. I was intrigued by the technique and found it challenging when I was at college. It's a relatively simple sauce but you do need to understand what is happening to the ingredients as you make it or you'll mess it up – as I did the first time I made it. In that moment I began to appreciate that to cook great food you need to know the techniques. There have been many similar lessons over the years!

This hollandaise is slightly different from the traditional one. I use olive oil instead of butter, which I suppose makes it a bit healthier (but not much!) and flavour it, judiciously, with the ingredients of tartare sauce. Tender, young leeks are the perfect complement.

BASS WITH LEEKS AND TARTARE HOLLANDAISE

Serves 4 as a main course

4 filleted bass portions, 160–180g each, scaled and pin-boned
light olive oil to drizzle
Cornish sea salt

For the tartare hollandaise
350ml olive oil
finely grated zest and juice of 1 lemon
4 large egg yolks
3 tablespoons water
1 large gherkin, finely chopped
1 tablespoon capers in brine, drained and chopped
1 tablespoon chopped curly parsley
1 tablespoon chopped chives
1 tablespoon chopped tarragon
1 tablespoon chopped chervil

For the leeks
12 young, tender leeks, trimmed and thoroughly cleaned

To finish
chopped chives, chervil and parsley
extra virgin olive oil

Set up a steamer or switch on your oven steamer if you have one.

To make the tartare hollandaise
Heat the olive oil in a pan over a low heat until warm, but not hot, then add the lemon zest and remove from the heat.

Place the egg yolks, water and lemon juice in a stainless steel bowl and set it over a pan of gently simmering water, making sure the bowl isn't touching the water. Whisk until the mixture triples in volume and is thick enough to leave a ribbon when the whisk is lifted.

Remove the bowl from the pan (save the hot water in the pan) and slowly whisk the olive oil into the egg yolk mix. Gradually increase the flow of oil until it is all incorporated, then season with salt to taste. Cover with cling film or a plate and keep warm.

To cook the leeks
Place the trimmed whole leeks in the steamer and steam for 5–6 minutes until cooked. Remove them from the steamer and slice into 3–4cm lengths. Keep warm.

To cook the fish
Trim the bass portions to neaten if necessary and season with salt. Lay the fish on a tray and drizzle lightly all over with olive oil. Cook in the steamer for 4–6 minutes, depending on thickness.

To assemble and serve
While the fish is steaming, put the bowl of hollandaise back over the pan of water and gently warm it. Add the gherkin, capers and herbs. Mix well and taste the sauce for seasoning, adding a little more salt if required.

Once the fish is cooked, remove it from the steamer and place on a board. Put the leeks back into the steamer to keep warm. Meanwhile, carefully remove the skin from the bass and season the flesh lightly with salt.

Share the sauce equally among 4 warmed plates and top each with a portion of bass. Take the leeks from the steamer and place on top of the fish. Finish with freshly chopped herbs and a drizzle of extra virgin olive oil. Serve straight away.

I don't need to tell you how good turbot is. It is well documented that most people consider this fish to be the best catch in UK waters. So, what do you serve it with? I'd say, preferably, not much. You really don't want to mask turbot's natural flavours.

Here I'm serving it with an unusual sauce made from celeriac, water, cream and lemon juice. It's not your typical fish accompanying sauce, but the flavour is fantastic, not least because celeriac is an excellent base for stock. The pickled Jerusalem artichokes add an extra surprise element and the smoked oil brings the whole dish alive.

TURBOT, CELERIAC, PICKLED JERUSALEM ARTICHOKES AND SPROUTING BROCCOLI

Serves 4 as a main course

4 filleted turbot portions, 160–180g each (from a 2kg fish)
olive oil for cooking
Cornish sea salt

For the pickled artichokes
100ml dry white wine
100ml white wine vinegar
80g caster sugar
100ml water
400g Jerusalem artichokes

For the celeriac and sauce
1 large or 2 small celeriac
juice of ½ lemon
about 400ml water (see recipe)
olive oil for cooking
150ml double cream
100g butter, in pieces

To assemble and serve
400g purple sprouting broccoli, trimmed of any tough ends
smoked oil (available from The Vinegar Shed)

To prepare the pickled artichokes
Put the wine, wine vinegar, sugar and water into a small pan with a good pinch of salt and bring to a simmer over a low heat, stirring to dissolve the sugar. Meanwhile, peel the artichokes and slice them thinly, using a mandoline. Place in a bowl and pour the simmering pickling liquid over them, making sure they are submerged. Cover the bowl with cling film and leave the artichokes to cool. (If you're not using them straight away, refrigerate and use within a week.)

To prepare the celeriac
Peel the celeriac, taking care to remove only the skin. Cut two 3cm thick slices from the thickest central part, halve and trim to the same size; reserve these slices in a bowl of cold water with the juice of ½ lemon added to avoid discolouration. Save all the trimmings for the stock.

To make the celeriac sauce
Chop up all the rest of the celeriac, then weigh it. Measure out the same volume of water.

Heat a large, heavy-based pan (I use a cast-iron pan) over a medium heat and add a drizzle of olive oil. When it is hot, add the chopped celeriac and colour all over, stirring from time to time to ensure it doesn't burn.

Try to get the celeriac as golden and caramelised as possible. Add the measured water and a pinch of salt, bring to a simmer and cook gently for 30 minutes.

Strain the sauce into another pan and place back on the heat. Simmer until it has reduced down to 6 tablespoons. Add the cream, stir and bring back to a simmer. Allow the sauce to bubble gently for 2 minutes, then take the pan off the heat. Keep warm (or cool and refrigerate the sauce if preparing ahead, ready to reheat for serving).

To cook the celeriac pieces
Place the reserved celeriac pieces in a saucepan and pour on just enough water to cover them. Add the butter and a pinch of salt. Bring to a simmer and cook gently for about 20 minutes until tender. Remove the celeriac from the liquid and set aside to cool.

To prepare for serving
Set up a steamer or switch on your oven steamer if you have one. Take the pickled artichokes out of the fridge and lay out enough slices on a plate to cover the 4 fish portions. Check the fish for any shavings of

...continued on page 166

bone (that could be left from filleting). Season the turbot portions with salt and drizzle lightly all over with olive oil. Place on a tray and set aside, ready for cooking.

To assemble and serve
Drain the celeriac slices and pat dry. Place a frying pan over a medium heat and add a drizzle of olive oil. When it is hot, add the celeriac slices and colour gently on both sides.

Meanwhile, put the purple sprouting broccoli into the steamer and cook for 3 minutes. Once the celeriac is golden, remove the pan from the heat and add the steamed broccoli, to keep it warm.

Place the turbot portions in the steamer and cook for 4–5 minutes, then remove and peel away the skin. Season the fish with a little salt and then lay the pickled artichoke slices on top, overlapping them slightly. Warm the celeriac sauce and add lemon juice and salt to taste, to liven up the flavours.

To serve, pour the celeriac sauce equally into 4 warmed deep plates and arrange the celeriac slices and purple sprouting broccoli on top. Place a portion of turbot on top and finish with a little smoked oil. Serve straight away.

Mostly, we associate lobster with summer flavours, but the meat is also good with autumnal ingredients. At this time of the year, lobsters are still in good nick and are usually at a fair price. The onion dressing has an addictive bitter-sweet taste that is great with the rich lobster meat, especially with the squeeze of lemon added at the end. The roast onion stuffed with lobster meat makes a great starter on its own. Filling the onions with autumn hen crab meat works a treat too.

LOBSTER WITH ROAST ONIONS AND CARROTS

First make the onion stock dressing
Heat a large pan over a medium heat and add a drizzle of olive oil. When it is hot, add the onions with the thyme, and cook, stirring occasionally, for about 15 minutes until softened and golden. Pour in the water, bring to a simmer and let simmer for 30 minutes. Strain the stock into another pan, squeezing the onions to extract as much flavour as you can. Return the stock to the heat and continue to simmer until reduced down to about 100ml.

Meanwhile, melt the butter in a pan over a low heat. Increase the heat to medium-high and cook until the butter is bubbling, turning brown, and has a nutty aroma. Immediately take off the heat and leave to cool. Carefully pour the brown butter into another pan, leaving the sediment behind. Keep the butter warm.

For the roast onions
Place the onion halves, cut side up, in a pan in which they fit snugly, side by side. Add the thyme, garlic and butter, then pour on just enough water to cover the onions. Add a good pinch of salt and bring to a simmer. Cook for about 20 minutes, until the onions are soft. Remove them from the pan and leave to cool slightly.

For the roast carrots
Place the carrots in a pan with the butter, thyme, cider vinegar and a small pinch of salt. Pour on enough water to just cover and bring to a simmer. Cook until the carrots are just tender, then remove to a plate. Simmer the cooking liquor until reduced to a glaze; set aside.

To steam the lobsters
Set up a steamer or switch on your oven steamer if you have one.

Take your lobsters from the freezer and place them on a board. Insert the tip of a strong, sharp knife firmly into the cross on the back of each lobster's head. (The lobster will be killed instantly, although it may continue to move a little; this is normal.)

Tie the lobster tail to the tip of the head, to straighten out the tail and keep it from curling up once cooked. Steam the lobsters for 6 minutes. Take them out of the steamer and leave to cool slightly.

Pull off the claws and crack them to extract the meat. Set aside (this will be used to stuff the onions). Cut the tails in half lengthways and remove the grit sack from the head and the intestinal track that runs the length of the tail. Set aside.

To stuff the roast onions
Carefully remove the inner layers of the onions, leaving an outer shell for stuffing, and chop the removed onion. Heat a frying pan over a medium-high heat and add a drizzle of olive

...continued on page 170

2 live Cornish lobsters, about 800g each, placed in the freezer for 30 minutes before cooking
Cornish sea salt and freshly ground black pepper

For the onion stock dressing
olive oil for cooking
1kg onions, peeled and chopped
4 sprigs of thyme
1 litre water
250g unsalted butter
1 tablespoon lemon juice

For the roast onions
2 medium white onions, peeled and halved crossways (through the equator)
2 sprigs of thyme
2 garlic cloves, peeled and crushed
50g unsalted butter
olive oil for cooking

For the roast carrots
4 medium carrots, peeled and trimmed
50g butter
2 sprigs of thyme
50ml cider vinegar
olive oil for cooking

For the spinach
200g spinach, washed and picked
a knob of unsalted butter

To finish
2 tablespoons chopped mixed fines herbes (parsley, tarragon, chives and chervil)

oil. When the oil is hot, carefully place the onion shells in the pan, cut side down, and cook for a few minutes until the edges are golden and lightly caramelised. Remove from the pan. Mix the lobster claw meat with the chopped onion centres and use to stuff the onion shells. Place them on a grill tray, ready to heat up at the same time as the lobster tails.

To finish the dressing

Put 4 tablespoons of the onion stock in a pan with 6 tablespoons brown butter and 1 tablespoon lemon juice. Heat, stirring to combine, and season with salt and pepper; keep warm.

To colour the carrots

Heat a frying pan over a medium-high heat and add a drizzle of olive oil. When it is hot, add the carrots and roast in the pan until golden and lightly caramelised.

To grill the lobsters

Preheat your grill to high. Lay the lobster tails on a grill tray, season with salt and pepper and spoon over some onion dressing. Grill the lobster for 2–3 minutes to finish the cooking.

To prepare for serving

While the lobsters are under the grill, warm up the carrots in their glaze. Wilt the spinach in a pan with the butter and season with salt. Pop the stuffed onions under the grill to warm them through. Add the herbs to the warm dressing. Drain the carrots and spinach.

To serve

Share the carrots and spinach among 4 warmed plates. Place a grilled half lobster tail and a stuffed onion on each plate. Spoon on the dressing and serve straight away.

CAMEL VALLEY VINEYARD
Our local winemaker

As well as its wonderful array of foods, Cornwall is becoming known for its range of wines. This is a real bonus for Restaurant Nathan Outlaw as it means we can source world-class wines locally.

Camel Valley Vineyard has been producing excellent wines since 1989. Situated in the small hamlet of Nanstallon, between Wadebridge and Bodmin in the heart of the Cornish countryside, Camel Valley Vineyard enjoys a wonderful aspect and south-facing slopes.

Ex-Royal Air Force pilot Bob Lindo and his wife, Annie, first bought their land to farm sheep and cows, but within a few years they realised that the location and soil were ideal for growing grapes. So, as many farmers do, they decided to diversify and try their hand at winemaking. Bob is largely self-taught, gleaning his early knowledge from books and practical experience. To begin with, he and Annie worked the vineyard themselves, calling on friends when they needed extra hands. Today they have a team in place to tend the vines, make the wine and look after visitors, though they are still actively involved in the business.

Annie has her own vineyard on their land, growing Seyval blanc grapes that she cares for personally, simply because she enjoys doing it. She is the only person to have winter-pruned all 5,000 vines by hand, and has been doing this for almost 30 years! She and her vineyard were the wine stars in the TV programme, *Caroline Quentin's Cornwall*, in 2017.

In 2002, their son, Sam, joined the family firm in a change of career, having started his working life in the City. He spent a year working in a winery in New Zealand and is now an accomplished winemaker in his own right.

The gamble of diversifying from cattle to grapes paid off for the Lindo family and Camel Valley Vineyard began to win prestigious awards for their wines. As well as their still wines, they began to produce sparkling wines by the traditional method, the first vineyard in the UK to attempt to do so. Again, the wine was a success and in 2005 they were awarded the International Wine Challenge Gold Medal for their Camel Valley 'Cornwall' Sparkling Wine.

Today Camel Valley Vineyard exports wines as far afield as Japan. They supply several large retail chains as well as a number of fine dining restaurants, the Tate Modern in London, British Airways First Class flights, Buckingham Palace and Clarence House. They are the first English winemaker to be awarded a Royal Warrant from His Royal Highness, The Prince of Wales, and the endorsement 'By Royal Appointment' can now be found on their wine labels.

Accolades have continued to accrue. Most recently, Bob was the recipient of a lifetime achievement award from the International Wine Challenge (IWC) 'for his outstanding contribution in helping drive the quality-focused rise of Britain's home-grown sparkling wines'. And Sam has won the award for UK Winemaker of the Year three times, and the International IWC Trophy for 'the Best Sparkling Rosé (including Champagne) in the world.'

We have been proud to offer Camel Valley Vineyard wines to our restaurant customers since 2010. Our Sommelier and Beverage Manager, Damon Little, says of their wines, 'In the past and at present we offer two Camel Valley sparkling wines, the Pinot Noir Rosé Brut and Annie's Anniversary Brut, as well as a still white wine known as Darnibole Bacchus. Judging the quality of wine is most certainly subjective, but over the years each and every vintage we have offered to our guests has never ceased to amaze. The quality and structure of Camel Valley wines is the deciding factor toward serving their wines not only at Restaurant Nathan Outlaw but across all our restaurants. In addition, the service level offered by the team is exemplary.'

I think that says it all!

I like the simplicity of this dessert. I have been making the vanilla cream and sweet wine jelly for a long time – since my first restaurant, in fact, when I served them with a raspberry sorbet and fresh berries. Recently I've paired them with passion fruit and I love the combination. It's light, yet rich at the same time, and the sweet wine and passion fruit are just great together. The vanilla cream is based on an Italian panna cotta, but has a lot less gelatine. I'm not a big fan of the popular panna cotta that you turn out of a mould, because it requires so much gelatine to do so. An Italian chef once told me that an authentic panna cotta doesn't have any gelatine and shouldn't be turned out. I like the sound of that…

VANILLA CREAM, SWEET WINE JELLY AND PASSION FRUIT

Serves 6

For the vanilla cream
2 sheets of bronze
  leaf gelatine
560ml whole milk
180ml double cream
2 vanilla pods, split
  lengthways
90g caster sugar

For the sweet wine jelly
5 sheets of bronze
  leaf gelatine
600ml sweet wine

For the passion fruit gel
225g frozen passion
  fruit purée
190g caster sugar
5g pectin
5g tartaric acid

**For the passion
fruit syrup**
3 passion fruit
50g caster sugar

To make the vanilla cream
Soak the leaf gelatine in a shallow dish of ice-cold water to soften. Pour the milk and cream into a pan and add the vanilla pods and sugar. Bring to a simmer over a medium heat, stirring to dissolve the sugar, then remove the pan from the heat. Immediately squeeze the excess water from the gelatine, then whisk it into the hot creamy milk until fully dissolved.

Leave to cool, then remove the vanilla pods and pour the vanilla cream equally into 4 serving bowls. Place in the fridge to set; this will take about 2 hours.

To make the sweet wine jelly
Soak the leaf gelatine in a shallow dish of ice-cold water to soften. Heat the wine in a pan until it is almost simmering, then remove from the heat. Immediately squeeze out the excess water from the gelatine, then add it to the hot wine and whisk until fully dissolved. Leave to cool.

Once cold, spoon the wine jelly evenly on top of the set vanilla creams. Carefully return to the fridge to set.

To prepare the passion fruit gel
Put the passion fruit purée and 180g of the sugar into a heavy-based pan and bring to the boil. Mix the pectin with the remaining 10g of sugar and add to the boiling liquor. Cook until the temperature reaches 106°C. Whisk in the tartaric acid and then pour the mixture onto a tray to cool.

Once cooled, transfer the mixture to a food processor and blend until smooth. Transfer to a disposable piping bag and refrigerate until ready to serve.

To make the passion fruit syrup
Halve the passion fruit and scoop out the seeds and pulp into a pan. Add the sugar and heat gently to dissolve, then bring to a simmer and cook until syrupy. Remove from the heat and leave to cool before serving.

To assemble and serve
Take the vanilla creams topped with sweet wine jelly from the fridge and pipe a blob of the passion fruit gel on top of each one. Finish with a few of the passion fruit seeds in syrup. Serve cold.

Raspberry and chocolate is a classic flavour combination that most of us enjoy. We are lucky enough to get fantastic raspberries right through to November in Cornwall, so they often feature on the menu. This raspberry ice cream is really a frozen mousse and it doesn't need to be churned, while the chocolate mousse is an old faithful that's appeared in different guises in all my restaurants. Technically it's a bavarois which is a set custard, but I'm happy to call it a mousse. The chocolate sugar tuiles are fragile and a bit tricky, but you could serve this dessert without them.

RASPBERRY ICE CREAM
AND DARK CHOCOLATE

To make the raspberry ice cream
Soak the leaf gelatine in a shallow dish of ice-cold water to soften. Put the raspberries and water into a pan and bring to the boil, then tip into a food processor and blend to a purée. Strain through a fine sieve into a clean pan, return to a medium heat and simmer until reduced by half.

Meanwhile, whisk the egg yolks and sugar together in a large bowl. Add the cream to the raspberry purée, stir to combine and bring back to a simmer. Pour the hot raspberry cream onto the egg and sugar mix, whisking as you do so. Immediately squeeze out the excess water from the gelatine and add it to the hot raspberry mixture, whisking until fully dissolved. Leave the mixture to cool, then cover with cling film and refrigerate to set.

Once set, whisk in the cream cheese. Spoon the mixture into a piping bag and pipe into 6 individual moulds. Freeze until firm, then remove from the moulds, wrap each one in cling film and return to the freezer until ready to serve. Clean the moulds.

To make the chocolate mousse
Soak the gelatine in a shallow dish of ice-cold water to soften. Pour the milk and 300ml of the cream into a pan and bring to a simmer. Meanwhile, whisk the egg yolks, sugar and cocoa together in a large

bowl. Pour the hot creamy milk onto the egg and sugar mixture, whisking as you do so. Immediately squeeze out the excess water from the gelatine and add it to the hot mixture with the chocolate, whisking until melted and smooth. Leave to cool.

Whip the remaining 200ml cream in a separate bowl until it begins to hold its shape, then fold through the cooled chocolate mixture. Spoon into a piping bag and place in the fridge until ready to serve.

To make the chocolate sugar
Put the sugar and glucose into a pan over a medium heat and heat gently; the mixture will start to colour and form a caramel. Cook until it reaches 158°C, then take the pan off the heat and add the chocolate. Beat with a spatula until the mixture is fully emulsified, then pour onto a non-stick silicone baking mat to cool.

When the chocolate caramel mixture is no longer sticky but still hot, place another non-stick mat on top and roll the caramel out to a thin sheet (to cool it quickly and make it easier to break up later). Leave until cold.

When cold, break up the mixture and place in a food processor. Blitz (noisily!) until it is as fine as possible.

...continued on page 180

Serves 6

For the raspberry ice cream
3 sheets of bronze leaf gelatine
300g raspberries
100ml water
5 medium egg yolks
120g caster sugar
400ml double cream
260g full-fat cream cheese, at room temperature

For the chocolate mousse
2 sheets of bronze leaf gelatine
100ml whole milk
500ml double cream
6 medium egg yolks
100g caster sugar
40g dark cocoa powder
100g dark chocolate (70% cocoa solids), chopped into small pieces

For the chocolate sugar tuiles
250g caster sugar
130g liquid glucose
90g good-quality milk chocolate, chopped into small pieces

For the raspberry syrup
200g raspberries
100g caster sugar

To finish
42 raspberries (in perfect condition)

To make the chocolate tuiles

First, you will need to make a template – a rectangular plastic ice-cream tub lid is ideal for this. Measure the circumference of the mould you have set the ice cream in (by holding a piece of string around the mould and checking it against a ruler), then add 5cm to this length. Check the height of the mould, too. Cut out a strip with these dimensions from the plastic lid and discard it. The lid with the plastic strip cut out is your template.

Now preheat your oven to 170°C/Fan 150°C/Gas Mark 3. Place the template on a large non-stick silicone mat on a baking tray. Using a fine sieve, sift about 3 teaspoons of the caramel dust into the template to create an even layer. Carefully lift off the template and repeat to shape another 5 caramel dust strips. Place in the oven for about 4 minutes to melt the dust and form caramel sheets. Remove from the oven.

When the caramel is no longer soft but still pliable, wrap each strip around a mould (the one used for the ice creams) and press the ends together to seal; the caramel will set quickly. If the strips set before you manage to shape them, pop them back in the oven briefly to soften again. Once shaped, they are ready to use (or you can store them in an airtight container, if making ahead).

To make the raspberry syrup

Put the raspberries and sugar into a pan over a medium heat to dissolve the sugar. When the mixture starts to bubble, give it a stir, then simmer for 5 minutes. Tip into a small food processor and blitz to a purée, adding a little water to loosen if necessary. Pass through a fine sieve to remove the pips. Leave to cool.

To assemble and serve

About 10 minutes before serving, take the raspberry ice creams from the freezer, unwrap and place one on each serving plate. Slot a tuile over each ice cream. Snip the end off the piping bag and pipe the chocolate mousse evenly over the ice cream. Top with fresh raspberries and a trickle of raspberry syrup. Serve immediately.

I am a big fan of these fruit jellies and we make them with all kinds of flavourful fruits in the restaurant. When we can get fresh blackcurrants with the perfect amount of sweetness and acidity, these are the ones I want on the menu for our customers.

Makes about 30

450g blackcurrant
  purée (fresh or frozen
  and defrosted)
380g caster sugar
10g pectin
5g tartaric acid
granulated sugar
  for coating

BLACKCURRANT JELLIES

Put the blackcurrant purée and 360g of the sugar into a heavy-based pan and bring to the boil. Mix the pectin with the remaining 20g of sugar and add to the boiling liquor. Cook until the temperature reaches 106°C. Whisk in the tartaric acid well and then pour the mixture onto a small tray and leave to cool.

When the blackcurrant mixture is completely cooled, place it in the fridge to set for 2 hours.

To serve, cut the blackcurrant jelly into squares, using a sharp knife. Roll them through the granulated sugar to coat evenly, shaking off the excess. Serve straight away.

Late Autumn

I like to use choux pastry to create tasty nibbles for our customers to enjoy with a drink while they browse the menu and these little flavour bombs are guaranteed to get a meal off to a great start. Filled with a smoked mackerel pâté flavoured with horseradish and served warm topped with a grating of Parmesan, they are so more-ish. You will want more than one, trust me!

SMOKED MACKEREL CHOUX BUNS

Makes 20 canapés

For the choux pastry
130g plain flour
1 teaspoon fine sea salt
220ml water
110g unsalted butter,
    in pieces
4 large eggs

For the smoked mackerel pâté
300g smoked mackerel
    fillet, skinned and
    pin-boned
juice of 1 lemon
2 tablespoons creamed
    horseradish
100g full-fat cream
    cheese
100g Greek-style
    yoghurt
freshly ground
    black pepper

To finish
smoked paprika to dust
100g Parmesan
    for grating

To make the choux pastry
Preheat the oven to 220°C/Fan 200°C/Gas Mark 7. Line a baking tray with a non-stick baking mat or silicone paper.

Sift the flour and salt together onto a piece of baking parchment. Put the water and butter into a saucepan and bring to the boil over a medium heat. When the butter has melted and the liquid is boiling, add the flour all at once and stir well to combine. Turn the heat down low and cook out the dough for 10 minutes, stirring occasionally. Remove from the heat and beat the mixture thoroughly for about 2 minutes until it comes away from the sides of the pan.

In a separate bowl, beat the eggs together, then gradually beat them into the choux mixture; make sure each addition is fully incorporated before adding the next.

Once all the egg is incorporated and the mixture is smooth and shiny, transfer it to a large piping bag fitted with a large plain nozzle.

To shape and bake the choux buns
Pipe small mounds of the choux pastry onto the prepared baking tray, leaving space in between for them to expand. Bake in the oven for about 10 minutes until golden brown.

When you remove the tray from the oven, make a small hole on the underside of each choux bun to allow the steam to escape. Place the buns on a wire rack and leave to cool.

To make the smoked mackerel pâté
Put the smoked mackerel into a food processor with the lemon juice and creamed horseradish and blend for 30 seconds, stopping to scrape down the sides of the bowl once or twice.

Add the cream cheese and yoghurt and blend for 1 minute until smoothly combined (the mixture needs to be smooth enough to pipe). Taste for seasoning, adding a little pepper.

Spoon the mackerel pâté into a piping bag fitted with a small plain nozzle, ready to pipe before serving (refrigerate if preparing ahead).

To assemble and serve
Heat your oven to 200°C/Fan 180°C/Gas Mark 6. Pipe the smoked mackerel pâté into the choux buns through the hole in the base and place them on a baking tray.

Sprinkle the choux buns with a little smoked paprika and place in the oven for 2 minutes to warm up. As soon as the buns come out of the oven, finely grate the Parmesan over the top. Serve immediately.

At this time of year, I get offered a few of the larger Dover soles, known as 'doormats', which are too big to be served as whole fish on the bone. They're good value for money, considering the superiority of this species. This terrine makes great use of them, combining them with young leeks and a crab dressing. You can make it a day ahead and keep it in the fridge – just remember to take it out an hour before serving to bring it to room temperature. When you're making a terrine like this, make sure you season everything well, otherwise the fish can taste a little bland.

DOVER SOLE AND LEEK TERRINE WITH CRAB DRESSING

Serves 6–8 as a starter

3 large Dover sole,
 gutted and skinned
20 young leeks, washed
 and trimmed of any
 tougher parts
1 sheet of bronze
 leaf gelatine
100ml fish stock
a little oil for brushing
Cornish sea salt
 and freshly ground
 black pepper

For the crab dressing
200ml shore crab stock
 (see page 290)
50ml agrodolce vinegar
100ml light olive oil

To prepare the terrine mould
Lightly oil a 26 x 10cm terrine mould, and line with 3 layers of cling film, leaving enough overhanging the rim to cover the terrine (once filled).

To cook the Dover sole
Set up a steamer or switch on your oven steamer if you have one. (As they are large, you may need to cook the fish one at a time in a steamer pan.) Season the sole well all over with salt and pepper and lay them on an oiled steamer tray. Steam the whole fish for 8–10 minutes until cooked. To check, insert a small knife into the thickest point around the head area. If you can pull the fish away from the bone cleanly with no visible rawness, the fish are ready.

Remove the tray from the steamer and leave the Dover sole to rest for 5 minutes, with a tray underneath to catch any juices.

To cook the leeks
While the fish are steaming, bring a pan of salted water to the boil. Add the leeks and cook for 4–5 minutes until just tender; do not overcook.

Drain the leeks and leave them to cool slightly; remove any parts that have become waterlogged (this sometimes occurs).

To make the terrine
While the leeks are cooling, soak the gelatine in a shallow dish of ice-cold water to soften.

Cut the fillets from the Dover soles and trim away any bones or sinew. Add any juices collected during resting to the fish stock and heat in a small pan until almost at a simmer. Remove from the heat. Immediately squeeze out the excess water from the gelatine, then add it to the hot stock, whisking as you do so, until the gelatine has fully dissolved. Season the liquor well with salt and pepper.

Using a pastry brush, brush the lined terrine with some of the fish stock. Place a layer of leeks on the base of the terrine and brush this with fish stock. Arrange a layer of Dover sole on top, leaving a clear margin along the sides. Fill the gaps along the sides with leeks. Brush the fish and leeks with fish stock. Repeat these layers twice more, then finish with a layer of leeks and a final brushing of stock. (You may have some fish fillet left over – a treat for the cook!)

To press the terrine
Bring the cling film overhanging the sides up and pull tightly (without tearing them). Now wrap the overhanging layers over the top

...continued on page 192

of the terrine to enclose it completely. Pierce the cling film with a pin 5 or 6 times all over (this will allow the excess stock and juice to escape when the terrine is being pressed). Now lay a flat tray (or something similar) that fits just inside the mould on the top of the leek and fish terrine, then place a few weights on top (food cans will do). Place in the fridge and leave to press for at least 4 hours, ideally overnight.

To unmould the terrine
Remove the weights and turn the terrine out of its mould onto a board. Carefully peel away the cling film, then re-wrap the terrine tightly in new cling film. Using a very sharp knife, slice the terrine into 6–8 generous slices. Transfer each slice to a serving plate and then remove the cling film. Leave the terrine to come to room temperature before serving; this will take about an hour.

To make the dressing
In a bowl, whisk the crab stock, vinegar and olive oil together and season with salt and pepper to taste.

To serve
I like to warm the dressing slightly before serving. Lightly oil the surface of each terrine slice and sprinkle with a little salt. Surround with the dressing and serve straight away.

At this time of the year, hen crabs are superb and full of brown meat, which I love. This is where the flavour is concentrated and when you cook a fresh crab, the brown meat is far superior to the pre-packed overcooked, processed option. This starter really shows off the quality of the hen over the cock crab. If you don't believe me, try it for yourself! The apple and cider flavours bring a lovely fruity acidity, which is perfect with the rich, clean crab taste. If you want to simplify the dish, serve the brown crab custard on its own, with some toasted sourdough.

HEN CRAB, CRAB CUSTARD AND APPLE

Serves 4 as a starter

For the crab
1 live brown hen crab, about 1kg, placed in the freezer 30 minutes before cooking
3 tablespoons Greek-style yoghurt
3 teaspoons chopped chives
Cornish sea salt and freshly ground black pepper

For the crab custard
1½ sheets of bronze leaf gelatine
light olive oil for cooking
2 shallots, peeled and finely chopped
200g brown crab meat (from above)
30ml brandy
200ml double cream
a pinch of cayenne pepper
2 tablespoons lemon juice

For the pickled apple slices
100ml cider
100ml cider vinegar
100ml water
100g caster sugar
1 large or 2 small Granny Smith apples

For the apple jelly
3 sheets of bronze leaf gelatine
150ml apple juice
150ml dry cider
20ml cider vinegar

To finish
extra virgin olive oil

To prepare the crab
Bring a large pan of water (big enough to hold the crab fully submerged) to the boil. Season the water generously with salt, to make it as salty as sea water. Once it comes to a rolling boil, lower the crab into the water and cook for 14 minutes.

Carefully lift the crab out of the pan, place on a tray and leave until cool enough to handle. Remove all the legs and claws from the cooked crab, by twisting them away from the body. Now, holding the crab in both hands, use your thumbs to push the body up and out of the hard, top shell or carapace. Remove and discard the dead man's fingers, stomach sac and hard membranes from the body shell.

Using a spoon, remove the brown crab from the carapace and put it into a bowl. Now cut the body in half, using a sharp knife, to reveal the little channels of white crab meat. Use a crab pick or the handle of a spoon to pick out all the crab meat from these crevices and put it into a separate bowl.

Using a heavy knife, break the claws with one hard tap if possible and pick out the white meat, prising out the cartilage from the middle of the claw. Do the same with the legs to extract the meat. Put 4 neat pieces of leg to one side for presentation. Once you have extracted all the white meat,

with clean hands, pick through it to search for any shell or cartilage. Cover the bowls of crab meat and refrigerate if preparing ahead.

To make the crab custard
Soak the gelatine in a shallow dish of ice-cold water to soften. Place a frying pan over a medium heat and add a drizzle of olive oil. When hot, add the shallots and cook for 2 minutes, stirring often. Add the 200g brown crab meat and brandy and cook for another minute. Pour in the cream and bring to a simmer.

Transfer the mixture to a blender and add the cayenne and lemon juice. Immediately drain the gelatine, squeeze out excess water and add to the blender. Blend for 30 seconds, then taste to check the seasoning and add a little more salt if required.

Pour the crab custard mixture into 4 serving dishes, sharing it equally, and place in the fridge to set for at least 2 hours.

To pickle the apple slices
Heat the cider, cider vinegar, water, sugar and a pinch of salt in a pan to dissolve the sugar and bring to the boil. Simmer for 2 minutes then take off the heat and leave until

...continued on page 196

cold. Meanwhile, using a mandoline, slice the apple(s) thinly and then cut each slice out with a plain cutter (just smaller in diameter) to neaten. Place the apple slices in the cold cider pickling liquor and leave until you are ready to serve.

To make the apple jelly
Soak the gelatine in a shallow dish of ice-cold water to soften. Pour the apple juice, cider and cider vinegar into a pan and place over a medium heat, adding a pinch of salt. When the apple liquor is almost simmering, take the pan off the heat. Immediately drain the gelatine, squeeze out the excess water and then add to the hot liquor, whisking until the gelatine is fully dissolved. Leave the jelly to cool, but not set.

To prepare for serving
Once the apple jelly is cool and the brown crab custards have set, spoon the jelly evenly over the custards. Carefully place the dishes back in the fridge and leave to set completely.

Meanwhile, to bind the white crab meat, add the yoghurt, chives and some salt and pepper. Mix together, then taste to check the seasoning and adjust as necessary.

To assemble and serve
Take the jelly-topped custards and crab meat out of the fridge at least 30 minutes before serving.

Drain the apple slices and lay one on each portion. Share the white crab equally between the dishes, spooning it on top of the apple disc. Lay another smaller, apple disc on the crab meat and top with a piece of leg or claw meat. Finish with a drizzle of extra virgin olive oil and serve at once.

CALUM GREENHALGH
Our crab and lobster fisherman

Port Isaac is a tiny fishing village with a fishing fleet numbering a mere handful of small day boats. As a consequence, the fishermen here are entirely dependent on the weather and tides. The fishing grounds around Port Isaac are quite awkward to fish and our fishermen would have to travel far out to catch enough to make a living. Fortunately, however, it's relatively easy to position crab and lobster pots around the coves, so the local fishing fleet is geared for catching crabs and lobsters.

Calum Greenhalgh is the solo skipper of the Mary D, a Starfish 8 fishing boat, 8 metres long. The future of our fishing industry is a concern for many fishermen, including Calum. Several years ago, he chose this single-handed slow boat, even though a lot of fishermen were buying bigger and faster boats. He wanted to reduce his carbon footprint and use fewer pots. It was an ethical decision that would make life more difficult for him, but would give him a clear conscience on sustainability.

Calum catches only enough to supply his regular customers and the small shop that he runs with his wife, Tracey, called Fresh From The Sea, a stone's throw from Restaurant Nathan Outlaw. Tracey prepares the crabs and lobsters and cooks them on the premises. They make the best crab sandwiches and lobster salads you'll ever eat!

As part of his quest to fish sustainably, when Calum catches a 'berried' female lobster (carrying eggs or 'roe'), he takes it to The National Lobster Hatchery in Padstow. The eggs are nurtured there until they hatch and the baby lobsters grow to a size that gives them an enhanced chance of survival at sea – about one thousand times that of eggs released by a female lobster in her natural habitat. Calum also helps to return the juvenile lobsters to Port Isaac Bay, when they are ready.

Brought up in Nottingham, Calum was originally introduced to fishing by Tracey's, family. It was her father who first took him out to sea on a fishing boat. Later, her grandfather, who Calum describes as 'an old man of the sea', took him under his wing and taught him everything he needed to know about fishing for a living. Calum enjoyed the life so much that he decided to make it his full-time occupation and he's now been fishing for over 30 years.

Around Port Isaac, he catches brown crabs, shore crabs, spider crabs and velvet crabs, all at different times of the year. And, of course, he catches lobsters and crawfish. Occasionally the odd triggerfish gets caught in a pot too, which is a treat when it happens!

Calum sets his pots and baits them according to what he's fishing for. Lobsters are lured by oily fish like mackerel, whereas crabs are looking for 'something fresh and bloody'. He returns to each pot daily, or every two or three days, depending on the time of year, to remove anything that might have been caught. In the autumn, Calum also fishes for mackerel and salts it to use as lobster bait in the summer.

The premium quality of Calum's crabs and lobsters is largely down to the way they are handled. Working alone, he is able to ensure full control over the fishing process. To start with, Calum is more selective than many other fishermen, taking only those crabs and lobsters that are likely to be of the finest quality. He gauges this using his experience, taking into account their weight, colour and the firmness of the shell, seeking out those who have been maturing in their shell for a while, but not too long. Once landed, Calum handles the shellfish carefully, keeps them cool and brings them straight to the kitchen. They are not subject to the typical lengthy storage and transport that causes stress to lobsters and crabs, affecting the quality of their meat. Having a fisherman like Calum on the doorstep means that our crabs and lobsters are of a quality that cannot be matched by bigger enterprises.

FRESH FRON
THE SEA

LOBSTER
&
CRAB

FROM
OUR
BOAT
TO
YOUR
PLATE

We usually pair red mullet with bold flavours, as this beautiful fish handles them so well. Here, the acidity from the pickled carrots and the saffron and basil flavours work exceptionally well with the unique oily flesh. If possible, prepare the carrots and basil oil a few days ahead, to allow time for the flavours to mellow. This dish is also very good prepared with bass.

RED MULLET, BASIL SALAD CREAM AND PICKLED CARROTS

Serves 4 as a starter

2 red mullet, 500–600g
  each, scaled, filleted,
  pin-boned and
  trimmed
light olive oil for cooking
Cornish sea salt
  and freshly ground
  white pepper

For the pickled carrots
8 baby carrots
200ml light olive oil
75ml white wine vinegar
2 garlic cloves, peeled
  and finely chopped
1 banana shallot, peeled
  and finely chopped
a pinch of saffron
  strands
3 teaspoons chopped dill

For the basil oil
40g basil leaves
30g flat-leaf parsley
  leaves
200ml light olive oil

For the salad cream
2 large egg yolks
2 teaspoons English
  mustard
2 teaspoons caster
  sugar
2 tablespoons
  lemon juice
150ml basil oil
  (from above)
150ml double cream

To prepare the pickled carrots
Peel the carrots and finely slice them lengthways, using a mandoline. Place in a shallow dish. Put the olive oil, wine vinegar, garlic, shallot and saffron into a pan and add a pinch of salt. Bring to a simmer over a medium heat. Pour the hot pickling liquor over the carrots and cover the dish with cling film, making sure they are submerged. Leave to cool.

To make the basil oil
Bring a large pan of salted water to the boil. Get a bowl of ice-cold water ready to refresh the herbs. Once the water is boiling, add the basil and parsley leaves and blanch them for 30 seconds. Immediately drain the herbs and immerse in the ice-cold water to cool quickly. Remove and squeeze out the excess water.

Put the herbs into a blender with the olive oil and a pinch of salt. Blend for 2 minutes, until the oil is green and the herbs are finely blitzed. Pour the herb oil through a very fine (or muslin-lined) sieve into a bowl. Keep chilled unless using straight away.

To make the salad cream
Put the egg yolks, mustard, sugar and lemon juice into a bowl and whisk together for 30 seconds. Now slowly pour in the basil oil, whisking constantly, until it is all incorporated and emulsified. Finally, whisk in the cream and season with salt and pepper to taste. Transfer to a disposable piping bag and keep in the fridge until ready to serve.

To prepare for serving
Before cooking the fish, drain the pickled carrots, saving the liquor for the dressing. Add the chopped dill to the liquor and taste for seasoning, adding salt and pepper if you wish.

To cook the red mullet
Heat a large non-stick pan over a medium-high heat. Season the red mullet fillets with salt. When the pan is hot, add a drizzle of olive oil and carefully lay the fillets in it, skin side down. Cook for about 3 minutes until the edges start to turn golden and the flesh appears to be cooked halfway through its depth. Take the pan off the heat, carefully flip the fish over and leave it to finish cooking in the residual heat while you start to assemble the dish.

To assemble and serve
Spoon some of the dill dressing onto each of 4 warmed serving plates and add a generous spoonful of salad cream. Place a red mullet fillet on each plate and finish with the pickled carrots. Serve immediately.

Scallops are coming to their best at this time of the year, but they can be difficult for the divers to get hold of if autumn storms take hold. I only use sustainable hand-dived scallops at the restaurant, so if the conditions are rough at sea they won't be on the menu.

This dish has wonderful flavours. Earthy sweet parsnips with different textures (pickled, roast and deep-fried) pair well with the sweetness of the scallops, and the curry sauce brings it all together perfectly.

SCALLOPS, PARSNIPS AND CURRY SAUCE

Serves 4 as a light main course

12 live medium
  scallops, removed
  from the shell
  and cleaned
olive oil for cooking
Cornish sea salt
  and freshly ground
  black pepper

For the curry oil
4 teaspoons mild
  curry powder
400ml light olive oil

For the pickled parsnip
1 medium parsnip,
  peeled
100ml dry cider
100ml cider vinegar
100g caster sugar
100ml water
1 tablespoon chopped
  coriander leaves

For the pan-roasted parsnip
2 medium parsnips,
  peeled and cut into
  1cm thick slices
50g unsalted butter
50g fresh root ginger,
  peeled and grated
olive oil for cooking

For the curry sauce
2 egg yolks
1 teaspoon mild curry
  powder
3 teaspoons cider
  vinegar
200ml sunflower oil
75ml apple juice

For the deep-fried parsnip
1 medium parsnip,
  peeled
sunflower oil for
  deep-frying

First make the curry oil (a day ahead)
Sprinkle the curry powder into a frying pan and toast over a medium heat for 2 minutes, without burning. Add the olive oil to the pan, heat for 2 minutes, then pour into a container. Cover and leave to infuse for at least 24 hours, then pass the oil through a muslin-lined sieve into a bowl.

For the pickled parsnip
Using a swivel peeler, shave the parsnip into long, fine ribbons and place in a bowl. Put the cider, cider vinegar, sugar and water into a small pan with a pinch of salt and bring to a simmer over a low heat, stirring to dissolve the sugar. Pour the hot liquor over the parsnip ribbons, making sure they are submerged. Cover with cling film to keep them submerged and leave to cool.

For the pan-roasted parsnip
Put the parsnip slices into a pan with the butter, ginger and a pinch of salt. Add water to cover and simmer until just tender, about 2 minutes. Remove from the pan and leave to cool.

To make the curry sauce
Put the egg yolks, curry powder and cider vinegar into a bowl and whisk for 30 seconds. Slowly add the oil in a thin, steady stream, whisking to make a thick, smooth mayonnaise. Season with salt and pepper to taste.

For the deep-fried parsnip
Using a swivel peeler, shave the parsnip into long, fine strips. Heat the oil for deep-frying in a deep-fryer or other suitable pan to 180°C. Add the parsnip strips and deep-fry for a minute until crisp and golden. Drain on kitchen paper and season with fine sea salt; set aside.

To prepare for serving
Drain off the liquor from the pickled parsnip then mix with the chopped coriander and season with sea salt. Whisk the apple juice into the curried sauce and taste to check the seasoning. Warm through gently, whisking as you do; do not boil. To finish the roast parsnips, heat a frying pan and add a drizzle of olive oil. When hot, add the parsnips and cook until golden all over; keep warm.

To cook the scallops
Heat a large non-stick frying pan over a medium-high heat and add a drizzle of olive oil. When the oil is hot, carefully lay the scallops in the pan, placing the side of the scallop down that would have been against the flat shell. Cook the scallops for 1½–2 minutes on each side until golden. Season with salt and pepper and serve straight away.

To serve
Pour the curry sauce equally into 4 warmed shallow bowls and place 3 pieces of roast parsnip in each bowl. Sit a scallop on each piece of roast parsnip. Pile some pickled parsnip in the centre of the scallops. Finish with the crispy deep-fried parsnip and a drizzle of curry oil. Serve at once.

When monkfish are nice and big, and their flesh is lovely and firm, I like to pan-roast them in this way. You need to treat monkfish rather like meat – resting it for 5–10 minutes before serving to enjoy it at its best. While resting, I sprinkle the fish with dried seaweed to impart a unique, almost truffle-like flavour. It's so good, I put it in the hollandaise sauce too. We gather the seaweed from outside the restaurant, dry it and then blitz it in a blender. I vary the veg here with the seasons, but this version – with roasted and puréed cauliflower and sprout tops – is my favourite.

MONKFISH WITH SEAWEED HOLLANDAISE, SPROUT TOPS AND CAULIFLOWER

Serves 4 as a
main course

1 monkfish tail, about
   2kg, skinned, filleted
   and trimmed
olive oil for cooking
2 teaspoons dried
   seaweed powder
Cornish sea salt

For the cauliflower
2 large cauliflowers
olive oil for cooking
50g unsalted butter

For the sprout tops
4 Brussels sprout tops
olive oil for cooking

For the seaweed
hollandaise
300ml olive oil
4 teaspoons dried
   seaweed powder
3 large egg yolks
2 tablespoons water
juice of 1 lemon
cayenne pepper
   to taste

Check the monkfish is trimmed of all sinew (if left on the fish this will be tough to eat). Cut the monkfish into 4 portions, cover and refrigerate.

To prepare the cauliflower
Cut the cauliflowers into florets and select 8 florets (roughly the size of a golf ball) for the roasted cauliflower. Trim these so they all have a flat side (to ensure they roast evenly). Save the trimmings. Finely slice all the remaining cauliflower (including the trimmings) for the purée.

To make the cauliflower purée
Heat a large pan over medium heat and add a drizzle of olive oil and the butter. When the butter is melted and bubbling, add the sliced cauliflower with a good pinch of salt. Cook for 3–4 minutes without letting the cauliflower colour, stirring often. Add a mug of water and place a lid on the pan. Cook for 8–10 minutes until the cauliflower is soft, adding more water if necessary. Remove the lid and continue to cook until the liquid has reduced down, almost completely.

Transfer the cauliflower to a blender and blitz to a very smooth purée. Taste for seasoning and add a little more salt if required. Transfer to a pan and keep warm or refrigerate in a suitable container if you're not using it straight away.

To make the seaweed hollandaise
Heat the olive oil in a pan over a low heat until tepid. Add the dried seaweed and keep warm.

Put the egg yolks, water and lemon juice into a heatproof bowl and set it over a pan of gently simmering water, making sure the bottom of the bowl isn't touching the water. Whisk until the mixture triples in volume and is thick enough to leave a ribbon trail when the whisk is lifted. Remove the bowl from the pan of water (keep it to warm the sauce back up). Add the tepid seaweed oil to the whisked mixture, little by little, whisking all the time, until it is all incorporated. Season with salt and cayenne pepper to taste. Cover with cling film and keep warm.

For the roast cauliflower
Bring a pan of salted water to the boil, add the cauliflower florets, bring back to the boil and cook for 3 minutes. Drain and leave to cool.

To cook the sprout tops
Bring a pan of salted water to the boil and add the sprout tops. Bring back to the boil and cook for 3 minutes, then drain and refresh in a bowl of

...continued on page 208

ice-cold water to cool quickly. Drain thoroughly and cut them in half.

To get the fish ready for cooking
Take the monkfish out of the fridge 30 minutes before you intend to cook it. Preheat your oven to 220°C/Fan 200°C/Gas 7.

To colour the vegetables
When you're ready to cook the fish, heat a frying pan over a medium-high heat and add a drizzle of olive oil. When it is hot, place the cauliflower florets, cut side down, in the pan and cook for 2–3 minutes until well coloured. Transfer to a warmed oven dish, turning the cauliflower as you do so; keep warm.

Return the frying pan to a medium-high heat and add a drizzle of olive oil. When it is hot, place the sprout tops cut side down in the pan and cook for 2–3 minutes until they look lovely and roasted. Take the pan off the heat, then turn the sprout tops.

To cook the fish
Heat a large non-stick ovenproof pan over a medium-high heat and add a drizzle of olive oil. When it is hot,

season the fish with salt and place in the pan. Colour the fish all over for 2 minutes, then place the pan in the oven and cook for about 4 minutes, depending on the size of the portions.

When the fish is just cooked, remove from the oven and sprinkle with the dried seaweed. Rest for 5 minutes.

To prepare for serving
While the fish is resting, place the sprout tops and roasted cauliflower in the oven to warm up. Heat the cauliflower purée in a pan over a low heat, stirring occasionally. Put the bowl of hollandaise back over the simmering water to warm up.

To serve
Spoon some seaweed hollandaise onto each of 4 warmed serving plates. Take the cauliflower florets and sprout tops out of the oven and put the monkfish back in for a minute.

Arrange the roasted cauliflower and sprout tops on the plates with a generous spoonful of cauliflower purée. Cut the monkfish portions in half and season with salt. Arrange on each plate and serve immediately.

This dish just screams autumn to me. I think it's the colour and the smell of pumpkin cooking – and, of course, autumn is the best season for wild mushrooms. Many chefs regard brill as a lesser alternative to turbot, but for me it's totally different in flavour and texture. The softer texture of brill makes it ideal for grilling as fillets, and the flesh handles bold flavours well, especially the wild mushrooms and red wine tartare dressing in this dish. For the dressing, all the classic tartare sauce ingredients – herbs, shallot, gherkin and capers – are combined with a red wine reduction and nutty brown butter. If you can't get brill, a lovely piece of filleted cod or hake from a large fish will work well too.

BRILL WITH ROAST PUMPKIN AND WILD MUSHROOMS

Serves 4 as a main course

For the brill
1 brill, about 2kg, scaled, filleted and portioned
light olive oil for cooking
Cornish sea salt and freshly ground black pepper

For the dressing
100ml red wine
100ml red wine vinegar
70g caster sugar
100ml water
250g unsalted butter
1 banana shallot, peeled and finely chopped
2 gherkins, cut into small dice
1 tablespoon baby capers, drained and left whole
2 teaspoons chopped chives
2 teaspoons chopped chervil
2 teaspoons chopped flat-leaf parsley
2 teaspoons chopped tarragon

For the pumpkin
600g peeled and deseeded pumpkin, cut into slim wedges
olive oil for cooking
4 garlic cloves, peeled and finely chopped
8 sprigs of thyme

For the wild mushrooms
4 handfuls of mixed wild mushrooms, cleaned and trimmed
olive oil for cooking
2 garlic cloves, peeled and finely chopped
4 teaspoons chopped flat-leaf parsley
a splash of red wine vinegar

To make the dressing
Put the wine, wine vinegar, sugar and water into a pan and bring to a simmer over a medium heat. Allow to bubble to reduce down until the liquid is syrupy, then remove from the heat; keep warm.

Melt the butter in a pan over a low heat, then increase the heat to medium-high. Cook until the butter is bubbling and turning brown, and has a nutty aroma. Immediately pour it into another pan or jug to stop the cooking; keep warm.

To cook the pumpkin
Preheat your oven to 220°C/Fan 200°C/Gas Mark 7. Heat a large frying pan (ideally cast-iron) over a medium-high heat and add a drizzle of olive oil. When hot, add the pumpkin wedges, together with the garlic and thyme, and colour on both sides until golden. Season with salt and pepper and transfer to an oven tray. Cook in the oven for 5 minutes until the pumpkin slices are tender. Remove from the oven and keep warm until ready to serve.

To cook the wild mushrooms
Heat your large frying pan over a medium-high heat again and add a drizzle of olive oil. When it is hot, add the wild mushrooms and cook them for 1 minute until lightly coloured. Don't overcrowd the pan;

if necessary, cook the mushrooms in two batches. Add the garlic and parsley and cook for another minute. Season with salt and pepper, and add a splash of red wine vinegar. Remove the mushrooms from the pan to a warmed plate and keep warm.

To prepare the fish for cooking
Preheat your grill to its highest setting. Check the fish for any residual scales and bone, or sinew. Oil the fish, season with salt and pepper and lay the fillets on a tray, ready to grill. Set aside while you finish the dressing.

To finish the dressing
Add 10 tablespoons of brown butter to the red wine reduction, together with the chopped shallot, gherkins, capers, herbs and some salt and pepper. Warm the dressing through over a low heat.

To cook the fish and serve
Place the fish under the grill and cook for 4–5 minutes, depending on thickness. Make sure the pumpkin and mushrooms are warm enough to serve (reheat briefly if necessary).

Divide the wild mushrooms and pumpkin among 4 warmed plates. Spoon roughly 3 tablespoons of dressing around each plate. When the fish is cooked, lay a portion on each serving. Serve immediately.

When the weather turns a little nippy, I like to serve up a warm baked dessert. All the stone fruit in Britain can be baked, but I'm particularly fond of cooking plums in this way. For this recipe, I'm serving a warm sponge with baked plums and a yoghurt sorbet flavoured with honey and bay leaves, which is a little unusual, but works a treat. I am lucky enough to be able to use local plums and honey, which at some point would have been connected by the bees when pollinating. You never know, they probably flew past the bay leaf tree too!

PLUM SPONGE, BAY AND HONEY YOGHURT SORBET

Serves 8

For the sponge
225g unsalted butter
2 vanilla pods, split
  lengthways, seeds
  scraped out and saved
225g egg whites (about
  5 large eggs)
100g light brown sugar
125g clear honey
90g ground almonds
90g plain flour, sifted
4 small plums, halved
  and stoned

For the baked plums
10 small plums,
  halved or quartered
  and stoned
100ml apple juice
150g clear honey
finely grated zest and
  juice of 1 orange

For the sorbet
200ml whole milk
175g clear honey
2 bay leaves
300g full-fat Greek
  yoghurt

First make the sorbet
Put the milk, honey and bay leaves in a pan, bring to a simmer and simmer, stirring, for 2 minutes. Take off the heat and set aside to cool and infuse with the bay. When cold, strain the milk through a sieve into a bowl and whisk in the yoghurt.

Churn the mixture in an ice-cream machine until firm, then transfer to a suitable container and freeze until ready to serve.

For the sponge
Preheat your oven to 200°C/Fan 180°C/Gas Mark 6. Line 8 individual round baking tins, 8cm in diameter and 3cm deep, with non-stick silicone paper or baking parchment.

Put the butter into a pan with the vanilla pods and melt over a low heat, then increase the heat to medium and cook until the butter starts to turn brown. Remove from the heat. Allow the butter to cool, then remove the vanilla pods.

For the baked plums
While the butter for the sponge is cooling, prepare the plums. Put the apple juice, honey, orange zest and juice into a pan and bring to the boil. Place the plums in a small oven dish or tray and pour the hot liquor over them. Cook in the oven at 200°C/Fan 180°C/Gas Mark 6 until the plums

start to collapse; this should take about 10 minutes, depending on the ripeness of the fruit. Remove the dish from the oven and leave the plums to cool in the liquor.

Drain the cooled plums and set aside, tipping the liquor into a pan. Bring to the boil over a medium heat and let it bubble to reduce until syrupy. Remove from the heat; keep warm.

To prepare and bake the sponge
Put the egg whites, brown sugar, honey and vanilla seeds into a large bowl and whisk together until evenly combined. Add the ground almonds and flour and mix well. Finally whisk in the cooled melted butter.

Spoon the sponge mixture into the prepared tins and place a plum half in the centre of each one. Bake in the oven for 18–20 minutes until golden. To check if the sponges are cooked, insert a knife into the centre of one; if it comes out clean, then the sponges are ready. Turn the sponges out of their tins.

To assemble and serve
Place a warm sponge on each warmed plate with a pile of cooked plums on the side. Spoon a neat quenelle of yoghurt sorbet on top of the plums and trickle some syrup from the poached plums around the plate. Serve straight away.

The inviting aromas that mulled pears release as they poach bring back childhood memories of Christmas flavours. For me, those warming spices – that go so well with poached autumn fruit and gingerbread – mark the changing of the season. This dessert is the perfect end to a meal: bitter-sweet chocolate cream, crunchy gingerbread crumb and boozy, spicy soft pears, topped with one of the tastiest ice creams I've ever made. Just the ice cream alone with a slice of warm gingerbread is great if you want to simplify the dish.

Serves 8

MULLED PEAR, BITTER CHOCOLATE AND GINGERBREAD ICE CREAM

For the gingerbread
115g unsalted butter
115g soft brown sugar
115g black treacle
1 large egg, beaten
175g plain flour
1 tablespoon ground
 ginger
1½ teaspoons ground
 cinnamon
a pinch of fine sea salt
140ml whole milk
1 teaspoon bicarbonate
 of soda

**For the gingerbread
ice cream**
150g gingerbread
 (from above)
375ml whole milk
175ml double cream
9 large egg yolks
175g caster sugar

For the pears
4 firm sweet pears
700ml red wine
160g caster sugar
1 cinnamon stick
10 cloves
15 juniper berries
2 bay leaves
10 black peppercorns
10 star anise

For the chocolate cream
180ml whole milk
130ml double cream
3 large egg yolks
25g caster sugar
120g dark chocolate
 (70% cocoa solids),
 chopped into
 small pieces

To finish
150g gingerbread
 (from above)

To make the gingerbread
Preheat your oven to 170°C/Fan 150°C/Gas Mark 3. Line a 26 x 12cm loaf tin with baking parchment.

Melt the butter, brown sugar and treacle together in a pan over a low heat. Remove from the heat and add the egg, flour, ginger, cinnamon and salt. Mix until thoroughly combined.

Warm the milk in another pan and stir in the bicarbonate of soda. Pour onto the spiced mixture and mix well until evenly incorporated.

Pour the mixture into the prepared mould and bake in the oven for 40 minutes or until a skewer inserted into the centre comes out clean. Remove the gingerbread from the tin and place on a wire rack to cool.

To make the gingerbread ice cream
Weigh 150g of the cooled gingerbread and crumble it into pieces. Pour the milk and cream into a pan and bring to a simmer over a medium heat.

Meanwhile, in a bowl, whisk the egg yolks and sugar together until smoothly combined. When the creamy milk comes to the boil, add the gingerbread crumbs and stir well. Bring back to a simmer and then pour onto the whisked egg and sugar mixture, whisking thoroughly to combine. Allow to cool.

Once cooled, churn the mixture in an ice-cream machine until thick. Transfer the gingerbread ice cream to a suitable container and keep in the freezer until ready to serve.

To cook the pears
Peel the pears and place them in a pan with all the other ingredients, making sure the pears are fully immersed in the liquor (top up with a little more red wine if necessary). Bring to a simmer and cook gently for 25–30 minutes until the pears are just soft; don't overcook them.

Using a slotted spoon, lift the poached pears out of their liquor and set them aside on a plate to cool.

Bring the poaching liquor back to a simmer over a medium heat and let it bubble to reduce by half. Remove from the heat, pour into a medium bowl and leave to cool.

Cut the poached pears in half and trim away the pips if there are any. Place them back in the cooled poaching liquid. Cover and keep in the fridge until ready to serve.

The poached pears are best left to steep in the liquor for a few days to take on all the flavours.

...continued on page 216

To make the chocolate cream

Pour the milk and cream into a pan and bring to a simmer over a low heat. Meanwhile, whisk the egg yolks and sugar together in a bowl, then pour on the hot creamy milk, whisking to combine. Add the chocolate and stir until fully melted. Pour the custard into a thermomix and cook until it reaches 80°C. Or return to the saucepan and cook, stirring constantly, over a low heat, until the custard registers 80°C on a cook's thermometer.

Have 8 individual serving dishes ready. As soon as the custard is ready, turn off the heat and blend on high speed for 30 seconds (using a hand blender if you are not using a thermomix). Immediately pour the custard into the dishes. Allow to cool, then place in the fridge to set; this will take about an hour.

To make the dried gingerbread crumb

Heat your oven to 120°C/Fan 100°C/ Gas Mark ½. Break 150g gingerbread into pieces and place on a baking tray lined with a non-stick silicone mat. Place in the low oven to dry out; this will take 2 hours.

Once the gingerbread is dried, transfer it to a food processor and blitz to crumbs. Keep in an airtight container until ready to serve.

To assemble and serve

Take the chocolate creams out of the fridge about 20 minutes before you intend to serve them.

Remove the pear halves from the liquor and cut each one into 6 or 7 equal slices, keeping them attached at the stalk end. Lay the pear slices on the chocolate cream, fanning them out decoratively.

Scatter 1 tablespoon of the dried gingerbread crumb onto each serving then add a quenelle of gingerbread ice cream. Serve straight away.

I have to confess I have a weakness for doughnuts – both making and eating them! Fortunately, my doughnut-making skills have improved over the years. My wife, Rachel, often teases me about the time I served doughnuts at my first restaurant, The Black Pig, on New Year's Eve. I thought I would make some little doughnuts to serve at the end of the meal with coffee. Let's just say, they were nothing like these! Something good always comes out of mistakes … at least that's how I see it. These cinnamon-scented doughnuts are best served warm.

APPLE AND CINNAMON DOUGHNUTS

To make the dough
Pour the water into a measuring jug and sprinkle in the yeast granules and sugar. Leave to activate and froth up; this should take 10 minutes. Put the flour, salt, butter, beaten egg and milk into a stand mixer fitted with the dough hook and mix for 30 seconds, then add the yeast liquid and mix on a medium speed for 5 minutes to form a smooth dough.

Transfer the dough to a floured bowl, cover with a damp cloth and leave to rise in a warm place until doubled in volume; this should take about 30 minutes.

Place the risen dough on a lightly floured surface and knock back to expel the large air bubbles and create a more even texture. Cut the dough into 15 equal pieces, each weighing 20g, and shape into small balls. Place each ball on a small square of silicone paper. Cover them loosely with a damp cloth and leave to prove in a warm place until doubled in size again, about 40 minutes.

To make the apple purée
Put the apples, butter and sugar into a heavy-based pan over a gentle heat. Cover and cook for 25 minutes until the apples are soft and reduced to a pulp, stirring occasionally. Remove the lid and let it bubble to reduce until the apple mixture becomes syrupy, stirring occasionally. Transfer to a bowl and set aside to cool. If you prefer a smooth purée, blitz using a hand-held stick blender until smooth.

For the cinnamon sugar
Simply toss the sugar and cinnamon together in a bowl to combine and set aside, ready to finish the doughnuts.

To fry the doughnuts
Heat the oil for deep-frying in a deep-fryer or other suitable deep, heavy pan to 180°C. When it is hot, deep-fry the doughnuts in batches, being careful not to overcrowd the pan: carefully lift each dough ball on the paper and lower it into the hot oil, holding the corner of the paper, then gently pull out the paper, leaving the dough in the pan. Deep-fry the doughnuts for 2–3 minutes until golden all over – you may need to jiggle them about to get an even colour all over.

Once cooked, lift the doughnuts out of the pan and drain them on kitchen paper. Place on a wire rack to cool slightly for a few minutes, then toss in the cinnamon sugar to coat.

To serve
The doughnuts are best served still warm from frying but if they have cooled, reheat them in an oven preheated to 180°C/Fan 160°C/Gas Mark 4 for a few minutes. Split the warm doughnuts three-quarters of the way through. Fill with the apple purée and serve immediately.

Makes 15

For the doughnuts
125ml warm water
7g dried yeast
40g caster sugar
500g plain flour, plus extra to dust
10g fine sea salt
50g unsalted butter, softened
1 large egg, beaten
200g whole milk
sunflower oil for deep-frying

For the apple purée
300g peeled and cored cooking apples (prepared weight), chopped
50g unsalted butter
100g caster sugar

For the cinnamon sugar
200g caster sugar
3 teaspoons ground cinnamon

Early Winter

What better way to start off a meal than with some freshly cooked and picked crab meat on warm toast? I like to add a little curry spice to it, and balance the richness with a spoonful of freshly made fennel pickle. You will need to prepare the curry oil a day or two ahead.

CURRIED CRAB ON TOAST

1 live brown crab, about 1kg, placed in the freezer 30 minutes before cooking

For the curry oil
4 teaspoons mild curry powder
400ml light olive oil

For the fennel pickle
1 red onion, peeled and finely sliced
1 fennel bulb, outer layer removed, halved and finely sliced
1 green chilli, halved, deseeded and thinly sliced
100ml white wine vinegar
50ml water
50g sugar
1 teaspoon sea salt
1 teaspoon ground cumin
1 teaspoon ground coriander seeds
2 teaspoons chopped coriander

For the mayonnaise
2 large egg yolks
2 tablespoons brown crab meat (from above)
finely grated zest and juice of 1 lime
350ml curry oil (from above)

To serve
3 teaspoons chopped coriander
wholemeal bread, thinly sliced

First make the curry oil (a day ahead)
Sprinkle the curry powder into a frying pan and toast over a medium heat for 2 minutes, without burning. Add the olive oil to the pan, heat for 2 minutes, then pour into a container. Cover and leave to infuse for at least 24 hours, then pass the curry-infused oil through a muslin-lined sieve into a bowl.

To make the fennel pickle
Place the red onion, fennel and chilli into a bowl. Put the wine vinegar, water, sugar, salt and spices into a pan and bring to the boil, then pour this hot liquor over the vegetables and push them down, to ensure they are fully submerged. Cover tightly with cling film to hold them down. Leave to cool.

When ready to serve, drain the vegetables and mix through the chopped coriander.

To cook and prepare the crab
Bring a large pan of water (big enough to hold the crab fully submerged) to the boil. Season the water generously with salt, to make it as salty as sea water. Once it comes to a rolling boil, lower the crab into the water and cook for 14 minutes. Carefully lift the crab out of the pan, place on a tray and leave until cool enough to handle.

Remove the legs and claws from the crab, by twisting them away from the body. Now, holding the crab in both hands, use your thumbs to push the body up and out of the hard, top shell or carapace. Remove and discard the dead man's fingers, stomach sac and hard membranes from the body shell.

Using a spoon, remove the brown crab from the carapace and put it into a bowl. Now cut the body in half, using a sharp knife, to reveal the little channels of white crab meat. Use a crab pick or the handle of a spoon to pick out all the crab meat from these crevices and put it into a separate bowl.

Using a heavy knife, break the claws with one hard tap if possible and pick out the white meat, prising out the cartilage from the middle of the claw. Do the same with the legs to extract the meat.

Once you have extracted all of the white meat, with clean hands, pick through it to search for any shell or cartilage. Cover the bowls of crab meat with cling film and place them in the fridge if you are preparing the crab in advance.

To prepare the mayonnaise
Whisk the egg yolks, brown crab meat, lime zest and juice together in a bowl. Slowly add the curry oil in a thin, steady stream, whisking continuously until all the curry oil is incorporated. Season with salt to taste.

To assemble and serve
Combine the white crab meat with the chopped coriander, adding a little of the mayonnaise to bind. Toast the bread slices and cut them into pieces (the shape and size you want).

Spoon the white crab meat onto the warm toasts and top each with a spoonful of the curried crab mayonnaise and some fennel pickle. Serve at once.

Brill has a great texture for curing – it is tender enough to eat raw and takes on the flavours of the cure extremely well. Here I'm using verjus (sour grape juice made from pressing unripe grapes) with salt and sugar to cure the fish. The acidity from the verjus is ideal and doesn't 'cook' the fish in the way that citrus would, as in ceviche for example. Grapes and fried pumpkin seeds add a nice textural contrast to the fish and the vibrant parsley oil dressing finishes the dish beautifully.

CURED BRILL, GRAPES AND PUMPKIN SEEDS

Serves 4 as a starter

600g very fresh brill fillet, skinned and trimmed of any sinew
Cornish sea salt and freshly ground black pepper

For the cure
200g sea salt
100g caster sugar
2 tablespoons chopped rosemary leaves
100ml verjus

For the parsley oil
30g flat-leaf parsley, leaves picked
30g curly parsley, leaves picked
200ml light olive oil

For the dressing
1 banana shallot, peeled and very finely chopped
2 teaspoons Dijon mustard
100ml verjus
150ml parsley oil (from above)

For the garnish
400ml sunflower oil for deep-frying
100g pumpkin seeds
8 green grapes, deseeded and sliced
8 red or black grapes, deseeded and sliced
1 lemon for zesting

To make the parsley oil
If possible, do this a day ahead. Bring a pan of salted water to the boil and have a bowl of iced water ready. Once the water is boiling, add all of the parsley and blanch for 20 seconds. Immediately scoop out the parsley and plunge into the iced water to cool quickly. Drain and squeeze out the excess water. Put the blanched parsley into a blender with the olive oil and blitz for 2 minutes. Transfer the parsley oil to a container, cover and leave to settle in the fridge for at least 3–4 hours, ideally overnight.

When the sediment has sunk to the bottom, strain off the oil through a muslin-lined sieve into a clean container. Refrigerate until ready to make the dressing.

To cure the brill
Put the salt, sugar and rosemary into a food processor and blitz thoroughly. Lay the fish on a tray and sprinkle evenly with the cure mixture. Turn the fish over a few times to ensure it is coated all over, then drizzle the verjus evenly over the fish.

Wrap the tray in cling film and place in the fridge for 2 hours, turning the fish halfway through.

To prepare the fish for serving
Once the curing time is up, wash off the cure mix and pat the fish dry with kitchen paper. Wrap the fish tightly in cling film and place in the freezer to firm up for 1 hour.

Unwrap the fish and place it on a very clean board. Using a sharp knife, slice the fish very finely and lay the slices straight onto the plates. The cured fish will be easier to slice because it is partially frozen; by the time you have sliced and plated it all it will have defrosted fully. (If you have more fish than you need for the plates, freeze it, wrapped well, for another time.)

To prepare the pumpkin seed garnish
Pour the oil into a small pan and add the pumpkin seeds. Heat slowly over a medium heat until the seeds start to puff up and rise to the surface. As soon as they start to pop, take the pan off the heat and skim the puffed pumpkin seeds off the surface of the oil with a slotted spoon. Place on a tray lined with kitchen paper and season them well with fine sea salt. Leave to cool.

To make the dressing
Put the chopped shallot into a bowl with the mustard and verjus. Whisk together and season with salt and pepper. Whisk in the parsley oil and leave the dressing to stand and come to room temperature for 10 minutes.

To serve
Spoon the dressing evenly over the 4 plates of sliced cured fish. Share the sliced grapes between the plates and scatter over the fried pumpkin seeds. Finely grate the zest of the lemon over each plate of fish to finish. Serve straight away.

At this time of year, when mackerel are at their biggest, sousing is a great way to prepare them. Full of flavour and more oily than ever, large mackerel really benefit from the acidity sousing lends. The accompanying green sauce, or 'salsa verde' as it is known, is full of vibrant, fresh-tasting flavours and works brilliantly with the oily fish. This is an ideal starter if you are entertaining, as it can pretty much all be prepared in advance, ready to assemble and serve. The dish also works well with sardines, herring or red mullet.

SOUSED MACKEREL, PICKLED ONION AND GREEN SAUCE

Serves 4 as a starter

2 large mackerel or
   4 smaller ones, filleted
   and pin-boned
50ml olive oil
2 shallots, peeled and
   finely diced
2 carrots, peeled and
   finely diced
2 garlic cloves, peeled
3 sprigs of thyme
100ml white wine
50ml white wine
   vinegar
a pinch of saffron
   strands
Cornish sea salt
   and freshly ground
   black pepper

For the pickled onion

1 red onion, peeled and
   cut into 8 wedges
100ml white wine
100ml white wine
   vinegar
100ml water
80g caster sugar
a pinch of saffron
   strands

For the green sauce

1 garlic clove, peeled
6 salted anchovy fillets
   in oil, drained
1 tablespoon capers
   in brine, drained
1 large gherkin
30g flat-leaf parsley,
   leaves picked and
   chopped
30g mint, leaves picked
   and chopped
50g rocket leaves
   chopped
1 tablespoon red
   wine vinegar
1 teaspoon English
   mustard
4 tablespoons extra
   virgin olive oil

For the dressing

6 tablespoons sousing
   liquor (from above)
4 tablespoons olive oil

To pickle the onion

Place the red onion in a bowl. Put the white wine, wine vinegar, water, sugar, saffron and a pinch of salt into a pan and bring to the boil, then pour this hot sousing liquor over the onion wedges and push them down, to ensure they are fully submerged. Cover tightly with a piece of cling film to hold them down. Leave to cool. Once cold, refrigerate. If possible, leave for 24 hours before using.

To prepare the mackerel

Check the fish fillets for pin-bones and season with salt. Heat a non-stick frying pan over a medium-high heat and add a drizzle of the olive oil.

When the oil is hot, lay the mackerel fillets skin side down in the pan and cook for 2 minutes until the skin starts to colour and turn golden at the edges. Carefully flip the fish over and cook for 30 seconds. Lift the fish fillets out of the pan and lay them in a dish in which they fit snugly.

Turn the heat down and add the rest of the olive oil to the pan. When it is hot, add the shallots, carrots, garlic and thyme and cook for 3 minutes. Add the wine, wine vinegar, saffron and some salt and pepper.

Pour the hot sousing liquor evenly over the fish, then cover the dish with cling film so that it holds the mackerel fillets down and keeps them submerged. Leave to cool.

Once cooled, the fish is effectively 'cooked' and can be served, but you can also keep it in the fridge for up to 2 days. When you remove it from the fridge, give it 30 minutes at room temperature to take off the chill or gently warm it under a low grill.

To make the green sauce

Chop the garlic and anchovy fillets together to a paste. Add the capers and gherkin and continue to chop until the mixture is as fine as you can get it. Chop the herbs and rocket together finely and then add them to the anchovy mixture. Add the wine vinegar, mustard and extra virgin olive oil and season with salt and pepper to taste. Cover and refrigerate until needed.

To assemble and serve

Lift the fish fillets out of the sousing liquor and arrange on 4 deep plates. Strain the sousing liquid through a sieve into a bowl (saving the veg in the sieve). For the dressing, measure 6 tablespoons of the sousing liquor and mix with 4 tablespoons olive oil. Add 3 tablespoons of the vegetables from the sieve to the dressing. Give it a good mix, taste and add a little salt if needed. Spoon the dressing and vegetables evenly over the fish.

Drain the pickled onion and arrange 4 or 5 individual onion petals on each portion of mackerel. Finish with a heaped teaspoonful of green sauce. Serve at room temperature.

I'm lucky to be able to get fantastic scallops where my restaurant is, and they are always a favourite when we put them on the menu. This dish, in particular, fills the kitchen with amazing smells when it is cooking. For best results, buy medium scallops rather than large ones, which are inclined to overcook and toughen on the outside before they are cooked through.

'Devilling' is a term that may be applied to anything in British food that has a bit of a kick to it and dates right back to the 1700s. I'm very much into food with a fiery kick to it, much to the annoyance of my wife and kids, who are forever telling me off for making things 'too hot!'

BAKED SCALLOPS, JERUSALEM ARTICHOKES, DEVILLED BUTTER

Serves 4 as a starter

12 live medium
scallops, removed
from the shell
and cleaned
200ml white wine
Cornish sea salt
and freshly ground
black pepper

For the artichokes
8 Jerusalem artichokes
juice of 1 lemon

For the devilled butter
300g unsalted butter,
cut into cubes and
softened
1 banana shallot,
peeled and finely
chopped
1 garlic clove, peeled
and chopped to a paste
2 teaspoons cayenne
pepper
1 teaspoon mustard
powder
2 tablespoons
Worcestershire sauce
3 anchovies in oil,
drained and chopped
to a paste
finely grated zest and
juice of 1 lemon
4 teaspoons chopped
parsley

For the breadcrumbs
200g good-quality
crustless white
bread, cubed
a handful of curly
parsley leaves
75g Parmesan, freshly
grated

To garnish
2 lemons, halved

To cook the Jerusalem artichokes
Half-fill a saucepan large enough to hold all of the artichokes with water and add the lemon juice. Peel the artichokes and add them directly to the water. Add a pinch of salt and bring to a simmer over a medium heat. Cook for 20–25 minutes until the artichokes are tender, then remove them from the pan and set aside to cool.

While the artichokes are cooking, preheat your oven to 220°C/Fan 200°C/Gas Mark 7, ready to cook the scallops, and prepare the devilled butter and breadcrumbs.

To make the devilled butter
Put the softened butter into a bowl and add all the other ingredients, seasoning with salt and pepper to taste. Mix together thoroughly until evenly combined, then spoon to a container. Cover and set aside.

To prepare the breadcrumbs
Put the bread cubes and parsley into a food processor and blitz until the bread is reduced to fine crumbs and the parsley is well incorporated. Add the grated Parmesan and blend for 20 seconds. Tip the crumbs out onto a tray and set aside.

To prepare the garnish
Heat a cast-iron griddle pan over a high heat. When it is hot, oil the lemon halves and season them with salt. Cook on the griddle for about 4 minutes, turning to colour well all over. Take the griddle pan off the heat and remove the lemons. Leave to one side, while you cook the scallops.

To assemble and bake the scallops
Cut the cooled Jerusalem artichokes in half and divide among 4 large ramekins or other individual baking dishes (i.e. 4 halves to each dish). Place 3 scallops on top of each portion and spoon 1 teaspoon of devilled butter on top of each scallop. Pour 50ml white wine into each dish around the scallops. Stand the dishes on a sturdy baking tray that won't buckle in the heat of the oven.

Bake in the oven for 3 minutes. Take out the tray and sprinkle the flavoured breadcrumbs evenly over the scallops. Return to the oven for a further 3 minutes.

To serve
Once cooked, place the baking dishes on warmed plates and serve straight away, with a grilled lemon half on the side of each plate.

ROCK SHELLFISH
Porthilly

Tim Marshall, of Rock Shellfish, is partly responsible for one of our most successful sauces at Restaurant Nathan Outlaw. In the early days, I wanted to create a rich shellfish sauce using local, sustainable shellfish. Tim told me that shore crabs were a real nuisance because they ate the baby mussels and oysters he was trying to grow. I knew that in France and Spain shore crabs were used in shellfish soups, so I decided to try them out in a shellfish sauce. Thus Porthilly Sauce, with its deep, rich and unique flavour, was born!

Rock Shellfish is situated in the tiny hamlet of Porthilly, just a few miles from the restaurant. Wonderful Pacific oysters and mussels are being grown there by the Marshall family. For five generations the family were dairy farmers but they decided to diversify around forty years ago to include fish farming too. Originally working just one small site on the Rock side of Camel Estuary, Tim and his son, Luke, now have four sites situated on either side of the estuary.

The addition of purification facilities to their premises around ten years ago means that Rock Shellfish can sell directly to local restaurants and food outlets, moving them from a purely wholesale business to one that can cater directly for retail customers too.

The company now grows around 1,500,000 Pacific oysters and 100 tonnes of mussels a year. However, approximately half these will be lost through natural causes before coming to market. Their shellfish is sold around the UK. It is also exported via a wholesaler, as far as Malta and China.

Pacific oysters are brought into the farm as tiny 'seed', which is sourced from a hatchery, each one measuring a mere 7 x 7mm on arrival. The seeds are placed in mesh bags and taken out into the Camel Estuary where they remain for 16–24 months before being harvested, provided they are large enough. The oysters are then purified before being sold to the consumer. During their time in the estuary, it is necessary to continuously monitor, grade and turn the oysters, to encourage them to grow and improve. It's definitely not a case of 'leave them to grow by themselves!'

The Marshalls' mussels are also farmed sustainably. They are removed from areas where they would not prosper as seed and relocated to the Camel Estuary where the sheltered conditions enable them to thrive and grow into a superior quality product. Tim's theory is that because Porthilly Bay is tidal, the sea water empties and refreshes completely each day, keeping it really clean, which can only be good for the shellfish he is farming. Once the mussels are ready – like oysters, some 16–24 months after being re-sited – they are harvested as long as they are large enough and purified before being deemed ready for consumption. Any that have not grown to size are returned to the estuary to continue growing.

Tim is keen to let people know about his produce. He says that to get the true flavour from oysters they should be chewed, not just swallowed as is widely thought. He also has a word of advice about storing shellfish. He says that rather than keep them in water, they should be placed in a bowl, covered with a damp cloth and kept in the bottom of the fridge. He also maintains that although shellfish can be eaten all year round, they are at their best consumed when the water they're growing in is cold.

Tim Marshall came to fishing almost by chance, taking over a failing business from someone else because he was looking to diversify his dairy farming and he had always liked fishing.

When asked why he still does it, his answer is that he likes doing it, the life suits him … 'and my wife needs new shoes!'

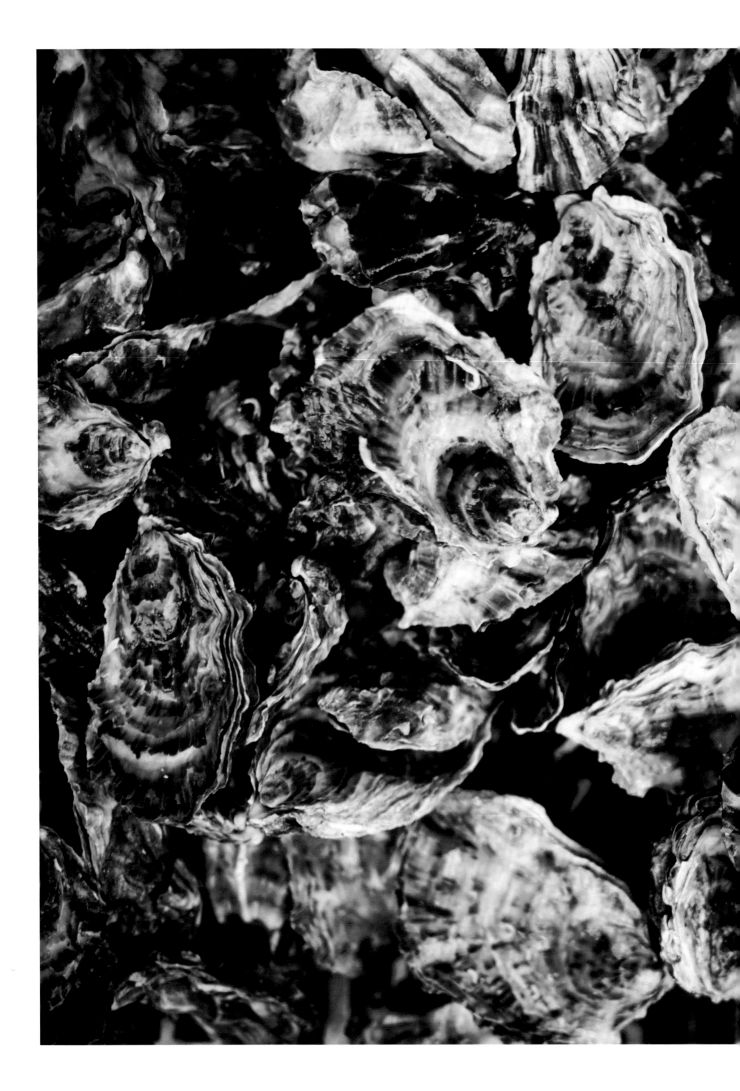

For me, the best way to cook and serve Dover sole is on the bone. Owing to its structural nature and tightly packed, almost meaty flesh, this fish needs to age a little before it is cooked. To experience its true flavour and wonderful texture, I think a Dover sole needs to be three days old when you cook it. The classic flavour combination of clams, parsley and garlic is the perfect complement.

DOVER SOLE WITH CLAMS, PARSLEY AND GARLIC

Serves 4 as a main course

4 Dover sole, 300–400g
  each, skinned,
  trimmed and
  heads removed
olive oil for cooking
Cornish sea salt
  and freshly ground
  black pepper

For the clams and sauce
400g live Palourde
  clams, well washed
olive oil for cooking
1 banana shallot,
  peeled and finely
  chopped
1 fennel bulb, outer
  layer removed,
  finely diced
1 large carrot, peeled
  and finely diced
2 garlic cloves, peeled
  and finely chopped
2 bay leaves
200ml white wine
50ml double cream
200g cold unsalted
  butter, diced
2 tablespoons curly
  parsley, picked
  and chopped
2 tablespoons flat-leaf
  parsley, picked
  and chopped
a few drops of lemon
  juice (optional)

For the roasted garlic aïoli
1 garlic bulb
400ml olive oil, plus
  a drizzle
2 large egg yolks
finely grated zest and
  juice of 1 lemon

Take the Dover sole out of the fridge to bring them to room temperature before cooking.

To prepare the roasted garlic aïoli
Preheat your oven to 220°C/Fan 200°C/Gas Mark 7. Wrap the garlic bulb in a piece of foil with some salt and a drizzle of olive oil. Place in an oven dish and bake for 1 hour until soft. Unwrap the garlic and leave until cool enough to handle, then separate the cloves and squeeze out the soft garlic pulp.

Put the egg yolks, lemon zest and juice and the roasted garlic pulp into a blender or food processor. Blitz briefly to combine, then, with the motor running on a low speed, add the olive oil through the funnel in a thin, steady stream until it is all incorporated and the aïoli is thick. Season with salt and pepper to taste and blend for 30 seconds. Transfer to a container, cover and refrigerate until ready to serve.

To prepare the clams and sauce
Place a large pan (that has a tight-fitting lid) over a medium-high heat. When it is hot, add a good drizzle of olive oil, then the shallot, fennel and carrot. Sweat for 2 minutes without colouring. Add the garlic and bay leaves and cook for another minute. Now add the clams and wine and put the lid on the pan. Cook for 2–3 minutes until the clam shells open. Tip the clams, along with the vegetables, into a colander set over a bowl to catch the juices.

Wipe out the pan and put it back on the heat. Tip the collected wine and clam juices back into the pan and simmer to reduce by half then add the cream. Now lower the heat and gradually whisk in the cold diced butter. The butter will emulsify into the juices to make the sauce base. When it is all incorporated, set the sauce aside; keep warm.

If you prefer, you can remove the clams from their shells. Either way, discard any that haven't opened. Set aside while you cook the fish.

To cook the Dover sole
Oil a large, shallow roasting tray (big enough to hold all 4 fish) and sprinkle with salt. Season the fish well with salt and lay on the tray (with the side the dark skin has been removed from uppermost). Oil the fish generously and bake for 10–12 minutes until cooked. Remove from the oven and set aside to rest while you finish the sauce; keep warm.

To assemble and serve
Warm the sauce gently, then add the clams, 3 tablespoons of the reserved vegetables and all of the chopped parsley. Taste the sauce for seasoning and acidity, adding a little salt and/or a few drops of lemon juice if you think it needs it. Carefully lift the fish from the roasting tray onto warmed plates.

Share the sauce, vegetables and clams equally among the 4 plates and finish with a good spoonful of aïoli on the side. Serve immediately.

John Dory, also known as St. Peter's fish, is a stunning fish. Whenever I get offered the larger fish, I'm really keen for people to try it, as the texture and flavour are fantastic. John Dory are rarely targeted by fishermen, they are more of a happy by-catch, but I'm sure no one complains when they are brought on board.

A great thing about John Dory is that it works with strong flavours as well as subtle ones. In this dish, I'm serving it on a warm salad of squid, salami, watercress and celeriac, dressed with a squid ink sauce. It's an unusual combination, but one that I enjoy … and so do our customers!

JOHN DORY WITH SQUID, WATERCRESS, CELERIAC AND SALAMI

Serves 4 as a
main course

2 medium John Dory,
 1kg each, or 1 large
 John Dory, about 2kg,
 filleted and trimmed
olive oil for cooking
Cornish sea salt
 and freshly ground
 black pepper

For the sauce
1 tablespoon olive oil
1 banana shallot,
 peeled and chopped
1 red pepper, cored,
 deseeded and chopped
1 celery stick, chopped
3 garlic cloves, peeled
 and crushed
1 apple, cored and
 chopped
2 teaspoons smoked
 paprika
2 teaspoons ground
 cumin
500ml fish stock (see
 page 288)
500ml shellfish stock
 (see page 290)
50g unsalted butter
4–5 teaspoons squid ink
a drizzle of agrodolce
 vinegar

For the squid salad
400g medium squid,
 cleaned, with tentacles
1 garlic bulb, halved
150ml olive oil
75ml agrodolce vinegar
1 red onion, peeled
 and sliced
1 small celeriac, peeled
 and finely sliced on
 a mandoline
150g salami (ideally
 with fennel seed)
a bunch of watercress,
 leaves picked
1 tablespoon chopped
 tarragon

To make the sauce
Place a large saucepan over a medium heat and add the olive oil. When it is hot, add the shallot, red pepper, celery, garlic and apple and sweat for 3 minutes. Stir in the smoked paprika and cumin and cook for 4 minutes, then pour in both the stocks and add the butter. Bring to a simmer and cook until the liquor has reduced down to a quarter of its original volume. Add the squid ink. Transfer the contents of the pan to a blender and blitz for 4–5 minutes until very smooth. Pass the sauce through a sieve into a clean pan and set aside.

To prepare the squid salad
Cut the squid body into long, thin slices and score the fins. Set aside with the tentacles.

Bring a large pan of salted water to the boil, add the halved garlic bulb and simmer for 5 minutes. Combine the olive oil and agrodolce vinegar in a medium bowl and season with salt and pepper. Add the squid to the pan of boiling water and blanch for

20 seconds, then remove with a slotted spoon, drain well and add to the oil and vinegar. Leave to cool. Once the squid is cooled, add the red onion, celeriac and salami and mix well. Leave for 1 hour to allow all the flavours to mingle.

To cook the John Dory
Preheat your grill to its highest setting. Oil a large, sturdy oven tray (big enough to hold all of the fish). Oil the fish fillets on both sides and season well with salt. Slide the oven tray under the grill and grill the fish for 5–6 minutes, without turning until it is just cooked.

To assemble and serve
While the fish is cooking, heat up the sauce and add a drizzle of agrodolce vinegar. Toss the watercress and tarragon through the squid and salami salad.

Pour the warm sauce equally onto 4 warmed plates and arrange the squid salad on top. When the fish is cooked, place on top of the salad and serve immediately.

CHRIS PRINDL
Artisan potter

Dining at Restaurant Nathan Outlaw isn't just about the food and service, it's about everything the customer encounters when they dine here. An integral part of that experience is beautifully crafted tableware that complements the food and frames it in an aesthetically pleasing way.

Chris Prindl of Prindl Pottery, located at Trebyan Forge near Lanhydrock, is responsible for every piece of crockery we use. The designs, which Chris creates especially for us, leave a lasting impression and customers often detour to his studio having dined with us.

Born in Germany, Chris lived in England and Japan as a child, then studied Japanese Language and History at Princeton, New Jersey. It was at the university, under the tutelage of Toshiko Takaezu that his love of throwing pots began. He became fascinated with making 'big pots' and after leaving Princeton, served an apprenticeship to a pottery located in the mountains of Yamagata in northeastern Japan.

Chris has been working from Trebyan Forge for the past eighteen years and says that throwing pots 'is still a magical thing to do'. Our collaboration began purely by chance when a photographer, who was working with me at the time, needed some plates for a photoshoot. I was so impressed by Chris' work that I asked him to make some small pieces for Restaurant Nathan Outlaw. Those designs – a cheese plate and a small chutney pot – are still in use here today.

Most of the pieces in the restaurant are porcelain, made from china clay originating from St Austell. Chris also works with stoneware clay from St Agnes. He fires the pieces in his kilns, which include traditional wood- and salt-fired kilns. He mixes his own glazes using a wide range of powdered clays, rocks, ashes and metals, and has developed several unique and beautiful finishes for his creations.

The process can be quite challenging as some glazes are unpredictable, firing differently according to the amount of oxygen present in the kiln. Too much moisture in the clay will cause the piece to explode when it is being fired, something that is frustrating when you've taken time to make a huge pot! However, Chris says he likes the challenge and tells me that inspiration and new ideas sometimes come about from these accidents!

At the restaurant, one of Chris' most popular designs is his 'proud spout teapots', as he calls them. They have a long spout for easy pouring and a large loop handle so they can be held comfortably. Customers comment on them with a smile and Chris admits that they were designed not only to pour well and look beautiful but also to have an aspect of amusement.

All of Chris' pieces are made to be functional as well as beautiful. The finish is of paramount importance but so is the ease of use. His teacups, for example, are very fine and delicate to look at but they have a weight to them that suggests they are not just for show. He thinks about the 'feelability', as his wife, Susannah, calls it. He wants his pieces to be things that people want to touch.

Several of Chris' larger pieces are on show in the restaurant. One of the latest additions is an indoor water feature: a tower of large pottery barrels inspired by traditional Japanese straw-covered sake barrels, in hues that complement the backdrop of the seascape through the window behind them. Each slightly irregular barrel balances on another and a gentle stream of water trickles down the stack. Chris and I had talked about the idea for several years before it came into being. The piece sits at the bottom of the stairs to the upper restaurant area and has become a talking point for staff and customers alike. I find the effect of the trickling water extremely calming.

When asked to describe the style of his work, Chris says he uses 'a Japanese approach to Western pots'.

And I'm very glad he does!

Red mullet that is landed in the winter is usually slightly bigger in size and has a rich, powerful, almost shellfish-like taste. Here I'm pan-frying the fillets to get a lovely crisp skin, and serving them with a velvety shrimp sauce, which works so well with the flavour of the fish. Chicory, which is also good at this time of the year, lends some acidity and bitterness to balance the dish nicely. The little shrimp fritters introduce a contrasting crisp texture and saltiness to the dish. If you can't get red mullet, you could use fillets of grey mullet or sea bass instead.

RED MULLET, CHICORY AND SHRIMP SAUCE, SHRIMP FRITTERS

Serves 4 as a
main course

2 red mullet, 800g–1kg
  each, filleted and
  pin-boned
olive oil for cooking
Cornish sea salt
  and freshly ground
  black pepper

For the roast shallots
8 round shallots, peeled
2 sprigs of thyme
1 garlic clove, peeled
  and crushed
olive oil to drizzle

For the pickled chicory
1 head of chicory,
  leaves separated and
  trimmed if necessary
125ml white wine
75ml white wine vinegar
75ml water
75g caster sugar

For the shrimp sauce
750ml shellfish stock
  (see page 290)
500ml fish stock (see
  page 288)
5 ripe tomatoes, chopped
5 sprigs of tarragon
50g unsalted butter

For the roast chicory
2 heads of chicory,
  trimmed of any
  damaged leaves then
  halved lengthways
2 tablespoons caster
  sugar
100g unsalted butter
200ml orange juice

For the shrimp fritters
200g gluten-free
  self-raising flour
200ml chilled
  sparkling water
oil for deep-frying
28 small shrimps,
  peeled

To serve
extra virgin olive oil

For the roast shallots
Preheat your oven to 220°C/Fan 200°C/Gas Mark 7. Place the shallots on a sheet of foil and add the thyme and garlic. Season with salt and pepper and add a drizzle of olive oil. Bring the edges of the foil up over the shallots and fold them together to make a sealed parcel. Cook in the oven for 15 minutes, until the shallots are soft. Leave them in the foil parcel until ready to serve.

For the pickled chicory
Place the chicory leaves in a bowl that is big enough to take them and the pickling liquor. Put the wine, wine vinegar, water and sugar into a small pan with a pinch of salt and bring to a simmer over a low heat, stirring to dissolve the sugar. Pour the hot liquor over the chicory leaves and cover with cling film to keep them submerged. Leave to cool.

To make the shrimp sauce
Put all of the ingredients into a pan and bring to a simmer over a medium heat. Simmer steadily until the liquor has reduced to about 300ml. Tip the contents of the pan into a blender and blitz for 2 minutes until smooth. Keep the sauce warm, or refrigerate if preparing ahead (ready to reheat for serving).

For the roast chicory
Heat a frying pan over a medium heat and add a drizzle of olive oil. When the oil is hot, carefully place the 4 chicory halves cut side down in the pan and cook for 2 minutes to colour and lightly caramelise them. Turn the chicory over and repeat on the other side. Sprinkle the sugar over the chicory and season with salt and pepper. Add the butter to the pan and flip the chicory halves back onto their cut surface.

Pour in the orange juice and simmer gently for 8 minutes, turning the chicory every 2 minutes. When the core is soft at the base, take the pan off the heat, leaving the chicory inside to finish cooking in the residual heat of the pan.

To prepare for serving
To finish the roast shallots, heat a little olive oil in a frying pan over a medium-high heat, add the shallots and colour all over until nice and golden. Drain off the liquor from the pickled chicory and gently warm the leaves. Warm the shrimp sauce through, if necessary. Heat the pan of roast chicory gently to warm it through.

For the shrimp fritters
In a large bowl, mix the flour with the sparkling water to make a smooth, light batter and season with salt and pepper. Line a tray with kitchen paper.

...continued on page 244

To cook the red mullet

Pat the fish skin dry with kitchen paper. Heat a large non-stick (or well-seasoned) frying pan over a medium heat. When it is hot, add a drizzle of olive oil and place the fish skin side down in the pan. Cook for 3 minutes until the fillets are golden at the edges. Carefully turn them over, take the pan off the heat and leave the fish in the pan to finish cooking in the residual heat for 2 minutes.

To cook the shrimp fritters

While the fish is cooking, heat the oil for deep-frying in a deep-fryer or other suitable deep, heavy pan to 180°C. Drop the shrimps into the batter to coat. You will need to cook them in 2 batches. One by one, drop the shrimps into the hot oil and fry them for a minute or so, until crispy. Remove with a slotted spoon, drain on the kitchen paper and sprinkle with salt. Keep warm for as little time as possible before serving.

To assemble and serve

Warm up the shrimp sauce, roast chicory and shallots. Pour the sauce equally onto 4 warmed plates. Lay 2 pickled chicory leaves on each plate and add a piece of roast chicory and 2 roasted shallots. Drizzle a little extra virgin olive oil on the shrimp sauce and then add the red mullet fillets. Finish with the hot, crispy shrimps. Serve immediately.

Sometimes, a good, well-made tart is just what is needed to finish a meal. At this time of year, when there isn't much fruit about, the humble pear comes into its own. When pears are baked into an almond sponge within a crisp pastry case they are fabulous. This is a familiar combination of flavours, but one that works so well. To my mind, the satisfaction of a dish like this is perfecting it. The more you make it, the better it becomes.

The amaretto ice cream is gorgeous with the pear and almond tart, but for a simple pudding, you could just serve it with the crumble and some poached pears.

PEAR AND ALMOND TART WITH AMARETTO ICE CREAM

Serves 8

For the pastry
200g unsalted butter, diced
180g icing sugar, sifted
1 large egg
140g egg yolks (about 7 large eggs)
500g plain flour, plus extra to dust

For the almond filling
250g unsalted butter, softened
250g golden caster sugar
2 large eggs, beaten
80g plain flour
250g ground almonds
finely grated zest of 1 lemon
1 teaspoon vanilla extract

For the pears
4 pears (I like to use Comice)
300ml water
100ml amaretto liqueur
150g golden caster sugar

For the amaretto ice cream
450ml whole milk
400ml double cream
150ml amaretto liqueur
8 large egg yolks
150g clear honey
a pinch of sea salt
100g amaretti biscuits, crushed

For the pear jam
500g pears
50g unsalted butter
30g golden caster sugar
50ml amaretto liqueur
juice of 1 lemon
1 vanilla pod, split and seeds removed

First make the amaretto ice cream
Pour the milk, cream and liqueur into a heavy-based pan and bring to a simmer over a medium heat. Meanwhile, whisk the egg yolks, honey and salt together in a bowl until pale and fluffy. Pour on the hot creamy milk, whisking well as you do. Wipe out the pan and pour the mixture back into it. Cook over a low heat, stirring all the time, until the custard is thick enough to coat the back of the spoon; don't let it boil.

Pour the custard through a sieve into a bowl set over a larger bowl of ice to cool quickly. Stir the custard as it cools then transfer it to an ice-cream machine. Churn until almost set then add the crushed amaretti and churn to combine. Transfer the ice cream to a suitable container and place in the freezer for 2–3 hours before serving.

To make the pastry
Using a stand mixer or electric hand mixer, cream the butter and icing sugar together in a bowl until pale and fluffy. Lightly beat the egg and egg yolks together, then gradually beat into the creamed mixture. Add the flour and stop mixing as soon as a dough is formed.

Tip the dough onto a lightly floured surface and knead briefly until smooth. Divide in half, shape each piece into a ball and flatten to a disc.

Wrap both pastry discs in cling film. Place one in the fridge to rest for at least 30 minutes; freeze the other to make a dessert for another day. Meanwhile, cook the pears.

To cook the pears
Put the water, amaretto and sugar into a pan, heat to dissolve the sugar and bring to a simmer. Peel the pears and place them in the pan, making sure they are immersed in the liquor. Bring to a simmer and cook gently for 25–30 minutes until the pears are just soft; don't overcook them. Lift the poached pears out of the liquor and set them aside on a plate to cool.

Bring the poaching liquor back to a simmer over a medium heat and let it bubble to reduce by half. Remove from the heat, pour into a medium bowl and leave to cool.

Cut the poached pears in half and trim away the pips if there are any. Place them back in the cooled poaching liquid. Cover and keep in the fridge until ready to serve.

To shape the tart cases
Roll the chilled pastry out on a lightly floured surface to the thickness of a £1 coin. Cut out 8 rounds of pastry

...continued on page 248

...ingredients continued on page 248

and use to line individual tart cases, about 8cm in diameter, pressing the pastry firmly into the edges of the tin and making sure there are no holes or cracks. Trim away any excess pastry around the rim. Place the pastry cases in the fridge to rest while you prepare everything else.

To make the pear jam
Peel, core and dice the pears then place in a pan with all the remaining ingredients. Cover and cook over a medium heat until the pears are soft. Remove the lid and continue to cook until the liquor has reduced and is syrupy. Transfer to a blender and blitz until smooth. Spoon the jam into a container and leave to cool.

To prepare the almond crumble
Preheat your oven to 200°C/Fan 180°C/Gas Mark 6. Line a baking sheet with a non-stick baking mat or silicone paper. Mix the flour, ground almonds and sugars together in a bowl and rub in the butter with your fingertips until the mixture looks like crumble.

Spread the crumble mixture out on the lined baking sheet and bake for 20–25 minutes until it is cooked and golden. Remove from the oven and lift the crumble (on the mat or lining paper) onto a wire rack to cool. (Leave the oven on to bake the tarts.)

To make the amaretto syrup
Put the liquid glucose, sugar, lemon zest and juice and the amaretto into a pan over a medium heat to dissolve the sugar. Let it simmer for 3 minutes, then pour the syrup into a bowl and set aside to cool.

To prepare the almond filling
Using a stand mixer or electric hand mixer, beat the butter and sugar together until pale and fluffy, then incorporate the beaten eggs a little at a time. Sift the flour and ground almonds together over the mixture, then add the lemon zest and vanilla extract and fold in carefully, using a large metal spoon or spatula, until evenly combined.

To assemble and bake the tarts
Take the pastry cases out of the fridge. Remove the poached pears from their poaching liquor, drain them and cut each half into 5 or 6 slices. Spread 2 teaspoons of pear jam in each pastry case and spoon the almond filling on top. Arrange a sliced pear half on each tart.

Bake the tarts in the oven at 200°C/Fan 180°C/Gas Mark 6 for about 30 minutes until cooked and golden. Meanwhile, make the apricot glaze.

For the glaze
Warm the apricot preserve and water together, then pass through a fine sieve into a small bowl; keep warm. When the tarts are ready, remove them from the oven and immediately brush the surface with the warm apricot glaze.

To serve
Spoon a dollop of pear jam onto one side of each plate. Add a neat little pile of almond crumble alongside. Place a warm pear tart on each plate and spoon a quenelle of amaretto ice cream on top of the crumble. Finish with a trickle of the amaretto syrup. Serve immediately.

For the almond crumble
100g plain flour
150g ground almonds
100g golden caster sugar
100g demerara sugar
100g unsalted butter, diced

For the amaretto syrup
100ml liquid glucose
50g golden caster sugar
finely grated zest of 1 lemon
75ml lemon juice
75ml amaretto liqueur

For the apricot glaze
4 tablespoons apricot preserve
2 tablespoons water

There is something about a custard tart that fascinates me. It's so simple, yet so perfect and I can't resist it. Through the year, I change what I serve it with, but this version is my favourite.

CUSTARD TART, ROAST QUINCE, QUINCE AND GINGER SORBET

Serves 8

For the roast quince
300ml orange juice
600ml water
300g soft brown sugar
3 star anise
4–6 quinces, depending on size

For the quince and ginger sorbet
500g roasted quince (from above)
500ml ginger beer
100g liquid glucose

For the pastry
200g unsalted butter, diced
180g icing sugar, sifted
1 large egg
140g egg yolks (about 6 large eggs)
500g plain flour, plus extra to dust
egg wash (1 egg, beaten with 1 tablespoon milk)

For the custard filling
600ml double cream
300ml whole milk
8 large eggs
200g golden caster sugar
nutmeg, for grating, to finish

To roast the quince
Preheat your oven to 170°C/Fan 150°C /Gas Mark 3. Put the orange juice, water, brown sugar and star anise into a pan, heat to dissolve the sugar and bring to a simmer. Meanwhile, peel and quarter the quince. Place in a roasting tray, pour on the hot liquor and lay a sheet of baking parchment on top. Roast in the oven for 2½ hours or until tender. Remove and leave to cool.

To make the sorbet
Weigh 500g of the roast quince (save the rest) and place in a pan with the ginger beer and liquid glucose. Bring to a simmer, take off the heat and tip into a blender. Blitz until smooth. Leave to cool, then churn in an ice-cream machine until thick. Transfer to a suitable container and keep in the freezer until ready to serve.

To make the pastry
With an electric stand or hand mixer, cream the butter and icing sugar together until pale and fluffy. Lightly beat the egg and egg yolks together, then gradually beat into the creamed mixture. Add the flour and stop mixing as soon as a dough is formed.

Tip onto a lightly floured surface and knead briefly until smooth. Divide the dough in half, shape each piece into a ball and flatten to a disc. Wrap both discs in cling film. Chill one in the fridge at least for 30 minutes; freeze the other for another tart.

Preheat your oven to 200°C/Fan 180°C/Gas Mark 6. Roll the pastry out on a lightly floured surface to the thickness of a £1 coin and use to line a loose-based 25cm round tart tin, pressing firmly into the edges. Prick the base with a fork and trim away the excess pastry. Line the pastry case with a scrunched-up piece of greaseproof paper and a layer of baking beans. Place in the fridge to rest for 20 minutes.

Bake the pastry case in the oven for 15 minutes, then remove the paper and beans and return the tart case to the oven for 5 minutes. Take out and brush the inside well with egg wash. Put back into the oven for 2 minutes to set. Slide the tart tin onto a wire rack to cool. Turn the oven down to 130°C/Fan 110°C/Gas Mark ¾.

To prepare the custard filling
Pour the cream and milk into a pan and bring to a simmer over a medium heat. Meanwhile, whisk the eggs and sugar together in a bowl, then pour on the hot creamy milk, whisking to combine. Pass through a sieve into a large jug and allow to cool.

Place the tart tin on a baking sheet in the oven and carefully pour the custard into the pastry case. Bake in the oven for 25–30 minutes until the custard is set, with a slight wobble in the middle. Remove the tart from the oven, grate some nutmeg over the surface and allow to cool.

To assemble and serve
Using a sharp, hot knife, cut the tart into 8 portions. Slice the reserved roast quince and arrange on serving plates with a slice of custard tart alongside. Place a neat scoop of sorbet on top of the roast quince and serve immediately.

A word of warning! This fudge is dangerously more-ish ... it's as simple as that. I challenge anyone to eat only one piece. The recipe makes quite a bit, but I am sure you won't find that a problem.

Makes about 60 pieces

75g unsalted butter
750g caster sugar
250g liquid glucose
215ml double cream
100g clotted cream
2 teaspoons sea salt
375g caramel milk
   chocolate, broken
   into pieces

CARAMEL CHOCOLATE AND **SEA SALT FUDGE**

Line a shallow baking tin, about 25 x 20cm, with non-stick silicone paper or baking parchment.

Put the butter, sugar, liquid glucose and both creams into a deep, heavy-based saucepan and place over a medium-low heat. Stir constantly until the butter has melted and the sugar is dissolved.

Now bring the mixture to a simmer over a medium heat, without stirring, and place a sugar thermometer in the pan. Once it registers 100°C, stir the mixture occasionally and continue to cook until it reaches 117°C.

Take the pan off the heat and beat in the salt and chocolate. Continue to beat until the chocolate is fully melted and emulsified into the mixture. Pour into the prepared tin and leave to set for a few hours.

Once the fudge has set, cut it into squares. Serve with an extra sprinkle of sea salt on top.

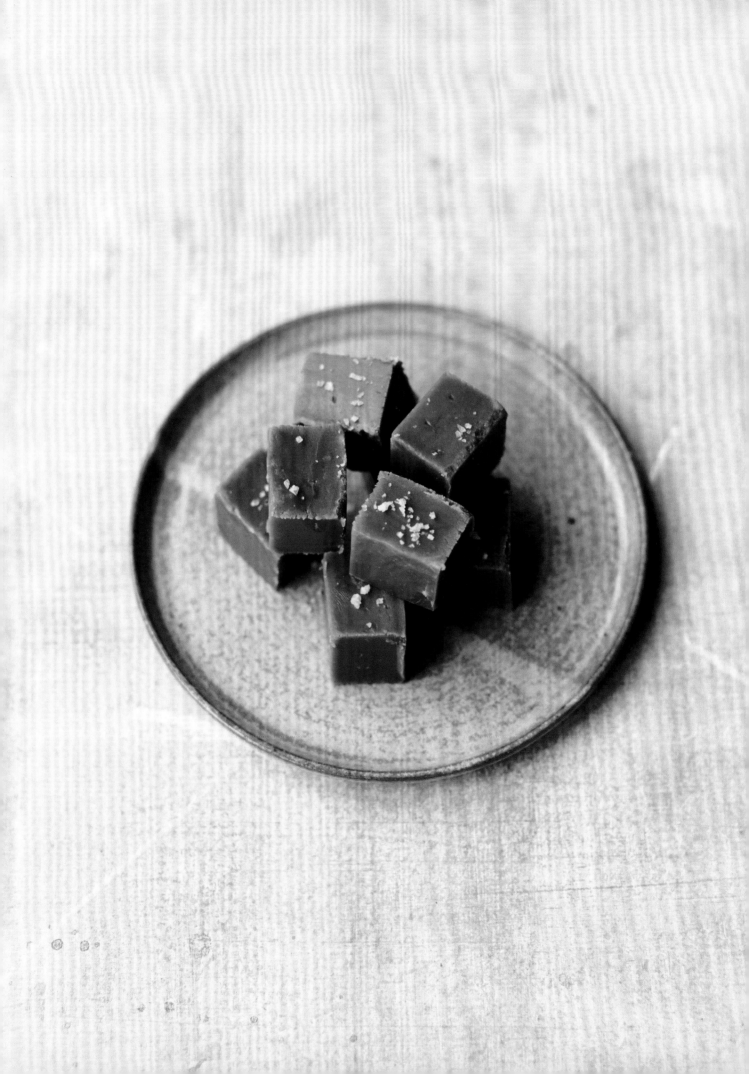

Late Winter

This dip is simple to make and so more-ish – my son would eat the whole lot in one go if I turned my back. The key, obviously, is the main ingredient. You want to buy good-quality smoked cod's roe that isn't too large and has a good, firm texture.

SMOKED COD'S ROE DIP WITH SOURDOUGH CRISPS

For the cod's roe dip
500ml light olive oil
4 garlic cloves
  (unpeeled)
100g good-quality
  crustless bread
about 100ml milk
400g smoked cod's
  roe, rinsed and
  membrane removed
40g Dijon mustard
juice of 2 lemons
smoked paprika
  to sprinkle
mixed dried seaweed
  to sprinkle
Cornish sea salt
  and freshly ground
  black pepper

For the sourdough crisps
½ large sourdough loaf
  (2 days old)
extra virgin olive oil
  to drizzle

To make the cod's roe dip
Heat the olive oil and garlic in a saucepan over a medium heat until the oil starts to bubble around the garlic cloves. Turn the heat down slightly (so the garlic doesn't fry), and cook gently for 20 minutes until the garlic is soft. Take the pan off the heat and leave to infuse and cool.

Meanwhile, break the bread into chunks and place in a bowl. Pour on the milk and set aside to soak. Once the oil is cold, remove the garlic cloves with a slotted spoon; reserve the oil. Peel the garlic cloves.

Put the smoked cod's roe, mustard, lemon juice and garlic into a blender or food processor. Squeeze the bread to remove excess milk, then add it to the blender and blitz for 1 minute.

With the motor running, slowly add most of the garlic-infused oil through the funnel until the mixture thickens and has the consistency of mayonnaise; save a little garlic oil for serving. Season the dip with salt and pepper to taste and blend for another 20 seconds. Scrape into a bowl, cover and refrigerate until needed.

For the sourdough crisps
Preheat your oven to 200°C/ Fan 180°C/Gas Mark 6. Slice the sourdough as thinly as possible and lay the slices out on a large baking tray. Drizzle with extra virgin olive oil and season with salt and pepper. Bake the sourdough slices in the oven for 10–15 minutes until crisp. They may crisp at different times, so take them out individually as they're ready and place on a wire rack to cool.

To serve
Sprinkle the dip generously with smoked paprika and seaweed. Finish with a drizzle of garlicky olive oil. Serve with the sourdough crisps on the side.

When scallops are super fresh, I think their flavour is best appreciated when they are eaten raw. This dish was created while we were creating different stocks from the amazing vegetables we were getting from one of our local growers. The onion stock, which forms the base of the dressing for this dish, was the most successful. It works so well with its touch of lemon juice and the chilli oil.

RAW SCALLOPS, ROAST ONION, PARSNIP CRISPS AND CHILLI OIL

Serves 4 as a starter

12 live medium
  scallops, removed
  from the shell
  and cleaned
fine Cornish sea salt

For the chilli oil
4 green chillies, halved
  and chopped
400ml light olive oil
1 teaspoon sea salt

For the onion stock
400g white onions,
  peeled and roughly
  chopped
olive oil for cooking
400ml water
juice of 1 lemon, or
  to taste

For the brown butter
250g unsalted butter

For the pan-roasted
onion
1 white onion, peeled
  and halved vertically
50ml white wine
50ml white wine
  vinegar
50g caster sugar
50ml water
olive oil for cooking

For the parsnip crisps
2 parsnips
sunflower oil for
  deep-frying
a good pinch of cayenne
  pepper

First make the chilli oil (a day ahead)
Put the chillies, olive oil and salt into a blender or food processor and blitz for 1 minute. Transfer to a saucepan and warm over a medium heat until the oil is hot. Remove and leave to cool. When cold, decant the oil into a container and leave for 24 hours.

To prepare the onion stock
Heat a large pan over a medium-high heat and add a drizzle of olive oil. When hot, add the onions and cook for 15 minutes, stirring frequently, until they are well caramelised. Pour in the water, bring to a simmer and let simmer for 20 minutes. Pass the stock through a sieve into a clean pan and return to the heat. Simmer to reduce to about 100ml. Leave to cool.

For the brown butter
In a pan over a medium heat, melt the butter. Continue to cook until it starts to turn brown, then remove from the heat and set aside to cool.

To prepare the onion
Heat the wine, wine vinegar, sugar and water together in a pan with a pinch of salt to dissolve the sugar then bring to the boil. Take off the heat and leave to cool. Once it is cool, put the halved onion into a boilable vac-pac bag with the pickling liquor. Seal the bag and immerse it in a pan of boiling water for 14 minutes.

Lift the bag out of the water and leave the onion halves inside to cool in the liquor. Refrigerate unless you are using straight away.

To make the parsnip crisps
Line a tray with kitchen paper. Peel the parsnips and cut them into matchsticks. Meanwhile, heat the oil for deep-frying in a deep-fryer or other suitable deep, heavy pan to 180°C. When hot, add the parsnips and fry until golden and crisp. Remove and drain on the kitchen paper. Season with salt and cayenne while still hot. Leave to cool.

To pan-roast the onion
Drain the onion halves, cut into wedges and pat dry on kitchen paper. Heat a frying pan over a medium-high heat and add a drizzle of olive oil. When it is hot, add the onion wedges and colour them well on all sides. Remove from the pan and cut off the root end, so the onion separates into petals. Set aside.

To assemble and serve
Using a sharp knife, carefully slice the scallops in half and arrange on 4 serving plates. Lay a pickled onion petal or two on each scallop half.

For the dressing, pour the onion stock into a small pan and carefully pour in the browned butter, leaving the sediment behind. Warm through, stirring occasionally, over a medium heat. Add lemon juice and season with salt to taste.

Spoon the dressing evenly around the plates. Drizzle 1–2 teaspoons chilli oil over each portion of scallops and finish with the crisp-fried parsnips. Serve immediately.

Lemon sole is such an underrated fish but I really don't understand why. It cooks quickly and is easily overdone, which may account for its lack of popularity. I find you get the best results if you gently grill the fillets with the skin on to protect the flesh, then pull the skin off just before serving. I have been serving versions of this dish since we opened. The sauce is unique: an oyster mayonnaise, thinned with a punchy cucumber and horseradish stock. It looks rich and creamy but is, in fact, light and fresh, as there is no cream or butter. Don't worry if it sounds too healthy – it's finished off with a deep-fried oyster!

LEMON SOLE WITH OYSTER, CUCUMBER AND DILL

First make the dill oil (a day ahead)
Bring a large pan of salted water to the boil and have ready a bowl of iced water. Once the water is boiling, add the dill and spinach and blanch for 30 seconds. Immediately drain and plunge into the iced water to cool quickly. Drain and squeeze out all the excess water.

Put the blanched dill and spinach into a blender with the olive oil and blitz for 2 minutes. Transfer the oil to a bowl, cover and leave to settle in the fridge for 24 hours.

When the sediment has sunk to the bottom, slightly warm the oil then strain through a muslin-lined sieve into a clean container. Refrigerate until needed (it will keep for a week).

To make the sauce
Put the cucumber and horseradish into a blender with the wine vinegar, sugar and a pinch of salt. Blitz for 2 minutes, then strain through a fine sieve into a bowl and set aside.

Place the egg yolks, lemon juice and oysters, with their juices, in a blender and blitz for 30 seconds. With the motor running, slowly add the olive oil until it is all incorporated and you have a thick mayonnaise. Set aside.

For the deep-fried oysters
Have the flour, beaten egg and panko breadcrumbs ready in three separate bowls. Pass the oysters through the flour, then the egg mix and finally the breadcrumbs to coat. Set aside.

To make the dressing
Mix the diced cucumber with the 8 tablespoons dill oil.

To cook the fish and oysters
Heat your grill to a medium-high setting. Heat the oil for deep-frying in a deep-fryer or other suitable deep, heavy pan to 180°C.

Oil the grill tray and sprinkle with salt. Lay the sole fillets, skin side down, on the tray, season with salt and turn them so the skin is face up. Cook under the grill for 4 minutes.

At the same, deep-fry the oysters in the hot oil for 1 minute until crispy and golden. Drain on kitchen paper and season with salt. Once the fish is cooked, remove the skin and sprinkle the fillets with a little salt.

To assemble and serve
Whisk the mayonnaise and cucumber stock together, then heat gently in a pan over a medium heat, whisking all the time; do not boil.

Pour the warm sauce into 4 warmed shallow bowls. Add a crispy oyster to each and arrange 2 sole fillets on top. Spoon on the cucumber dressing and finish with the diced lemon and a crispy oyster. Serve immediately.

Serves 4 as a starter

2 lemon soles, about 500g each, filleted
light olive oil for cooking
Cornish sea salt

For the dill oil
30g dill leaves
60g spinach leaves
200ml light olive oil

For the cucumber and horseradish sauce
1 large cucumber, chopped
50g fresh horseradish, peeled and grated
50ml white wine vinegar
1 tablespoon caster sugar
2 large egg yolks
Juice of 1 lemon
4 oysters, shucked, juices retained
250ml light olive oil

For the deep-fried oysters
8 oysters, shucked and drained, juices retained
plain flour to dust
1 large egg, beaten with 1 tablespoon milk
100g panko breadcrumbs
oil for deep-frying

For the dressing
1 large cucumber, peeled and diced
8 tablespoons dill oil (from above)

To finish
1 lemon, peel and pith removed, segmented and diced

I am always trying to come up with new crab dishes. Port Isaac, where Restaurant Nathan Outlaw is situated, has a fleet of five boats, all fishing for crab. So, it is pretty much always available, as long as the boats can go out. In my opinion, this crustacean is at its best during the winter, when you can get great hen crabs, which are full of brown meat, and the odd spider crab too. I love Asian food and this has influenced this dish a little. Ginger, garlic, spring onions and fresh coriander enhance the sweet crab meat beautifully and saffron is used to flavour the pickled beetroot.

CRAB WITH PICKLED BEETROOT AND GINGER DRESSING

Serves 4 as a starter

For the crab
1 live brown crab, about
  1kg, placed in the
  freezer 30 minutes
  before cooking
about 3 tablespoons
  Greek yoghurt
2 tablespoons chopped
  coriander
4 spring onions,
  trimmed and sliced
juice of 1 lemon, or
  to taste
Cornish sea salt
  and freshly ground
  black pepper

For the pickled beetroot
1 large raw beetroot
1 banana shallot,
  peeled and finely
  chopped
50g freshly peeled root
  ginger, sliced
2 garlic cloves, peeled
  and sliced
200ml light olive oil
75ml white wine vinegar
a pinch of saffron
  strands

For the ginger juice
200g freshly peeled
  root ginger, chopped

For the ginger dressing
2 tablespoons ginger
  juice (from above)
4 tablespoons light
  olive oil
3 tablespoons beetroot
  pickling liquor
  (from above)

For the ginger and
coriander yoghurt
100g full-fat Greek
  yoghurt
2 tablespoons ginger
  juice (from above)
1 tablespoon chopped
  coriander

To pickle the beetroot
Peel and finely slice the beetroot, using a mandoline. Using an 8cm plain round cutter, cut 12 neat rounds from the beetroot slices.

Put the shallot, ginger, garlic, olive oil, wine vinegar and saffron into a small saucepan and add a pinch of salt. Bring to a simmer over a medium heat.

Lay the beetroot slices evenly in a dish and pour the hot pickling liquor over them. Cover with cling film, making sure the beetroot slices are submerged. Leave to cool.

To cook and prepare the crab
Bring a large pan of water (big enough to hold the crab fully submerged) to the boil. Season the water generously with salt, to make it as salty as sea water (this ensures that the flavour of the crab isn't lost during cooking). Once it comes to a rolling boil, lower the crab into the water and cook for 14 minutes.

Carefully lift the crab out of the pan, place on a tray and leave until cool enough to handle.

Remove all the legs and claws from the cooked crab, by twisting them away from the body. Now, holding the crab in both hands, use your thumbs to push the body up and out of the hard, top shell or carapace. Remove

and discard the dead man's fingers, stomach sac and hard membranes from the body shell.

Using a spoon, remove the brown crab from the carapace and place it in a container (you won't need it for this dish so cover and refrigerate or freeze for another use – it's good on toast).

Now cut the body in half, using a sharp knife, to reveal the little channels of white crab meat. Use a crab pick or the handle of a spoon to pick out all the crab meat from these crevices and put it into a bowl.

Using a heavy knife, break the claws with one hard tap if possible and pick out the white meat, prising out the cartilage from the middle of the claw. Do the same with the legs to extract the meat. Once you have extracted all the white meat, with clean hands, pick through it to search for any shell or cartilage. Cover and refrigerate if preparing ahead.

To prepare the ginger juice
Blitz the root ginger thoroughly in a small blender with a little water (just enough to get it going). Tip the pulp into a square of muslin over a bowl, gather up the edges and squeeze tightly over the bowl to extract as much juice as possible.

...continued on page 264

To make the ginger dressing
Measure 2 tablespoons of the ginger
juice and mix with the 4 tablespoons
olive oil and 3 tablespoons beetroot
pickling liquor. Season with salt to
taste and set aside.

For the coriander and ginger yoghurt
In a bowl, stir the yoghurt with
2 tablespoons ginger juice and the
chopped coriander to combine.
Season with salt to taste. Cover and
refrigerate until ready to serve.

To finish the crab
Fold enough of the plain yoghurt
through the white crab meat to
combine the mixture delicately, then
stir through the coriander and spring
onions. Add lemon juice and season
with salt and pepper to taste.

To assemble and serve
Drain the pickled beetroot and
lay one disc on each serving plate.
Cut the remaining beetroot into
matchsticks. Place a spoonful of the
coriander and ginger yoghurt on
top of the beetroot discs, then pile
the white crab meat evenly on top.
Arrange the beetroot matchsticks
in a pile on top of the crab. Drizzle
1 tablespoon of the ginger dressing
over each portion and serve.

THE FISHERMEN'S MISSION

When I came to Cornwall, like much of the population, I wasn't aware how difficult the life of a fisherman can be. I now realise the struggles and dangers they face every day, just to make a living and put fish on our plates. Fishing is the most dangerous peacetime occupation in the UK. Statistically, someone who starts fishing at the age of sixteen and continues until they are sixty-five stands a one in fourteen chance of dying at sea.

Most UK fishermen are self-employed, many working alone or in crews of just two or three. Each time they go out to sea, their lives are put at risk because of the sea's unpredictable nature. Even the most experienced fisherman can fall foul of an unexpected swell of waves or suffer an accident while out at sea, ending up in a precarious position.

The Fishermen's Mission is a Christian-based charity, that works tirelessly to help both active and retired fishermen and their families by offering support, whether that be emotional, spiritual, practical or financial.

When the charity started in 1881, the objectives were to 'preach the Word and heal the sick'. Using a small fleet of their own boats, charity workers would visit fishermen while at sea, providing food and medicine where needed. Moving with the times, during the 1900s the charity set up accommodation centres for fishermen, so those far from home could be guaranteed a bed and some home comforts. However, with the decline of the fishing industry in the 1980s and 1990s, more help was needed for those fishermen and their families where the main breadwinner had been forced to retire or found themselves out of work.

In the UK, there are currently around 13,000 fishermen, most of whom fish from boats under 10 metres in length, from their home port or with facilities on board. The Fishermen's Mission has opened mini-centres where assistance is available around the clock. It now also provides support through outreach work and welfare officers are located all around the coastline of the UK.

Recently, through a scheme piloted in Cornwall, the charity has partnered with health professionals to offer health checks on the harbourside and these have, quite literally, saved lives. The arrangement has now been rolled out nationwide.

In addition to their community. role, The Fishermen's Mission works closely with the industry to promote safe fishing and better working conditions.

As the charity doesn't receive funding from the Government or the National Lottery, it relies totally on donations, fund-raising and just one charity shop in Helston to carry out its work. For every £1 donated, 88p is used directly for services. Many of its supporters, recognising the dangers faced to bring fish into the kitchen, are in the restaurant or food business, and I'm proud to be one of them.

Here, in Cornwall, the team are familiar faces throughout the forty-nine ports and coves they cover, on hand to offer help and support, no matter how complex the circumstance or how desperate the times. Welfare is the cornerstone of all they do and they have an eye to the safety and wellbeing of the active fishermen in equal measure to concerns regarding loneliness and poverty. Their time is shared between working with active fishermen and their families, and those who are retired. If the worst should happen, they will be there to help with the trauma of losing a loved one to the sea.

Whatever happens, 'the team from The Fish Mish', as they are fondly called, will be there to help. In their words, it's 'Christianity with sleeves rolled up'.

In winter, you can find some stunning big cod that has wonderful pearly white flesh when cooked and a great texture too. For me, baking is the best way to cook thick filleted portions from big cod. It is a much gentler way of cooking than frying and the fish flakes beautifully into large pieces once cooked. I like to top the fish with a breadcrumb, herb and Parmesan crust before it goes in the oven.

Cuttlefish is something we should all be embracing and cooking. Not only is it sustainable, it's as good to eat as squid, if not better. In this dish, I braise it until tender and then add some creamy white beans and a zingy lemon, garlic and parsley dressing. It's great with the baked cod.

Serves 4 as a
main course

COD, CUTTLEFISH AND BEANS, LEMON AND GARLIC DRESSING

4 filleted portions
of cod, about 120g
each, pin-boned
and skinned
olive oil for cooking
Cornish sea salt
and freshly ground
black pepper

For the cuttlefish
1kg cuttlefish, cleaned
light olive oil for cooking
1 white onion, peeled
and finely diced
2 garlic cloves, peeled
and chopped
1 tablespoon thyme
leaves
500ml red wine
3 tomatoes, halved
400ml fish stock (see
page 288)
150g drained tinned
(or freshly cooked)
borlotti beans
2 tablespoons chopped
curly parsley

For the crust
200g good-quality
crustless white bread
(2 days old), cubed
2 garlic cloves, peeled
and finely chopped
3 tablespoons chopped
curly parsley
50g Parmesan,
freshly grated

For the dressing
finely grated zest and
juice of 1 lemon
a handful of curly
parsley, finely
chopped
1 garlic clove, peeled
and finely chopped
6 tablespoons extra
virgin olive oil

To cook the cuttlefish
Cut the cuttlefish into 2cm slices and pat dry. Heat a large saucepan and add a drizzle of olive oil. When it is hot, add the onion, garlic and thyme and cook for 2 minutes. Pour in the wine, add the tomatoes and bring to the boil. Let it bubble over a medium heat until reduced by half. Pour in the fish stock and bring to the boil.

Heat a frying pan over a high heat and add a drizzle of olive oil. When the oil is hot, fry the cuttlefish in batches, to avoid overcrowding the pan. Cook each cuttlefish batch for 2–3 minutes, season with salt and pepper, then drain in a colander.

Now add the cuttlefish to the stock base and bring to a simmer. Cook gently for 1½–2 hours, until tender. Add the borlotti beans to the pan and cook for a further 10 minutes. Season with salt and pepper to taste and remove from the heat.

To prepare the crust
Put the bread, garlic and parsley into a blender or food processor and blitz for 3 minutes to green crumbs. Add the Parmesan and blitz for another 30 seconds. Tip out onto a tray and leave to one side.

To make the dressing
In a bowl, mix the lemon zest and juice, parsley and garlic together with the extra virgin olive oil and season with salt and pepper to taste. Set aside.

To cook the fish
Preheat your oven to 220°C/Fan 200°C/Gas Mark 7. Oil the cod portions and season with salt and pepper. Place on a baking tray lined with non-stick silicone paper. Sprinkle the crust evenly on top of the fish and bake in the oven for 8–10 minutes until just cooked, depending on the thickness of the fish portions.

While the fish is cooking, heat up the cuttlefish stew and add the chopped parsley. Share it among 4 warmed plates. Drizzle with the dressing and then top with the crusted cod portions. Serve immediately.

King of the sea, turbot, with a decadent champagne sauce and caviar … what's not to like? At the restaurant, I serve this on special occasions, and on request. Everyone needs a little extravagance from time to time. I make an amazing sauce from the turbot head, champagne, butter and caviar. It's pretty special this one! I like to serve the dish with stewed leeks and a cauliflower purée.

TURBOT, CHAMPAGNE AND CAVIAR

Serves 4 as a main course

4 filleted turbot portions, about 150g, skin on (head reserved for the sauce)
oil for cooking
Cornish sea salt

For the sauce
1 turbot head, gills and blood removed
1 white onion, peeled and roughly chopped
1 leek (white part only), thoroughly washed and sliced
1 celery stick, diced
1 fennel bulb, roughly chopped
3 garlic cloves, peeled, halved and germ removed
500ml champagne
2 bay leaves
2 sprigs of thyme
100ml double cream
100g unsalted butter, cubed
2 tablespoons chives, chopped
2 tablespoons parsley, chopped
1 tablespoon tarragon, chopped
100g caviar

First make the sauce
Preheat your oven to 220°C/Fan 200°C/Gas Mark 7.

Place the turbot head in a roasting tray with all the vegetables and the garlic and roast for 30 minutes.

Once cooked, remove the turbot head and vegetables from the tray and put them into a cooking pot big enough to hold everything comfortably. Pour on the champagne and top up with enough water to ensure the turbot head and vegetables are just covered. Add the bay leaves and thyme sprigs and bring to a simmer. Skim off any impurities from the surface and cook gently for 30 minutes.

Strain the liquor through a sieve into a clean pan; discard the turbot head, vegetables, garlic and herbs. Place the pan over a medium heat and let the liquor bubble gently to reduce down to about 200ml; this will take about an hour.

Add the cream to the reduced liquor and simmer for 5 minutes. Strain the sauce into a clean pan and set aside while you cook the fish.

To cook the fish
Set up a steamer or switch on your oven steamer if you have one. Oil the turbot fillets and season them with salt. Place in the steamer and cook for 6 minutes.

Meanwhile, gently heat up the sauce. Once the fish is cooked, leave it to rest while you finish the sauce.

To finish the sauce
Bring to a simmer and whisk in the butter, a piece at a time. Add the chopped chives, parsley, tarragon and caviar, then taste to check the seasoning and adjust as necessary.

To serve
Peel away the skin from the fish, season the fillets with a little salt and place them on warmed plates. Spoon the sauce over the turbot portions and serve immediately, with stewed leeks and a cauliflower purée, or other accompaniments of your choice, on the side.

Not long ago, hake was a fish in danger from overfishing, owing to its popularity in Spain, Italy and France, but weirdly, it was not so in demand in the UK. Now it's making a big come back in Cornwall, with boats targeting hake that is sustainable. I love it, and more of our customers are beginning to as well. Once cooked, it has a great texture; it's also a versatile fish. If it's cooked simply – grilled or pan-seared, as below – it seems to handle robust flavours with ease. In its raw state, it can be quite fragile and the quality can be variable, so I would only recommend buying from a good fishmonger, who you trust. This is a lovely winter dish with some intense, warming flavours: smoked meaty mushrooms, a velvety saffron and garlicky potato purée, pickled mushrooms and a tangy red wine dressing. They work a treat with the hake … enjoy!

HAKE AND MUSHROOMS WITH ROAST GARLIC AND SAFFRON POTATO PURÉE

First prepare the smoked mushrooms
Set up your smoker for cold smoking. Lay the mushrooms on the smoking rack and smoke for 1 hour.

Once the mushrooms are smoked, place them in a pan with the butter, thyme, garlic and a pinch of salt. Add just enough water to cover the mushrooms and lay a circle of greaseproof paper over them. Cook gently for 20 minutes, then remove the mushrooms from the liquor with a slotted spoon; save the liquor. Slice the mushrooms in half and cut each half into 4 wedges. Lay these mushroom wedges in an ovenproof dish and spoon over some of the reserved cooking liquor.

For the potato purée
Preheat your oven to 220°C/Fan 200°C/Gas Mark 7. Split the garlic bulb into individual cloves. Take a square of foil and scrunch up the sides. Put the garlic cloves into the foil bag, sprinkle with salt and drizzle with olive oil. Seal the foil bag, place on an oven tray and cook in the oven for 30 minutes.

Meanwhile, put the potatoes into a pan of cold salted water, bring to a simmer and cook until soft, about 15 minutes. Drain the potatoes and leave them in the colander to dry for a few minutes.

Once the garlic is cooked, open the foil bag and leave the cloves until cool enough to handle, then peel.

Put the potatoes into a food processor with the saffron, roasted garlic and egg yolks. Blend until smooth, adding the 150ml olive oil in a steady stream through the feeder tube. Once the oil is all incorporated, stop the machine and add the wine vinegar and a little salt. Blend for 2 minutes, then taste and adjust the seasoning if required. Transfer to a bowl and cover the surface with cling film. Keep warm.

To make the dressing
Put the red wine, wine vinegar, water and brown sugar into a pan, heat gently to dissolve the sugar, then bring to a simmer. Let it bubble to reduce until thick and syrupy.

Meanwhile, melt the butter in a pan over a low heat and add the thyme.

...continued on page 274

Serves 4 as a main course

4 filleted portions of hake, about 160g each, trimmed
olive oil for cooking
Cornish sea salt and freshly ground black pepper

For the smoked mushrooms
2 large portobello mushrooms, peeled
100g unsalted butter
2 sprigs of thyme
2 garlic cloves, peeled and crushed
wood chips for smoking

For the potato purée
1 large garlic bulb
150ml light olive oil, plus extra to drizzle
500g floury potatoes, peeled (300g peeled weight)
½ teaspoon saffron strands
4 large egg yolks
50ml white wine vinegar

For the dressing
200ml red wine
100ml red wine vinegar
100ml water
100g soft brown sugar
250g unsalted butter
3 sprigs of thyme

For the sautéed mushrooms
olive oil for cooking
200g mixed wild and cultivated mushrooms
1 round shallot, peeled and finely chopped
1 garlic clove, peeled and finely chopped
2 tablespoons sherry vinegar
1 tablespoon chopped parsley

To garnish
12 red grapes, sliced
a handful of wild sea beet, steamed

Increase the heat to medium-high and cook until the butter is bubbling, turning brown, and has a nutty aroma. Immediately remove from the heat and leave to cool. Carefully pour the brown butter into another pan, leaving the sediment and thyme behind. Keep the butter warm.

To sauté the mushrooms

Heat a frying pan over a medium heat and add a drizzle of olive oil. When it is hot, add the mushrooms and cook for 1 minute. Add the shallot and garlic and cook for another minute, adding a little more oil if needed. Deglaze the pan with the sherry vinegar and season with salt and pepper. Finally, before serving add the chopped parsley. Keep warm.

To cook the hake

Preheat your oven to 220°C/Fan 200°C/Gas Mark 7. Make sure the skin on the hake is dry; pat dry with kitchen paper if necessary. Heat a non-stick (or well-seasoned) ovenproof frying pan over a medium heat. When it is hot, add a drizzle of olive oil, then place the fish, skin side down, in the pan. Cook, without moving, for 2–3 minutes until golden at the edges. Transfer the pan to the oven, keeping the fish skin side down, and cook for 3 minutes. Remove from the oven and carefully turn the fish over. Leave the fish in the pan to finish cooking in the residual heat.

To prepare for serving

Just before serving, place the smoked mushrooms in the oven for a few minutes to warm through, then sprinkle with a little salt. To finish the dressing, mix the red wine reduction and butter together in a pan and season with salt and pepper to taste.

To serve

Spoon the potato purée equally into the centre of 4 warmed serving plates. Place the hake on top and spoon the sautéed and smoked mushrooms around. Give the dressing a stir with a whisk, then spoon it around the fish and mushrooms. Finish with the grapes and sea beet. Serve hot.

Bitter-sweet, rich chocolate mousse, a chocolate cake with a hint of stout, creamy milk ice cream and zingy, sweet blood oranges: think Jaffa cake, but fresher and tastier. It sounds good but tastes even better!

Serves 6

DARK CHOCOLATE MOUSSE, STOUT CAKE, MILK ICE CREAM AND BLOOD ORANGE

For the stout cake
250g unsalted butter, softened
400g soft brown sugar
1 vanilla pod, split lengthways, seeds extracted
2 large eggs, beaten
275g self-raising flour
75g cocoa powder
140g Greek-style yoghurt
250ml stout

For the chocolate crumble
100g plain flour
1 teaspoon sea salt
150g ground almonds
150g soft dark brown sugar
100g unsalted butter, softened
40g cocoa powder

For the milk ice cream
550ml whole milk
50ml double cream
30g liquid glucose
425g condensed milk

For the chocolate mousse
2 sheets of bronze gelatine
100ml whole milk
300ml double cream
6 large egg yolks
100g caster sugar
40g cocoa powder
100g dark chocolate (70% cocoa solids), chopped
200ml double cream

For the stout syrup
200g liquid glucose
finely grated zest of 1 orange
100ml stout
50g soft dark brown sugar

To garnish
2 blood oranges, cut into segments (all peel and pith removed) and halved

First make the stout cake
Preheat your oven to 180°C/Fan 160°C/Gas Mark 4. Line the base and sides of a 20cm round cake tin, 6cm deep, with baking parchment.

Using a stand mixer fitted with the paddle attachment, cream the butter, sugar and vanilla seeds together until pale and fluffy, then slowly beat in the eggs. Sift the flour and cocoa together and fold into the mixture. Add the yoghurt and stout and fold in until evenly combined.

Spoon the mixture into the prepared tin and bake for 30 minutes, until a skewer inserted into the centre comes out clean. Transfer the cake to a wire rack to cool. Keep the oven on.

For the chocolate crumble
Line a baking tray with a non-stick silicone mat. Using the stand mixer and paddle attachment, mix all the ingredients together well until there is no visible sign of the butter. Tip the mix onto the lined tray and spread out evenly. Bake for 20 minutes, then give it a stir and bake for a further 10 minutes until golden. Set aside to cool. Once cold, break it up a bit and keep in an airtight container.

To make the milk ice cream
In a pan, bring the whole milk, cream and glucose to the boil, then take off the heat and leave to cool. When cold, whisk in the condensed milk. Pour into an ice-cream machine and churn until thick. Transfer the ice cream to a suitable container and keep in the freezer until ready to serve.

To prepare the chocolate mousse
Soak the gelatine in a shallow dish of ice-cold water to soften. Pour the milk and cream into a pan and slowly bring to a simmer over a medium heat, Meanwhile, whisk the egg yolks and sugar together in a bowl, then whisk in the cocoa. Pour on the hot creamy milk, whisking to combine.

Pour the custard back into the pan and cook, stirring constantly, until it registers 70°C on a cook's thermometer. Remove from the heat. Immediately squeeze the excess water from the gelatine, then whisk it into the custard. Add the chocolate and whisk until melted and smooth.

Pour the mixture into a bowl set over a larger bowl of ice and stir until cool. When cool, lightly whip the cream in a separate bowl until soft peaks form, then fold it into the mousse mixture. Transfer to a piping bag and keep in the fridge until ready to serve.

To make the stout syrup
Bring all the ingredients to a simmer in a pan over a medium heat and give the syrup a good whisk. Remove from the heat and leave to cool.

To assemble and serve
Cut 6 equal slices from the cake and moisten them with some of the syrup. Place on 6 plates. Pipe the chocolate mousse next to the cake and add a little pile of crumble. Arrange 4 or 5 blood orange segments on each plate and drizzle more syrup around. Place a spoonful of milk ice cream on top of the cake. Serve immediately.

Winter is not a good time for local fruit and there are days in Cornwall when you wish you could have stayed in bed, because the weather is so horrible. So, in step the sunshine puddings! If you've eaten at my restaurant in the winter you may well have tried this mango and lime ice cream, sandwiched between coconut tuiles and served with a passion fruit and mango jam and a toasty coconut sorbet. The combination of tropical flavours isn't new, but it's a lovely, original dessert … give it a go.

MANGO ICE CREAM SANDWICH WITH **TOASTED COCONUT SORBET** AND **LIME SYRUP**

Serves 8

For the mango ice cream
250g ripe fresh mango flesh or frozen mango purée, defrosted
finely grated zest of 2 limes
50ml lime juice
3 sheets of bronze leaf gelatine
400ml double cream
5 medium egg yolks
120g caster sugar
260g full-fat cream cheese, at room temperature

For the coconut sorbet
100g desiccated coconut
200ml coconut milk
100g caster sugar
120ml liquid glucose
50ml white rum
300g full-fat yoghurt

For the passion fruit and mango jam
250g ripe fresh mango flesh or frozen mango purée, defrosted
4 ripe passion fruit, halved, pulp and seeds scooped out
25ml white rum
50g caster sugar
50g unsalted butter

For the coconut tuiles
55g desiccated coconut
100g egg whites (about 3 medium eggs)
100g caster sugar
100g plain flour, sifted

For the lime syrup
200ml liquid glucose
100g caster sugar
finely grated zest of 2 limes
100ml lime juice

To finish
1–2 ripe fresh mangoes, peeled and sliced away from the stone

For the mango ice cream
Put the mango into a blender or food processor with the lime zest and juice and blend until smooth. Transfer to a pan and bring to a simmer over a medium heat. Let simmer until reduced by half. In the meantime, soak the gelatine in a dish of ice-cold water. Add the cream to the reduced mango purée and return to a simmer.

Meanwhile, whisk the egg yolks and sugar together in a bowl. Pour on the hot mango cream, whisking as you do. Immediately squeeze the excess water from the gelatine, then whisk it into the hot mango mixture until fully dissolved. Leave to cool, then cover and refrigerate.

Once the mixture is chilled, whisk in the cream cheese and spoon into a piping bag. Place 8 metal rings, about 6cm in diameter and 3cm deep, on a tray and line with cling film, leaving enough overhanging to cover the surface. Spoon the ice cream mixture into the rings and fold over the cling film. Place in the freezer for a few hours until firm.

To make the coconut sorbet
Preheat your grill to medium-high. Spread the desiccated coconut out on the grill tray and toast under the grill until golden, stirring a few times; this should take 4–5 minutes.

Remove from the grill and set aside to cool on the tray.

Put the coconut milk, sugar, liquid glucose and rum into a pan and bring to a simmer. Add half the toasted coconut and allow to cool; put the rest of the toasted coconut in a bowl. Once the sorbet mix is cold, whisk in the yoghurt. Pour into an ice-cream machine and churn until thick. Transfer to a suitable container and freeze for a few hours until firm.

Half an hour before serving, scoop individual balls of sorbet, using a hot wet spoon, flatten one surface (to create a dome shape) and drop them one at a time into the bowl of coconut, turning to coat. Place on a small tray and return to the freezer once you have 8 balls of sorbet, to firm up.

For the passion fruit and mango jam
Place all the ingredients in a pan over a medium heat and stir until smooth, then cover and cook gently for about 25 minutes until the mango is soft. Transfer to a food processor and blend until smooth. Pass the mixture through a fine sieve into a container and leave to cool, then cover and chill in the fridge.

...continued on page 280

To prepare the coconut tuiles

Preheat your grill to medium-high and the oven to 200°C/Fan 180°C/Gas Mark 6. Line a baking tray with a non-stick silicone mat. Scatter the coconut on a grill tray and grill until golden, stirring every 30 seconds to colour evenly. Allow to cool.

Whisk the egg whites and sugar together in a bowl until evenly mixed. Add the toasted coconut and flour and stir to combine. Using a palette knife, spread the mixture thinly and evenly on the lined baking tray. Bake in the oven for 8–10 minutes until golden all over.

When you take the tray from the oven, mark your desired tuile shapes with a plain cutter or sharp knife. Set aside to cool. Once cooled, the biscuits should snap where marked, with a little help. Keep in an airtight container until ready to assemble.

To make the lime syrup

Heat all the ingredients together in a pan over a medium heat. When the syrup comes to the boil, remove from the heat and set aside to cool.

To assemble and serve

Take the ice creams out of their moulds and remove the cling film. Sandwich each ice cream disc between two coconut tuiles. Put a blob of the passion fruit and mango jam in the centre of each plate and place an ice-cream sandwich on top.

Arrange the mango slices overlapping on the ice-cream sandwich and drizzle the lime syrup over the fruit and around the plate. Carefully place a dome of sorbet on top of the mango. Serve immediately.

One of my head chefs, Tim Barnes, has worked with me for seven years now, but when he first started he was struggling to get any sleep when he got home at night. We couldn't work out why until it dawned on us that Tim had been eating all the trimmings and spare slices of espresso tart. By the end of each night he'd consumed an awful lot of caffeine – equivalent to six shots, at least! Don't be put off: you don't need to eat as many as Tim to get your espresso tart fix, one or two will do you!

ESPRESSO CUSTARD TARTS

Makes 12

For the pastry
430g plain flour, plus
  extra to dust
20g caster sugar
4g fine sea salt
4g baking powder
170g unsalted butter,
  diced and softened
120–180ml milk

For the custard filling
9 large egg yolks
90g soft brown sugar
420ml double cream
120ml freshly made
  espresso coffee, cooled

For the crystallised pistachios
100g caster sugar
25ml water
100g freshly shelled
  roasted and salted
  pistachio nuts

To make the pastry

Mix all the dry ingredients together in a bowl then, using your fingers, rub in the butter until the mixture resembles a crumble mix. Add 120ml of the milk and mix with a table knife to a smooth dough, adding as much of the remaining milk as you need to bring the dough together; don't overwork it. Wrap in cling film and chill for 1 hour.

For the custard filling

Whisk the egg yolks and brown sugar together in a bowl until creamy. Heat the cream and espresso in a saucepan to a simmer. Pour onto the egg mixture, whisking continuously. Pass the mixture through a fine sieve into a jug and set aside.

To shape the pastry cases

Unwrap the pastry and roll out on a lightly floured surface to the thickness of a £1 coin. Using an 8cm cutter, cut out 12 circles and use these to line 12 individual mini tart cases, about 6cm in diameter and 1cm deep. Place in the fridge to rest for 30 minutes. Meanwhile, preheat your oven to 200°C/Fan 180°C/Gas Mark 6.

To bake the pastry cases

Line the pastry cases with a double layer of heat-resistant cling film and fill with lentils or rice (baking beans are too big!). Pull the edges of the cling film up and twist together to make little parcels in the pastry-lined tins. Bake in the oven for 15 minutes then take them out and remove the lentil or rice parcels. Reduce the oven temperature to 140°C/Fan 120°C/Gas Mark 1. Return the pastry cases to the oven and bake for a further 5 minutes.

Fill the pastry cases with the coffee custard, then carefully return to the oven for 15 minutes until they are set with a slight wobble in the centre. Transfer to a wire rack to cool.

For the crystallised pistachios

Place the sugar and water in a heavy-based saucepan (ideally stainless steel so you can see the colour of the syrup) and bring to the boil. Continue to cook over a medium heat until the sugar just starts to turn golden. Immediately add the shelled pistachios and remove from the heat. With a sturdy wooden spoon, stir the mixture quickly and vigorously until the sugar begins to crystallise and coats the nuts.

Tip the nuts out onto a tray, breaking up any large clusters and allow to cool. When cold, the nuts can be kept in an airtight container.

To serve

Chop the crystallised pistachios up a bit and sprinkle them over the surface of the espresso custard tarts. Serve warm or at room temperature.

THE STAFF
A great core team

When I opened my first restaurant, The Black Pig, there were just four of us, and I was both cooking and taking turns washing up. Today, our restaurants have a team of staff numbering over fifty.

Currently, at Restaurant Nathan Outlaw, we have a kitchen team of six, plus a kitchen porter, and a front-of-house team of eight. I spend a large amount of my time here and cook on a regular basis, which some find surprising. In fact, I am never happier than when prepping fish!

I've always maintained that it is the staff who make the restaurant what it is. For this reason they are chosen very carefully, particularly for their attitude and desire to make customers feel at ease. The training of staff is continuous, with many gaining qualifications recognised in the hospitality industry, as well as attending frequent in-house sessions. Each time a change is made on the menu, all the staff try the dish and learn about the ingredients and cooking method, so they can answer any questions customers may have. The same is true when new wines come onto the wine list.

I am willing to consider applications from anyone so long as they show a passion for the work and a keenness to learn. The common bond throughout the staff team is the desire to offer the very best they can, whether that be in terms of cooking or hospitality.

For over a decade, my core team at Restaurant Nathan Outlaw has been with me, contributing significantly to the consistency of the offering and the relaxed ambience enjoyed by our customers. In addition to the actual restaurant staff, I must mentioned other vital personnel who work behind the scenes. My accountant and PA, who are also family members, and the General Manager of the company, all help to make things run smoothly.

While I always seek to recruit staff from the local area, it's not always possible, for several reasons. Firstly, there is a general shortage of trained chefs in the UK at the current time and with Cornwall's main economy being hospitality, there just aren't enough local chefs to go around. Add to that the need to recruit the very best staff to keep up the standard required of a two-Michelin-starred restaurant and things become even more problematic!

In the case of front-of-house positions, sadly, most people don't recognise this as a worthwhile career, so finding locals who are serious about this type of work is particularly difficult. At present, two of our chefs and three front-of-house staff are Cornish.

Secondly, Port Isaac is a lovely, quaint village, but it does have to be pointed out to potential workers from outside Cornwall that it is almost 300 miles from London and quite remote, so they aren't going to be able to 'pop up East' on their days off!

Finding accommodation can be tricky too. While Port Isaac has lots of lovely holiday lets, there are very few long-term rental properties available and house prices are expensive – so out of the reach of most of the staff. Although we have a staff house, it is impossible to find a room for everyone (especially as we have another restaurant, Outlaw's Fish Kitchen, in the village too). The nearest town, with some possibilities of accommodation for staff is Wadebridge, but that means travelling by car as there is very little public transport, especially during the hours our staff need to travel to and from work!

As a consequence of all this, we tend to have a multi-national staff – currently South African, German, Italian, Danish and British, as well as some from Cornwall. Fortunately, it seems to work pretty well!

© Chris Hewitt

Basics

VEGETABLE STOCK

Makes about 2 litres

Finely chop all of the vegetables and place them in a large saucepan with the garlic, spices and salt. Pour on enough cold water to cover. Bring to a simmer over a medium heat and simmer for 30 minutes.

Remove from the heat then pour the wine into the stock and add the herbs. Set aside to cool.

For best results, leave the stock to infuse overnight in the fridge.

Strain the cooled stock to remove the vegetables, spices and herbs. It is now ready to use.

The stock is best used the day after it is made or it can be frozen for up to 2 months.

2 onions, peeled
6 carrots, peeled
6 celery sticks
2 leeks, trimmed
2 garlic cloves, peeled
 and crushed
10 white peppercorns
1 star anise
2 teaspoons fennel
 seeds
a pinch of sea salt
500ml dry white wine
a sprig of thyme
a handful of parsley
 stalks

FISH STOCK

Makes about 500ml

Preheat your oven to 200°C/Fan 180°C/Gas Mark 6. Line a roasting tray with silicone paper. Lay the fish bones and/or cod heads in the lined roasting tray. Roast for 30 minutes, then turn the bones over and roast for another 10 minutes.

Transfer the roasted fish bones to a stockpot and pour on enough cold water to cover. Bring to a simmer over a medium heat and skim off any

impurities from the surface. Allow to simmer for 30 minutes.

Remove from the heat and strain the stock through a sieve into another pan. Bring back to a simmer and let it bubble to reduce by half. Remove from the heat and allow to cool.

The stock is now ready to use. You can store it in the fridge for up to 3 days or freeze it for up to 2 months.

1kg turbot, brill or
 sole bones and/or cod
 heads, washed and all
 blood removed

SHELLFISH STOCK

Makes about 500ml

Preheat your oven to 200°C/Fan 180°C/Gas Mark 6. Put the frozen prawns on a roasting tray and roast for 30 minutes.

Meanwhile, heat a large pan over a medium heat and add a little olive oil. When it is hot, add the onions, carrots, tomatoes, garlic and orange zest and sweat gently for 5 minutes until softened and lightly coloured.

Once the prawns are roasted, chop them roughly and add to the pan. Pour on enough cold water to cover everything and add the orange juice. Bring to a simmer and simmer for 1 hour.

Strain through a sieve into another pan and simmer to reduce by half. Take off the heat and allow to cool.

The stock is now ready to use. You can store it in the fridge for up to 2 days or freeze it for up to a month.

Shore crab stock
Replace the prawns with 1kg live shore crabs. Prepare for cooking as for live brown crab (see page 20). Roast for an extra 15 minutes.

Lobster stock
Replace the prawns with 1kg lobster shells and heads.

1kg frozen shell-on
  prawns
olive oil for cooking
2 onions, peeled and
  chopped
3 carrots, peeled and
  chopped
6 ripe tomatoes, chopped
6 garlic cloves, peeled
  and chopped
finely pared zest and
  juice of 1 orange

VINAIGRETTE

Makes about 250ml

Whisk the ingredients together in a bowl or shake in a screw-topped jar to emulsify, seasoning with salt and pepper to taste. Use as required.

50ml white wine
  vinegar
1 teaspoon Dijon
  mustard
200ml light olive oil
Cornish sea salt
  and freshly ground
  black pepper

FERMENTED STARTER DOUGH

Makes enough for
4 loaves

This is the 'starter dough' I use to make most of my breads. It gives an amazing depth of flavour.

To create the fermented fruit juice, a couple of days before making your bread, open a 400g tin of peaches or pears. Tip into a bowl, cover and leave to ferment for 2 days. Transfer the fermented fruit and juice to a blender and blitz until smooth, then pass through a sieve into a jug.

Put the flour, yeast and fermented juice into an electric mixer fitted with the dough hook and mix on a high speed until a smooth dough has formed. Transfer the dough to a lidded container.

The fermented 'starter' dough will live in the fridge happily for up to 5 days, but check that it doesn't become over-active. Use as required.

160ml fermented peach
  or pear juice
  (see method)
280g white bread flour
15g fresh yeast

Index

A

almonds

and pear tart 246

and raspberry biscuits 148

sugared 108

amaretto ice cream 246

apples

and blackberry tart 142

and cinnamon doughnuts 218

with crab 194

Arctic Roll, Raspberry Sorbet and

Sugared Almonds 108

artichoke *see* globe artichoke;

Jerusalem artichoke

asparagus 64

and crab 20

scallops, samphire and smoked

butter hollandaise 60

aubergine purée with

triggerfish 98

B

Baked Hake, Creamed Corn,

Pickled Red Onions and

Peppercorn Sauce 134

Baked Scallops, Jerusalem

Artichokes, Devilled Butter 228

bananas ice cream 40

basil salad cream with red

mullet 202

bass

griddled with mash, courgette

and hazelnuts 100

with leeks and tartare

hollandaise 162

beans and cuttlefish, cod, lemon

and garlic dressing 268

beetroot pickled 262

biscuits

almond and raspberry 148

pistachio tuiles 72

roast onion and Cheddar

straws 152

shortbread custard creams 44

blackberries and apple tart 142

blackcurrants

jellies 182

pavlova, bitter lemon sorbet and

clotted cream 144

brandy

and chocolate truffles 112

snaps 80

bread

crab scones 50

fermented starter dough 290

sourdough crisps 256

bream *see* gilt head bream

brill

cured, grapes and pumpkin

seeds 224

with roast pumpkin and wild

mushrooms 210

broad beans

haddock and smoked haddock

potatoes 66

with scallops and braised

fennel 94

broccoli sprouting with turbot 164

Brussels sprouts with monkfish

and seaweed hollandaise 206

Buse, Jax 64

butter

devilled 228

smoked hollandaise 60

C

cakes

plum sponge 212

stout 276

Camel Valley Vineyard 172

Caramel Chocolate and Sea Salt

Fudge 252

carrots

with lobster and roast onions 168

pickled with red mullet 202

cauliflower

with bream, fennel and

dumplings 128

with monkfish and seaweed

hollandaise 206

caviar turbot and champagne 270

celeriac

with John Dory, squid, watercress

and salami 236

with turbot, artichokes and

broccoli 164

ceps and oxtail sauce 130

champagne

strawberry sorbet 106

turbot and caviar 270

cheese Cheddar and onion

straws 152

cherries with chocolate tart 72

chicory with red mullet and

shrimp fritters 242

chillies

with marinated gurnard 18

oil 258

chocolate

bitter sauce 36

bitter with mulled pear 214

and brandy truffles 112

caramel and sea salt fudge 252

dark mousse 276

and raspberry ice cream 178

tart, cherries, pistachio ice

cream 72

cider sorbet 142

cinnamon mousse 142

clams with Dover sole, parsley and

garlic 234

coconut sorbet 278

cod cuttlefish and beans, lemon

and garlic dressing 268;

see also salt cod

cod's roe smoked dip with

sourdough crisps 256

Q

quince and ginger sorbet 250

R

raspberries

and almond biscuits 148

ice cream and dark chocolate 178

ice cream sandwich 80

sorbet 108

Raw Gilt Head Bream, Tomato
Water and Samphire 86

Raw Scallops, Roast Onion, Parsnip
Crisps and Chilli Oil 258

Raw Wild Gilt Head Bream with
Pea and Mint 52

red mullet

with basil salad cream and
pickled carrots 202

chicory and shrimp sauce, shrimp
fritters 242

and red pepper tart with smoked
paprika 118

squid salad, courgette and
fennel 68

red onions pickle 134

red peppers

and red mullet tart with smoked
paprika 118

sauce 54

rhubarb

and orange trifle 76

and rye ketchup 16

Ripley, Paul 30

Roast Onion and Cheddar
Straws 152

Rock Shellfish 230

rye and rhubarb ketchup 16

S

saffron

aïoli 96

roast garlic potato purée 272

salads squid 68

salami with John Dory, squid,
watercress and celeriac 236

salmon cured, seaweed salad
cream and cucumber relish 58

salsify with lemon sole and green
mayonnaise 34

salt cod and lobster scampi 90

samphire

and gilt head bream 86

with plaice and mussels 32

scallops, asparagus and smoked
butter hollandaise 60

sardines and tomato ketchup 98

sauces

bitter chocolate 36

celeriac 164

ceps and oxtail 130

curry 204

green 226

lobster 90

peppercorn 134

Porthilly 158

red pepper 54

rye and rhubarb ketchup 16

saffron aïoli 96

sardine and tomato ketchup 98

seaweed salad cream 58

shrimp 242

smoked butter hollandaise 60

tartare hollandaise 162

see also dressings; mayonnaise

scallops

asparagus, samphire and smoked
butter hollandaise 60

baked, Jerusalem artichokes,
devilled butter 228

with braised fennel and broad
beans 94

parsnips and curry sauce 204

raw, roast onion, parsnip crisps
and chilli oil 258

scones crab 50

seafood 30, 160, 230

stock 290

seasons 102

seaweed

hollandaise with monkfish 206

salad cream, cured salmon 58

shellfish *see* seafood

Shortbread Custard Creams 44

shrimp sauce and fritters 242

Smoked Cod's Roe Dip with
Sourdough Crisps 256

smoked haddock potatoes 66

smoked mackerel

choux buns 186

fritters and gooseberry pickle 84

sole *see* Dover sole; lemon sole

sorbet

bitter lemon 144

cider 142

honey yoghurt 212

quince and ginger 250

raspberry 108

strawberry champagne 106

toasted coconut 278

soups wild garlic 22

Soused Mackerel, Pickled Onion
and Green Sauce 226

squid

with John Dory, watercress,
celeriac and salami 236

marinated with ink and tarragon
dressing 122

salad with red mullet 68

staff 284

Stein, Rick 30, 88

stock 288, 290

strawberries with elderflower
custard and champagne
sorbet 106

sustainability 30

ACKNOWLEDGEMENTS

When I first saw this book in print after a year of working on it, I was stunned at how wonderful it looked. In essence, it's my restaurant on paper and I'm extremely proud of both. Of course, neither my restaurant or this book would be what they are without the huge team of special people I have behind me, so I'd like to take this opportunity to thank them.

Firstly, there would be no Restaurant Nathan Outlaw book and, in fact, no Restaurant Nathan Outlaw full stop if it wasn't for my wife, Rachel. There is no way I could keep my head straight and focus on the restaurants and writing if it wasn't for her. My best friend and love, the one that keeps my feet on the ground and makes sure I haven't got my head in the clouds. I love you x

Jacob, my son, and Jessica, my daughter, who both make me proud every day and actually did help with peeling a few vegetables and picking some herbs for this book. Oh, and both did a bit of washing up. Love you both too x

Sharon 'Mum' Outlaw aka co-writer/PA. Thank you for all your hard work with this book. It would not have happened for sure if you hadn't been here to help me and get out and chat to all our wonderful suppliers and friends. You make me look good! Forever grateful x

Big love and thanks to Tim Barnes, Jim Preston-Evens, Zack Hawke, Alex Murtagh, Ian Dodgson and Danny Madigan for all helping with the preparations for this book over the year it took to produce. Without each of you, I couldn't have done it.

Special mentions and thanks to the 2018 team who all helped in their own wonderful ways – Steffi and Damon Little, Anna Davey, Kelly Parsons,

Emma Meech, Karl Lucking, Joshua Henry, Rosie Barclay, Trille Lassen, Dave Waters, Alessandro Avellino, Mattia Tonelli, Manny De Souza, Max Allen and Jilly Wright.

All the staff, past and present, at Restaurant Nathan Outlaw and Outlaw's Fish Kitchen, thank you and I hope you enjoy seeing the book.

Pete Biggs, Andrew 'Ginger' Sawyer, James Rhodes.

Clive 'Dad' Outlaw, thanks for being you and lighting the spark in me to cook and love what I do!

David Loftus, what can I say that I haven't already said to you about your amazing photographic capture of my food? I will always be grateful for your support with what I do. A million big thank yous!

All the team at Absolute: Jon Croft and Meg Boas for believing in me and supporting this book and making it happen. Marie O'Shepherd for everything you have done and really understanding me and my restaurant and getting it onto these wonderful pages. Hope you enjoyed your trips to Port Isaac. Emily North, thanks for supporting this book and being there to push the project along and make sure we got there on time, I think? Ha! Ha!

Thanks to Janet Illsley, my editor, who has supported me for years and manages to make sense of my recipes, always questioning me on some of my more 'adventurous' methods! Forever grateful Janet x

© Chris Hewitt

ABOUT THE AUTHOR

Originally from Kent, Nathan now calls Cornwall his home and is a proud ambassador of all things Cornish. His style of cooking is one of simplicity but with complex flavour combinations using local, seasonal, responsibly-sourced ingredients. Nathan was proud to be named the AA Chef's Chef of the Year 2014/15, Restaurateur of the Year 2017 at The Catey Awards (voted by those in the industry) and Chef of the Year at the Food & Travel Awards 2017 (voted for by readers).

Having attending Thanet College in Kent, Nathan worked with several chefs including the late Peter Kromberg, Gary Rhodes, Eric Chavot and John Campbell. However, his love for seafood cookery was ignited when he came to Cornwall as a young chef to work with Rick Stein.

Nathan currently has two restaurants in Cornwall. In early 2015, Restaurant Nathan Outlaw relocated from Rock to the historic fishing village of Port Isaac and retained its two Michelin stars. It was awarded the number one spot of the 'Top 50 Restaurants in the UK' in the Waitrose and Partners *Good Food Guide 2018*, for the second consecutive year having scored a perfect 10 for cooking for the past three years. Outlaw's Fish Kitchen, also in Port Isaac, offers diners small plates of seafood in an informal setting. It holds one Michelin star.

In London, Nathan's latest venture at The Goring Hotel, in the heart of Belgravia, will open in May 2019, bringing the very best of sustainable Cornish seafood to London.

Nathan actively supports the education and training of future chefs and front of house staff, often taking time to work individually with younger members of staff. He is also in demand at industry conferences in Britain and abroad, where his expertise is valued both by those training and by experienced chefs.

Nathan's easy manner, enthusiasm and obvious passion for his work make him a hit with audiences of all ages and he regularly appears on TV programmes such as *Saturday Kitchen* and *Masterchef: The Professionals*.

Nathan has written several cookery books. His first, *Nathan Outlaw's British Seafood* was named 'Best Cookery Book' by Food and Travel Awards 2013; this was followed in 2014 by *Nathan Outlaw's Fish Kitchen* and in 2016 by *Nathan Outlaw's Everyday Seafood*. His last, a collection of favourites from his kitchen at home, *Nathan Outlaw's Home Kitchen* was published in April 2017.

Credits

Publisher Jon Croft
Commissioning Editor Meg Boas
Senior Editor Emily North
Art Director & Designer Marie O'Shepherd
Junior Designer Anika Schulze
Photographer David Loftus
Editor Janet Illsley
Production Controllers Gary Hayes and Marina Asenjo
Proofreader Margaret Haynes
Indexer Zoe Ross